James M. MacDonald

Two Centuries in the History of the Presbyterian Church, Jamaica, L.I.

The oldest existing church, of the Presbyterian name, in America

James M. MacDonald

Two Centuries in the History of the Presbyterian Church, Jamaica, L.I.
The oldest existing church, of the Presbyterian name, in America

ISBN/EAN: 9783337324704

Printed in Europe, USA, Canada, Australia, Japan

Cover: Foto ©Lupo / pixelio.de

More available books at **www.hansebooks.com**

TO

NATHAN SHELTON, M.D.,

FOR MORE THAN FIFTY YEARS A PRACTISING PHYSICIAN IN JAMAICA, AND FOR MORE THAN FORTY YEARS

A Ruling Elder

IN THE

PRESBYTERIAN CHURCH

OF THAT PLACE,

This Volume

IS RESPECTFULLY INSCRIBED.

CONTENTS.

CHAPTER I.

Preliminary.

POLITICAL HORIZON TWO CENTURIES AGO — CROMWELL — CHARLES II. — CONDITION OF THOUGHT AND KNOWLEDGE — BAXTER, BUNYAN, OWEN, HOWE, ELLIOTT — HARVARD COLLEGE — NEWSPAPERS — MINISTERS IN NEW YORK AND BROOKLYN — SCHOOLMASTERS — THE FIRST IN JAMAICA — RELIGIOUS HORIZON — THE FIRST COMPANIES OF PURITANS LEAVE ENGLAND — CHARLES AND LAUD — THE SCOTTISH COVENANT AND CIVIL WAR — PRESBYTERIANS AND CAVALIERS — CHARLES II. INVITED TO THE THRONE — HIS INGRATITUDE TO THE PRESBYTERIANS — JEREMY TAYLOR — ACT OF UNIFORMITY — ATTEMPT TO ESTABLISH PRELACY IN SCOTLAND — MONUMENT IN GRAYFRIARS CHURCHYARD — REVOLUTION 1688 — A "MUSTARD SEED" — THE "EAGLE WING" — PROVIDENCE OF GOD, ... PAGES 17–24

CHAPTER II.
1656–1670.

SETTLEMENT OF JAMAICA — PETITION — LEAVE GIVEN BY GOVERNOR AND COUNCIL — FIRST ENTRY IN THE RECORDS — DECLARATION OF PROPRIETORS — TALL TREES TO BE SPARED — THE TENTHS — YEMACAH — SELLING STRONG DRINK TO INDIANS PROHIBITED — CARE AS TO THE CHARACTER OF SETTLERS — FIRST MAGISTRATES APPOINTED — EARLY PREACHING — ARRANGEMENTS FOR A MINISTER — A MINISTER'S HOUSE TO BE BUILT — MR. WALKER — BEATING THE DRUM ON SABBATH DAYS — AGREEMENT WITH MR. WALKER — MEETING-HOUSE TO BE BUILT — MR. WALKER REQUESTED TO PROCURE ORDINATION — REMOVES TO CONNECTICUT — HIS DESCENDANTS — STYLE OF DWELLINGS — FOOD — CATTLE — HABITS — INDUSTRY — WOMAN — INCREASE IN WEALTH — COMPARATIVE ESTATES OF INDIVIDUALS — DANIEL DENTON — HIS HISTORY — SETTLEMENT OF ELIZABETHTOWN, N. J. — SOCIAL LIFE OF THE PEOPLE — SABBATH AND WORSHIP — DRESS — FUNERALS — THE BURYING GROUND, ... 25–52

CHAPTER III.
1670–1692.

REV. JOHN PRUDDEN — A CONVENIENT PEW TO PREACH IN — PERMISSION GIVEN TO MR. PRUDDEN TO BUILD ON THE MINISTER'S LOT — THE TOWN "FURTHER THE COMING INTO A CHURCHWAY" — MR. PRUDDEN LEAVES — REV. WM.

WOODROP — FORTY ACRES APPROPRIATED FOR THE USE OF THE MINISTER IN 1676 — MR. PRUDDEN RETURNED, AND ARTICLES OF AGREEMENT WITH HIM — "RULES OF THE GOSPEL IN THIS TOWN" — WAS THE CHURCH PRESBYTERIAN OR CONGREGATIONAL? — REV. RICHARD DENTON — TESTIMONY OF DUTCH MINISTERS THAT HE WAS A PRESBYTERIAN — PRESBYTERIANS AT FLUSHING AND NEWTOWN — DR. WOODBRIDGE'S HISTORICAL DISCOURSE — GOV. STUYVESANT TO THE MAGISTRATES OF HEMPSTEAD — PRESBYTERIANS IN NEW ENGLAND — COTTON MATHER'S ACCOUNT OF MR. DENTON — CHURCH GOVERNMENT ACCORDING TO THE SYNOD OF DORT — MR. PRUDDEN'S PETITION TO THE GOVERNOR TO ALLOW HIM TO BE MINISTER OF CONGREGATIONALISTS — MR. P. BECOMES A PRESBYTERIAN — GEORGE SCOT — ARCHIBALD RIDDELL — THE TOWN VOTES IN FAVOR OF PRESBYTERIAN ORDINATION IN 1700 — REV. GEORGE M'NISH — THE CHURCH FOSTERED BY THE DUTCH PRESBYTERIANS — THE OLDEST CHURCH OF THE PRESBYTERIAN NAME IN AMERICA — VOTE RESPECTING THE ERECTION OF A MEETING HOUSE IN 1689 — MR. PRUDDEN GOES TO NEWARK — HIS DEATH AND EPITAPH, 53–80

CHAPTER IV.
1692–1699.

FIRST MOVEMENT TOWARDS ERECTING THE STONE MEETING HOUSE — APPLICATION TO THE ASSEMBLY — VANE A TARGET TO BRITISH SOLDIERS IN THE REVOLUTION — DATE ON IT — STYLE OF THE BUILDING — JEREMIAH HOBERT — GEORGE PHILLIPS — HIS "DYOTT" PAID FOR — PEOPLE SEND TO THE "MAIN" FOR A MINISTER — MR. JONES, LATE OF DANBURY — SUBSCRIPTION LIST FOR THE SUPPORT OF A MINISTER — VOTES OF THE TOWN RESPECTING MEETING HOUSE AND MR. PHILLIPS — THE GOV. PETITIONED RESPECTING THE SETTLEMENT OF MR. HOBERT — DISPUTE RESPECTING MEETING HOUSE SETTLED — ACCOUNT OF MR. HOBERT — HOUSE FINISHED,.. 81–93

CHAPTER V.
1700–1724.

JOHN HUBBARD — ORDAINED IN THE PRESBYTERIAN WAY — VESTRYMEN AND CHURCHWARDENS ELECTED — SILAS WOOD, ESQ. — REV. MR. THOMAS, HEMPSTEAD — COTTON MATHER ON JAMAICA — CHIEF JUSTICE SMITH ON THE JAMAICA TROUBLES — "WATCH TOWER," LIVINGSTONE, SCOTT AND SMITH — CORNBURY'S ORDERS TO INQUIRE INTO THE RIOT, AND TO MR. HUBBARD TO VACATE THE PARSONAGE — ORDER TO WARDENS AND SHERIFF TO SELL THE CORN — ORDER TO LAY TAX AND FINE THE WARDENS AND VESTRY FOR REFUSING — REV. MR. BARTOW'S ACCOUNT OF THE RIOT — MR. HUBBARD'S DEATH — REV. P. GORDON BURIED UNDER THE CHURCH — REV. W. URQUHART — REV. F. GOODHUE'S CALL AND COMMISSION — HIS EARLY DEATH — ELEGANT LATIN LINES ON HIM — REV. G. M'NISH CALLED — THE CHURCH TAKEN POSSESSION OF BY THE PRESBYTERIANS — ACCOUNT OF MR. M'NISH — THE PERSECUTION CONTINUES — MEMORIAL OF THE PEOPLE TO THE GOVERNOR — S. CLOWES INFORMS OF THE RIOT IN 1710 — ORDERS AND FINES IN RESPECT TO IT — REV. THOS. POYER — MEMORIAL OF THE CLERGY IN RESPECT TO HIM — GOV. HUNTER, COL. MORRIS AND COL. HEATHCOTE ON THE CHURCH DIFFICULTIES — SUBJECT BROUGHT BEFORE THE QUEEN IN PRIVY COUNCIL — THE LAWSUIT — MR. M'NISH'S CHARACTER AND SERVICES — HIS

DEATH — REV. ROBERT CROSS — EJECTMENT SUIT DECIDED AGAINST MR. POYER — GOV. BURNET TO BISHOP OF LONDON — MR. POYER AND MR. CAMPBELL TO SECRETARY — THE CHURCH RECOVERED, ... 94–153

CHAPTER VI.
1724–1774.

A FREE SCHOOL — THE TOWN TAKE POSSESSION OF THE CHURCH — MR. CROSS CALLED TO PHILADELPHIA — THE PEOPLE STRENUOUSLY OPPOSE HIS REMOVAL — HIS REMOVAL — HIS EPITAPH — WALTER WILMOT — PUT IN POSSESSION OF THE PARSONAGE — MRS. WILMOT — HER DEATH — MR. WHITEFIELD VISITS THE PLACE — HIS PREACHING ON REGENERATION TROUBLES MR. COLGAN — EFFECT — MR. WILMOT'S DEATH — EPITAPH — MR. COLGAN REJOICES — DAVID BOSTWICK — TOWN FORMALLY SURRENDERS CHURCH PROPERTY TO THE PRESBYTERIANS — THE RECORD — MR. BOSTWICK CALLED TO NEW YORK — COMMITTEE OF SYNOD MEET AT JAMAICA ON HIS REMOVAL — MR. BOSTWICK APPOINTED TO SUPPLY NEW YORK — COMMITTEE OF SYNOD MEET AT PRINCETON — VOTE FOR HIS REMOVAL — HIS MINISTRY IN NEW YORK — HIS PUBLICATIONS, CHARACTER AND DEATH — ELIHU SPENCER — ORDAINED AS A MISSIONARY TO THE INDIANS — HIS KNOWLEDGE OF THE INDIAN LANGUAGES — SETTLES AT ELIZABETHTOWN — REMOVES TO JAMAICA — CHAPLAIN IN THE FRENCH AND INDIAN WAR — SETTLES AT ST. GEORGE'S DEL. — REMOVES TO TRENTON, N. J. — HIS READY TALENT — EPITAPH — HIS DESCENDANTS — B. BRADNER — WM. MILLS — NUMBER IN COMMUNION — REVIVAL OF RELIGION — EFFECT OF AN ACCOUNT OF THE REVIVAL AT EASTHAMPTON — MR. WHITEFIELD VISITS JAMAICA, THE SECOND TIME — PREACHES IN AN ORCHARD — A TRACT BY MR. MILLS — MR. SEABURY VS. MR. WHITEFIELD — MR. MILLS DECLINES A CALL TO PHILADELPHIA — HIS DEATH — HIS DISEASE — HIS CHILDREN — HIS MSS. — PEOPLE STILL RESIST THE TAX TO SUPPORT THE EPISCOPAL MINISTRY — MR. BLOOMER ON THE POLITICAL TROUBLES OF 1776 — SHUTS HIS CHURCH FOR FIVE SUNDAYS UNTIL THE KING'S TROOPS ARRIVE, ... 154–189

CHAPTER VII.
1775–1815.

MATTHIAS BURNET ORDAINED — MARRIES IN JAMAICA — THE REVOLUTION — PRESBYTERIAN MINISTERS SUPPORT THE CONTINENTAL CONGRESS — REVOLUTIONARY INCIDENTS — MR. BURNET HAS INFLUENCE WITH THE LOYALISTS — SAVES THE PRESBYTERIAN CHURCH FROM DESTRUCTION — HIGHLANDERS ATTEND HIS PREACHING — THE SCOTCH WOMAN AND HER BOTTLE OF WATER — MR. ONDERDONK'S REVOLUTIONARY INCIDENTS — ELIAS BAYLIS ARRESTED — SENT TO THE PROVOST — SINGS IN PRISON — HIS DEATH — OTHER WHIGS SEIZED — WHIGS RETURN AT THE CLOSE OF THE WAR — MR. BURNET LEAVES, AND SETTLES AT NORWALK — DEATH — GEORGE FAITOUTE INSTALLED — ONE OF THE ORIGINAL TRUSTEES OF U. H. ACADEMY — THE OLD STONE CHURCH TAKEN DOWN, AND A NEW ONE BUILT — MR. FAITOUTE'S DEATH, ... 190–211

CHAPTER VIII.
1815–1862.

H. R. WEED — REMOVES TO ALBANY — S. P. FUNCK — DISSENSION — REV. A. NETTLETON — GREAT REVIVAL — DISSENSION HEALED — MR. NETTLETON'S METHOD — E. W. CRANE — HIS USEFUL MINISTRY — DR. MURRAY'S SKETCH OF HIM — HIS DEATH — J. M. MACDONALD — THE NEW ERA IN THE HISTORY OF THE CHURCH UNDER MR. WEED'S MINISTRY — THE HIGHLY PROSPEROUS STATE OF THE CONGREGATION IN 1841 — INCIDENTS IN MR. MACDONALD'S MINISTRY — P. D. OAKEY, ... 212–225

CHAPTER IX.
Hortatory.

STATISTICS OF THE PRESBYTERIAN CHURCH IN THE UNITED STATES — INFLUENCE OF A SINGLE CHURCH — MEN DIE, TRUTH ENDURES — THE LIFE OF SOCIETY — ERROR AND SIN TRANSMITTED — LOSSES AND GAINS, OR THE TRANSIENT AND PERMANENT IN HISTORY — SIGNS OF THE TIMES — THE MISSIONARY SPIRIT OF RICHARD BAXTER — HOPE FOR OUR COUNTRY IN ITS PRESENT TRIALS — PRINCIPLES RECEIVED FROM THE PRESBYTERIAN FATHERS — LOYALTY — RELIGIOUS INSTRUCTION OF YOUTH — FREEDOM OF CONSCIENCE — CHOICE OF RULERS — HOW WE MAY BEST SERVE THE FUTURE — KING DAVID — ABEL — THE CHAIN OF EXPERIENCE — MR. AMOS DENTON — FAITH AND PRAYER, ... 226–238

ADDENDA

I. RATE LIST OF JAMAICA IN 1683 — II. RETURN OF MARRIAGES, BAPTISMS AND BURIALS FOR SEVEN YEARS PRECEDING 1688 — III. RATE LIST OF JAMAICA, FEB. 1708–9 — IV. LETTER OF THE REV. GEORGE HALE, PENNINGTON, N. J. — V. PRESBYTERIES WITH WHICH THE CHURCH HAS BEEN CONNECTED — VI. CATALOGUE OF THE MINISTERS — VII. CATALOGUE OF THE ELDERS — VIII. DEACONS — IX. TRUSTEES OF THE CONGREGATION — X. NUMBER OF COMMUNICANTS ANNUALLY REPORTED TO PRESBYTERY — XI. LIST OF MINISTERS WHO HAVE GONE FORTH, ETC. — XII. LIST OF VESTRYMEN, ETC. — XIII. CONTEMPORARY MINISTERS OF JAMAICA — XIV. THE FIRST INDIAN DEED FOR THE TOWNSHIP, ... 239–259

APPENDIX.

PRELIMINARY ARRANGEMENTS — OPENING EXERCISES — MURAL TABLETS — SERMON BY DR. MACDONALD — INTERLOCUTORY MEETING OF MINISTERS IN FORMER CONNECTION WITH THE CHURCH — SERMON BY REV. J. M. KREBS, D. D. — SERMON BY REV. W. P. BREED — COMMUNION — LETTERS FROM DR. WEED AND OTHERS — CONCLUDING ADDRESS BY THE PASTOR, REV. P. D. OAKEY — "NEW YORK OBSERVER," "PRESBYTERIAN,".................. 261–329

PREFACE.

The following note will serve to explain to the public the origin of this volume:

    JAMAICA, L. I., January 8, 1862.
To Rev. James M. Macdonald, D. D.:

 DEAR SIR:—The undersigned, a committee of the Elders, Deacons and Trustees, beg leave to thank you for the very able and interesting discourse delivered yesterday, commemorative of the 200th anniversary of the Presbyterian church in this place; and, believing that the important matter therein contained should be preserved in a permanent form, ask the favor of a copy for publication.

  Very sincerely and truly yours,
    P. D. OAKEY,
    JNO. J. ARMSTRONG,
    LAURENS REEVE,
    JNO. D. SHELTON.

 Shortly after this was received, the Session and Trustees, through the Pastor, Rev. Mr. Oakey, requested that a new and enlarged edition of the History of the Church, which was published in 1847, might be prepared. This work was accordingly undertaken; and the historical matter referred to in the above note, and other matter new, or deemed too important to be allowed to pass into oblivion, will be found incorporated in the following pages.

 As in the former publication, of which this can scarcely be called a new edition, the author felt constrained to express his special acknowledgments to

Henry Onderdonk, Jr., Esq., author of "Revolutionary Incidents of Long Island," for directing him to sources of valuable information, he is in this called upon to renew his acknowledgments to that gentleman for similar services, and especially for securing for him an accurate copy of all the minutes relating to the church, found in the ancient Town Records of Jamaica. These minutes, nearly entire in the order of their dates, are here preserved.

Thanks are also due to Dr. E. B. O'Callaghan of Albany, for kindly furnishing two of the oldest documents in the book, one of which he translated from the Dutch; and to Charles Shaw, Esq., for perfecting, from his own recollections, the rough sketch of the stone church, left by the late Judge Lamberson, an engraving of which appears in this volume.

The Indian deed for the first purchase of land by the original settlers, was discovered too late to be inserted in the proper place. It, with other important documents, will be found in the *Addenda*.

The Appendix, containing an account of the recent bi-centennial celebration was prepared, under the direction of a committee appointed for that purpose, by the Trustees and Elders of the congregation.

This history, it is thought, will be possessed of some interest outside of the particular community to which it relates, as it presents the evidence (if it might not rather be called *proof*) of its being the oldest existing church of the Presbyterian name in America.

PARSONAGE-HOUSE, LIBRARY PLACE,
    PRINCETON, N. J., May 8th, 1862.

INTRODUCTION.

Jamaica, on Long Island, was settled, under the Dutch rule, in 1656. The English, laying claim to the same territory, it was surrendered to them in the year of our Lord 1664.

After the Revolution in England, in 1688, a great change took place in the Colonial government. A General Assembly was allowed, which consisted of deputies, chosen by the freeholders of each County, to whom, together with the Governor and the Council, the legislative power was intrusted.

In 1692, Colonel Fletcher arrived, with a commission to be Governor of the Colony. He very soon manifested great zeal to form a "religious establishment;" and, whilst the government was in his hands, a new policy was adopted, in respect to ecclesiastical affairs, which, at length, produced much dissension, and operated with disastrous effect on the Presbyterian churches in Hempstead and Jamaica. The recommendation of the Governor was for "the settling of an able ministry," but no intimation was given that the Church of England was to be exclusively supported by law. The majority of the Assembly were entirely disinclined to the scheme; but, as the model of the Church of Holland had been secured to them, by one of the articles of surrender, it is not probable they suspected Fletcher of his design to introduce uniformity of religion, or to have the Church of England exclusively supported by law. The Governor warmly rebuked them, asserting that the same law which secured to them the privileges of Englishmen, did "provide for the religion of the Church of England." Fletcher was a bigot to the Episcopal form of Church government.*

In September, 1693, a new Assembly met. The determination of the Governor at length induced the house to yield; and a bill was "brought in for settling the ministry, and raising a maintenance for them in the City and County of New York, Counties of Richmond and Westchester and Queens County." The bill was drawn by James Grahame, Esq., the Speaker of the Assembly, who was the only member of that body who belonged to the Church of England. As the inhabitants of Jamaica were, at that time, seeking to erect a new house of worship, and had applied to the Assembly for an Act to enable them to raise money for the work, Colonel Fletcher and Grahame, perceiving the Assembly inclined to pass such an Act, thought it a favorable opportunity to press their favorite measure for a religious establishment, and accordingly brought in the bill aforesaid. It was artfully framed, and prescribed a method of induction that " would not do well for the Dissenters, and but lamely for the Church, tho' 'twould do with the help of the Governor."† The bill passed and was sent to the Governor

---

* Smith, I. p. 128.
† Colonel Lewis Morris' MS Letter to the Ven. Soc.

and Council, who immediately returned it, with an amendment to the effect that ministers should be "presented to the Governor to be approved and collated." The members of the house refused to pass the amendment. Fletcher was so highly exasperated, that he summoned the representatives forthwith to the council chamber, and told them that he had "the power of collating or suspending any minister in his government." Smith thinks that it can only be attributed to the simplicity of the times that the members of the Assembly peaceably put up with that man's rudeness. The charter of privileges granted by the Duke of York to the inhabitants of New York provided that all "persons which profess in Godlynesse Jesus Christ" might "from time to time, and at all times, have and fully enjoy their judgments and consciences in matters of religion throughout all the province." The same charter confirmed "the respective Christian churches now in practice within the Citty of New Yorke, Long Island, and other places of this province," "that they shall be held and reputed as PRIVILEDGED CHURCHES, AND ENJOY THEIR FORMER FREEDOMS OF THEIR RELIGION, IN DIVINE WORSHIP AND CHURCH DISCIPLINE."

In the spring of 1695, the Assembly declared, in explanation of the Act of 1693, "That the vestry-men and church-wardens have power to call a DISSENTING Protestant minister, and that he is to be paid and maintained as the Act directs." This was done on account of the attempt to interpret the Act as made for the sole benefit of the Church of England. The design of the Governor, and the secret of all his zeal, for "settling the ministry," was now made evident; for he rejected the interpretation of the Assembly, and decided that the act applied solely to the ministry of that church.

Lord Cornbury was appointed to succeed the Earl of Bellomont in the government, and he arrived in the Colony early in the year 1702. In his zeal for "the Church," he was not behind any of his predecessors, and therefore he was a fit instrument to carry out the policy of Governor Fletcher. "His persecution of the Presbyterians very early increased the number of his enemies; the Dutch, too, were fearful of his religious rage against them, as he disputed their right to call and settle ministers, or even schoolmasters, without his special license." "We never had a Governor so universally detested, nor any who so richly deserved the public abhorrence. In spite of his noble descent, his behavior was trifling, mean, and extravagant. It was not uncommon for him to dress himself in a woman's habit, and then to patrol the fort in which he resided. Such freaks of low humor exposed him to the universal contempt of the people; but their indignation was kindled by his despotic rule, savage bigotry, insatiable avarice, and injustice, not only to the public, but even his private creditors; for he left some of the lowest tradesmen, in his employment, unsatisfied in their just demands."[*]

Such was the man whom the Presbyterians of Jamaica long had cause to remember. To honor his memory[†] must be to disregard the most authentic tes-

---

[*] Smith, I. pp. 190, 194.
[†] See a Discourse by the Rev. W. M. Carmichael, D. D., delivered at Hempstead, 1841.

timony as to his true character. "Cornbury became so obnoxious to the inhabitants of this province that they sent a complaint to England against him. The queen in consequence of this complaint displaced him."* "Lord Cornbury did more to bring disgrace upon the administration of the Colony than all his predecessors together. There was never probably a Governor of New York so universally detested, and who so richly deserved it."† Grahame says, " in every quarter of the province the Governor offered his assistance to the Episcopalians, to put them in possession of the ecclesiastical edifices that other sects had built, and to the disgrace of some of the zealots of Episcopacy, this offer was in various instances accepted, and produced the most disgusting scenes of riot, injustice, and confusion."

* Notes on Brooklyn, by the Hon. G. Furman, p. 108.
† Thompson, II. 108.

HISTORY

OF THE

PRESBYTERIAN CHURCH,

JAMAICA, L. I.

CHAPTER I.

Preliminary.

POLITICAL HORIZON TWO CENTURIES AGO—CROMWELL—CHARLES II.—CONDITION OF THOUGHT AND KNOWLEDGE—BAXTER, BUNYAN, OWEN, HOWE, ELLIOTT—HARVARD COLLEGE—NEWSPAPERS—MINISTERS IN NEW YORK AND BROOKLYN—SCHOOLMASTERS—THE FIRST IN JAMAICA—RELIGIOUS HORIZON—THE FIRST COMPANIES OF PURITANS LEAVE ENGLAND—CHARLES AND LAUD—THE SCOTTISH COVENANT AND CIVIL WAR—PRESBYTERIANS AND CAVALIERS—CHARLES II. INVITED TO THE THRONE—HIS INGRATITUDE TO THE PRESBYTERIANS—JEREMY TAYLOR—ACT OF UNIFORMITY—ATTEMPT TO ESTABLISH PRELACY IN SCOTLAND—MONUMENT IN GRAYFRIARS CHURCHYARD—REVOLUTION 1688—A "MUSTARD SEED"—THE "EAGLE WING"—PROVIDENCE OF GOD.

IN England, two hundred years ago, the people were feeling the throes of that mighty convulsion, which attended the long struggle between her sovereigns and their parliaments, and which issued at length in binding up together "the rights of the people and the title of the reigning dynasty." In 1660, two years before the establishment of a Christian congregation in this place, Charles II. had been restored to the throne. From 1649, when his father was executed, the government had been administered by a Council of State and the Parliament until 1653, when Oliver Cromwell dissolved the parliament and assumed the reins of government. Oliver was at the zenith of his greatness in 1656, when the first settlers came to Jamaica. England, from the insignificant position she had held for half a century, rose to be one of the most formidable powers of the world; her naval victories, under Blake and Dean over De Ruyter and Tromp, established her title as mistress of the seas.

Charles II. came to the throne with no mean abilities, with amiable qualities, and from "a school of bitter experience," which might have made him a great and good monarch. He was greeted by his subjects with a love and devotion such as none of his predecessors had known. But addicted, immoderately, to sensual indulgence and frivolous pleasures, incapable of friendship, without gratitude for favours, insensible to reproach, without desire for renown, with an utter detestation for business, he relinquished the direction of public affairs, and allowed himself to become a mere puppet in the hands of the worthless parasites who gathered around him. He spurned from the foot of the throne loyal subjects, without whose aid he never could have gained it. The vices of the court were not long in infecting the morals and manners of the people. Enforced decorum and sanctity under the Puritan rule, when the restraint was taken off and an example which discouraged no excess was set in high places, was soon followed by the opposite extreme, and the people became greedy for licentious pleasures and frivolous amusements. The writings of infidels, in which the obligations of morality were relaxed and religion was degraded, as in the pagan systems of old, into a mere affair of state, were eagerly welcomed by courtiers and fine gentlemen. The play-houses were re-opened and crowded, and became seminaries of vice. The female character was degraded and the education of high-born women neglected, as it had never been since the revival of learning, and as it has never been since. In literature France gave law to the world. The fountains of the great deep of evil seemed to be broken up, and to be flooding the land; and as the years of this reign progressed the national virtue sunk to the lowest point.

In 1662, Newton was yet to make his great discoveries. It was not, it is said, till 1666 he first conceived the idea of gravitation, by seeing an apple fall from a tree, which led to his theory of planetary motion—a theory which required nearly another century, before it was confirmed beyond a doubt. Chemistry, botany, geology, and even geography were almost unknown sciences. A fact so important to medical science as the circulation of the blood had been known to physicians but five years, and the Royal Society of England had just come into existence. The full strength and elevation of the French language was just then being demonstrated by the celebrated writers who flourished under Louis XIV.; but "it may be doubted," says Lord Macaulay, "whether any one of the forty members of the French Academy had an English volume in his library, or knew Shakspeare, Jonson, or Butler by name." The Augustan era of Spanish literature was already past, and German literature was a thing of the future. The world was yet to receive that imperishable monument of Milton's fame, the Paradise Lost. Bunyan was lying in Bedford jail with his Bible and Fox's Book of Martyrs, composing his immortal allegory. Baxter had a few years before, whilst a chaplain in the army, with no other books than the Bible and a Concordance written the Saints' Rest, and was yet to compose the greater portion of his voluminous productions. The most important works of the great Dr. Owen had not then been published. John Howe was yet to produce those writings, which are still so highly valued in the religious world. John Wesley had not been raised up, as by the visible hand of God, to withstand the prevailing indifferentism and infidelity of his day. Protestant missions among the heathen were unknown. The Indian Testament of John Elliott had just been printed; his Indian Bible was not completed. No English copy of the Scriptures had been printed in America. The authorized version had been finished only fifty years before.

In 1662, there was but one college in the colonies, and not a single newspaper until nearly forty years after this date. Tea was unknown, as it was also in the mother country. No settlement had been made in Pennsylvania, South Carolina, and Georgia. The Mississippi River had not been navigated, except by the canoes of the Red Men; nor was it even known to the civilized world. The entire white population of New England did not probably exceed fifty thousand. Brooklyn, now a city of more than two hundred and fifty thousands, contained a population of less than one hundred and forty persons. It had one Dutch church,* having one elder and twenty-four members. New

---

* Dominic Selyns Letter to the Classis of Amsterdam, 1660, in Doc. Hist. of New York, vol. iii., p. 109.

Amsterdam, now New York, with its eight hundred thousand, had about fifteen hundred inhabitants,* not two hundred and fifty of whom were capable of bearing arms. A dozen butchers could supply its shambles. A house and garden, at the corner of the present Wall and Pearl streets, could be bought for $220. The rent of a house of the better class was $80 per annum; the rent of an ordinary house, fifteen beaver skins, or $36. Beaver skins were the most stable article of currency, valued at six guilders, or $2.40.† In addition to the two ministers in New York, the one at Albany, and the one at Brooklyn, the Dutch had but two ministers in the entire province of New Netherlands, one at Middelwout (Flatbush), and one at Æsopus (Kingston).‡ Schoolmasters were still fewer. In 1657, there were but three in all the Dutch and English villages in the province. The earliest record of one in Jamaica is in 1676,§ when by vote of the town, Richard Jones was allowed to use the meeting-house, provided he swept it out and arranged the seats for the Sabbath.

When that struggle to which the English constitution is indebted for its principles of liberty, as I have said, was at its height, the settlement of Jamaica was made. The storm which arose during the reign of James I., and drove the first companies of Puritans from their native shore, in its next sweep drove his successor from the throne, and prostrated that throne

---

* Letter of Burgomasters to W. I. Co., in 1664, in Valentine's Man. 1860. p. 592.
† Valentine's Manual for 1860. Historical Minutes, &c.
‡ Letter of Dominie Selyns.   § Town Records.

in the dust. The attempt of Charles and Laud to force on the people of Scotland the English liturgy, gave to England her liberty. They formed the celebrated covenant to maintain their ecclesiastical rights and immunities, and took up arms against the king. Civil wars ensued, which ended in the execution of Charles and the elevation of Cromwell to power. Ten years, however, had not elapsed, when the sense of evils, and the fear of greater ones to come, brought about an alliance between the Cavaliers and the Presbyterians, and led to the restoration. The Presbyterians occupied a middle position between the high church prelatic party, who aimed to restore absolute monarchy, and the Independents and other sectaries, who would have destroyed all royal authority. A new parliament met at Westminster, in which the Presbyterians formed the majority. Charles II. was invited to return, and was proclaimed king with a pomp never known before. For a time he affected to treat, perhaps really desired to treat, the Presbyterian clergy, who had given such proof of loyalty, with respect and kindness. But his councillors and ministers were bent on enforcing the prelatic system by the strong hand of power. The ministers in Ireland had the honorable pre-eminence of being the first to suffer in the three kingdoms. Immediately after the restoration, in 1661, the celebrated Jeremy Taylor, Bishop of Down and Connor, under a law which, it was claimed, the restoration brought again into force, in the most summary manner declared thirty-six of the Presbyterian churches located within his diocese, vacant. The year 1662 was perhaps memorable beyond any other in the history of the Presbyterian Church. In that year, on the 19th of May, was passed the Act of Uniformity, which went into force on the 24th of August, by which two thousand Presbyterian ministers, including such men as Baxter, Bates and Calamy were ejected from their ecclesiastical preferments. In October of the same year, Charles II. gave orders prohibiting the meeting of Synods, Presbyteries and Kirk sessions, and establishing prelacy in Scotland. Sharp, Lauderdale and Claverhouse entered on their bloody work. On a monumental stone in the Grayfriars churchyard, Edinburgh, may be seen an inscription, which states, that between 1661 and 1688, 1800 persons are computed to have suffered death for their faith. The revolution in 1688 was important, not so much for the overthrow of the Stuarts as for rescuing the fundamental laws of the realm from their sad and long perversion, and settling the principle that the king has no divine right to disregard those fundamental laws.

But observe, as may be done at this distance of time, looking back on the map of the past, the wonderful movements of Divine Providence. Whilst the Presbyterian Church was struggling for its very existence in fatherland, and all the power of the State was employed to eradicate it from the soil, a little seed had been wafted to these shores, and was sending forth a shoot in the newly-cleared wilderness which has now grown to a size in comparison with which the parent stock is like one of the lesser trees of the forest. The tempest which in 1636 swept the EAGLE WING,* with

---

* See Foote's Sketches of North Carolina, pp. 104-108.

its Presbyterian colony, under the lead of such ministers as John Livingston, Robert Blair, James Hamilton and John McClelland back to Lockfergus, and the order of King Charles which prohibited the departure of the vessel a few years afterwards on a similar voyage, bore back and detained the spirits of the revolution to do a work in Scotland, Ireland, England, which was necessary to be done before the way could be prepared for the new development of liberty and industry in these modern times, on this continent. Well has it been remarked that

"PRINCIPLES, NOT MEN, MUST GOVERN THE WORLD UNDER THE PROVIDENCE OF GOD."

CHAPTER II.

1656–1670.

SETTLEMENT OF JAMAICA — PETITION — LEAVE GIVEN BY GOVERNOR AND COUNCIL — FIRST ENTRY IN THE RECORDS — DECLARATION OF PROPRIETORS — TALL TREES TO BE SPARED — THE TENTHS — YEMACAH — SELLING STRONG DRINK TO INDIANS PROHIBITED — CARE AS TO THE CHARACTER OF SETTLERS — FIRST MAGISTRATES APPOINTED — EARLY PREACHING — ARRANGEMENTS FOR A MINISTER — A MINISTER'S HOUSE TO BE BUILT — MR. WALKER — BEATING THE DRUM ON SABBATH DAYS — AGREEMENT WITH MR. WALKER — MEETING-HOUSE TO BE BUILT — MR. WALKER REQUESTED TO PROCURE ORDINATION — REMOVES TO CONNECTICUT — HIS DESCENDANTS — STYLE OF DWELLINGS — FOOD — CATTLE — HABITS — INDUSTRY — WOMAN — INCREASE IN WEALTH — COMPARATIVE ESTATES OF INDIVIDUALS — DANIEL DENTON — HIS HISTORY — SETTLEMENT OF ELIZABETHTOWN, N. J. — SOCIAL LIFE OF THE PEOPLE — SABBATH AND WORSHIP — DRESS — FUNERALS — THE BURYING GROUND.

JAMAICA was settled during the administration of Peter Stuyvesant. The leading proprietors came from Hempstead, which had been settled in 1644. The petition to the Governor and Council, as will be seen below, is dated 10th of March, 1656, whilst the first entry in the Records of Jamaica is dated 18th of February, 1656. This apparent discrepancy is probably to be accounted for by a confusion between old and new style, or by the use in one instance of the *new*, and in the other of *old* style. The year, according to old style, began March 25th till 1752. The Dutch Governor and Council in answering the petition, and the petitioners in addressing them, would seem to make use of new style regarding the year as having commenced in January, whilst Mr. Denton, the clerk of Jamaica, with English pertinacity, adheres to old style, regarding it as having commenced March 25th, and of course continuing till that date. Several of those whose names are attached to the petition, viz: Jackson, Ireland, Spragg and Carle did not remove to Jamaica.

To the Right Worshipfull Peter Steevesant, Esquire, Governor Generall of the N. Netherlands with the Councell of State there Established.

The humble petition of us subscribed sheweth that where as wee have Twice already petitioned soe are bold once againe to petition un to your worship & honourable Councell for a place to improve our Labours upon; for some of us are destitute of either habitation or possession others Though inhabited yett finde that in the place where they are they cannot comfortably subsist by their Labours & endeavours. By which means they are necessitated to Looke out for a place where they may hope with gods Blessing upon theyr Labours more comfortably to subsist, The place they desire & have alreadie petitioned for is called Conorasset & Lies from a river which divideth it from Conarie see to the Bounds of heemstead & may containe about twentie families this place upon incouragement from your worship by our messenger that presented our petition sent the second tyme wee have purchased from the Indians & are not willing to Remove out of the jurisdiction iff wee may bee tollerated to possesse our purchase & whereas we are desirous To settle our selves this spring wee humbly crave that this place may bee confirmed unto us with as much expedition as may be soe with Apprecation of all happiness to your worship and honoured Councell wee humbly take our leave who are your humble petitioners.

Heemstead the 10th of March 1656.

ROBERT JACKSON,	ABRAHAM SMITH,
NICHOLAS TANNER,	THOMAS IRELAND,
NATHANIEL DENTON,	THOMAS CARLE,
RICHARD EVERIT,	EDWARD SPRAG,
RODGER LINAS,	JOHN ROADES,
DANIEL DENTON,	ANDREW MESSENGER,
JOHN LAZAR,	SAMUEL MATHEWS.

From N. Y. Col. MSS. VI: 336, 337.

[REPLY.]*

On the preceding Petition is it ordered as follows:

The Director & Council having seen the request of the petitioners, at present inhabitants of the town of Heemsteede, & subjects of this Province, do consent that the Petitioners may begin a new Town according to their plan in this respect, between the land by us called Canaresse & the Town Heemsteede, on such Freedoms, Exemptions & special ground briefs as the Inhabitants of N. Netherland generally enjoy, as well in the possession of their lands as in the election of their Magistrates, on the same footing & order as is customary in the towns Middelborch, Breuckelen, Midwout & Amersfoort. Done at Fort Amsterdam in New Netherland, March 21, 1656.

P. STUYVESANT.

NICASIUS DE SILLE
LA MONTAGNE.
COR. VAN TIENHOVEN.

a. R. XII; 337, 339.

The first entry in the records of Jamaica is in these words:

* Translated from the Dutch Records, by E. B. O'Callaghan, Esq.

A town meeting held at ye town ye 18th off Feb., 1656.*

Daniell Denton chosen to write & enter all acts & orders off public concernment to y^s town, & is to have a daie's work a man for ye sayd employment.

It is voted and concluded by ye town y^t whosoever shall fell any trees in ye highways shall take both top & body out off ye highway.

It is further voted & agreed upon by ye town y^t whosoever shall kill a wolf within ye bounds off ye town, shall have fivetcen shillings a wolff.

Likewise it is agreed upon by ye town y^t whereas they have the Little plains by purchase & patent w^t in their limits, to maintain their right & priviledge in ye sayd place from any such as shall goe to deprive y^m off it, & so to make use off it as they shall see cause.

Records I. p. 1.

MEMORANDUM.

The town have given Mr. Robert Coe & his son, Benjamin Coe, each off y^m a home lot.

The town have alsoe given Nicolas Tanner, Abraham Smith, John Lazar, Samuel Smith, Morace Smith, & William Thorne, each off y^m a house lot lying upon ye west quarter.

The town have granted Andrew Messenger, Samuel Mathews, Thomas Wiggins, Richard Chasmore, Richard Harkert, Richard Everet, Henry Townsend, Richard Townsend, John Townsend & John Roades, each off y^m a house lot lying upon ye north quarter.

Records I. p. 1.

---

* New style, March 1st, 1657. By an act of Parliament in 1752, the Gregorian reformation of the calendar was adopted. The eleven days excess was suppressed in September of that year, and the beginning of the year transferred from the 25th of March to January 1.

To Sam'l Dein, Nath. Denton, Geo. Mills, Rodger Linas, Dan'l Denton & Sam'l Andrews each a house lot on ye South quarter. Records I. p. 2.

November ye 25th, 1656, Stylo Novo.*

These presents declareth y^t wee whose names are underwritten, being true owners, by vertue off purchase from ye Indians & grant from ye Governor & Council given & granted ye 21st of March, 1656, I say wee, who are ye true owners by vertue of purchase, & our associates, our names being underwritten, living at ye new plantation near unto ye bever pond, comonly called Jemaica, I say wee in consideration of our charge & trouble in getting & settling off ye place, have reserved unto ourselves ye full & just sum off ten acres off planting land a man, besides ye home lots in ye nearest & convenientest place y^t can be found, & soe likewise 20 acres of medowing * * every man taking his lot according to their first right. Witness our hands this day & date above written.

ROBERT COE,	RODGER LINAS,	RICH. TOWNSEND,
NIC. TANNER,	SAMUEL MATHEWS,	RI. HARKERT,
NAT. DENTON,	JOHN LAZAR.	RI. CHASMORE,
AND. MESSENGER,	RICHARD EVERET,	GEO. MILLS,
DANIELL DENTON,	JOHN TOWNSEND,	JOHN ROADES,
ABRA. SMITH,	HEN. TOWNSEND,	

Records I., p. 2.

Jan. 13th, 1657. It is this day granted by ye town that Mr. Robert Coe & his son Beniamen shall take up, possesse & enioy ten acres off land a piece at ye rear off their home lots.

* New style is here designated. This probably is an earlier date than "ye 18th off Feb. 1656," the latter being old style. After the first town meeting the document was copied for preservation, & *stylo novo* added to explain the seeming discrepancy. Washington was born Feb. 11th, 1731, old style, but on Feb. 22d, 1732, new style.

Feb. 27, 1658. It is agreed upon by the towne y^t according to a former order y^t ye first proprietors & there associates shall have ten acres off planting land a piece in ye most convenient place wch they shall chuse, so y^t ye shall now vew & have their lots layd out according to ye sayd order.

Theese men following doe conclude to have there lots eastward, John Townsend, Rich. Townsend, Henry Townsend, John Roades, Nathaniel Denton, Daniel Denton, Richard Everet, Richard Harkert, George Mills.

These men following take up y^{ere} ten acre lots westward, Nicholas Tanner, Andrew Messenger, Samuel Mathews, John Lazar, Richard Chasmore, Abraham Smith, Rodger Linas.

Richard Townsend and Nicolas Tanner are chosen to lay out the ten acre lots, & to have 2d an acre for y^{ere} labour.

It is voted & agreed upon by ye town y^t Daniel Denton shall bee town clark for ye ensuing year, & to have of some 30 st.* and of others a gilder.

Heny Townsend, Richard Townsend, and Daniel Denton have each of y^m a ten acre lot lying to ye northward off ye way y^t goes to Hemstead on ye side ye Rocky Hollow next adioining to ye home lots upon ye north east quarter. Heny Townsend lying ye first & next adioining to ye north east quarter, Daniel Denton ye next, & Richard Townsends ye 3d & east off ye three.

These ten acre lots above speciffied are given and granted to ye afforesayd men by ye town, and layd out according to order. Records I. pp. 5, 6.

Nov. ye 22d, 1658. A town meeting called, & agreed, & concluded upon by the town that ye medows shall bee layd out for the purchasers, 17 lots, 20 acres a lot. Rich-

* St.—stivers.

ard Everet, Rodger Linas, Richard Harker, and John Lazar chosen to lay out ye medow, & have 3d an acre for their labor. Records I. p. 4.

In the deed of purchase obtained from the Indians are the following singular words: "One thing to be remembered, that noe person is to cut downe any trees wherein Eagles doe make their nests." The tribes on this part of the island had been subdued in the fierce and cruel wars under Captain Underhill, Ensign Opdyke, and Peter Cock; and the occupation of their lands, purchased for some trifling consideration, was undisputed. The Dutch government, in its "ground-briefs," claimed of the inhabitants of New Netherlands "the tenth part of all the revenue that shall arise from the ground manured with the plow and hoe, in case it be demanded before it be housed, gardens and orchards not exceeding one Holland acre excepted."*

The name given to this town by the original settlers was Jemaica, evidently derived from Yemacah, (so written in the Town Records and not *Jemeco* as by Thompson,) the name of a branch, or a few families, of the Rockewa tribe of Indians, who resided along the small stream, running from Beaver Pond, and at the head of the bay. The Dutch government conferred on the settlement the name of Rusdorp, which occurs frequently in the early records, and was probably used exclusively in conveyances of property. After the surrender of the colony to the English, Jamaica soon came to be exclusively used.

* Thompson, II., 6.

—— —— 30th. It is y⁸ day voted, ordered and agreed upon by this town of Rustdorp, that no person or persons whatsoever, within this town, shall sell or give directly or indirectly, to any Indian or Indians whatsoever, within or about y⁶ said town, any strong licker or strong drinke whatsoever or of what sort soever, either much or little, more or less, upon the forffeiture off fifty Guilders [nearly twenty dollars] for every offence.

Jan. 21st, 1659. One Benjamin Hubard, who had bought a house-lot, without the approbation or knowledge of the town, was required to bind himself "to behave so in the town y⁴ he no waies prejudice his neighbours, by any unlawful or bad courses; and y⁶ said Benjamin doth engage himself iff he shall fullfill not all and every particular in y⁶ premises, to surrender up his lot again to the town."

Records I. p. 6.

Town made choice of Four men to be presented for magistrates to y⁶ Governor, viz:

Mr. Coe, Rich. Everet, Samuell Mathews and Luke Watson.

Nath'l Denton to present y^m to y⁶ Governor Aug. 6, 1659.

Sep. 9th, 1659. Sam'l Mathews, John Townsend & Ben. Coe, chosen assistants for a Court for this yeare.

Records I. p. 8.

The inhabitants early manifested a desire to have a minister of the Gospel settled among them. The minister of Hempstead no doubt often visited, and preached to them. Dominie Drisius, one of the Dutch ministers of New York, preached at Jamaica, January 8, 1661, "to correct the irregularities of Quakers and other Itinerant fanatics."* It is quite certain that pub-

---

* Mr. Onderdonk's MS Notes.

lic worship was regularly established as early at least as 1662.

Wee whose names are underwritten doe by these presents promise & engage that if any meeting or conventicles of quakers, shall bee in this town of Rustdorp, then we will give information to ye authority set up in this place by the Governor, and alsoe assist the authority of the town against any such person or persons called quakers, as need shall require. Witness our hands this 11th day of February, 1661. Stylo novo.

RICHARD EVERITT,   ANDREW MESSENGER,
NATH. DENTON,   BENIEMEN COE,
ABRA. SMITH,   GEORGE MILLS,
SAMUEL MATHEWS,   WILLIAM FOSTER.

[The rest of the names are illegible, it being the last page of the 1st vol.]   Records, I. p. 120.

62, March ye 6th. The town doe give Abraham Smith 30s ffor beating ye drum a year.

It is ordered by ye town y^t ye rates ffor ye minester shall bee leavied upon medowes ffor ye minester.

Records p. 14, vol. I.

It is ffurther ordered & agreed by ye town y^t ye townsmen [torn off in the original] shall look affter ye procuring off a minester.   Records p. 15.

March ye 13th, 62. It is ordered y^t those wch doe not appear at ye beating off ye drum y^t day & goe to burn ye woods, shall pay 2s. 6d. to those wch goe.

It is further ordered by ye town to build a house ffor ye minester off 36 ffoot long.

It is ordered and agreed by ye town y^t John Baylie shall keep an Ordinary in ye town of Rusdorp, for ye entertaining of strangers, and also to sell drink, and that noe man shall have liberty to sell drink, whether beer or liquors, or any sort of wine, within this town only the Ordinary

keeper aforesaid, and y^t he shall forthwith set upon ye work to provide for strangers, and to give entertainment to such strangers as shall come.
Records I. p. 15.

Aprill ye 11th 62. It is ye day ordered by ye town y^t A minester's house shall bee built, 26 foot long & 17 foot wide according as is agreed by covenant betwixt ye town & Andrew Messenger & his Son, Richard Darling, who have taken ye building of ye house of ye town and are to pay twentie-three pounds in bever pay y^t is to say, wheat, at sixe shillings, & indian corn at three shillings sixe pence ye bushell; to bee payd after ye work is done as soon as ye corn is merchantable & ye town doe ingage every man to pay & bring in what shall come to their shares, at such time & to such place as y^o [it] shall be appointed within ye town of Rustdorp.

Goodman Messenger hath promised to take Sam. Mills his rate for ye minester's house, in indian corn.
Records I. p. 16.

April ye 11th 1662. Articles of agreement concluded & agreed upon betwixt the town of Rusdorp on ye one party and Andrew Messenger and his son Richard Darling on ye other.

The town have hired ye aforesayd Andrew Messenger, & Richard Darling to build a house for ye Minester of twentie-six feet long & seaventeen foot broad to bee ten foot high in ye stood [stud] betwixt ioint and ioint ye house to bee well claboarded ye sides & ends, ye roof to bee well & sufficiently shingled w^t three foot shingle; two chimnies to bee made in ye house, one belowe for a lower room & another for ye chamber. Two floores of ioice & boards to be layd one above in ye chamber thoroughout ye house & another under foot: to bee well iointed & sufficiently layed above & below; a partition to bee made handsomely & well smoothed & ——— alsoe a payr of stears, well & stronglie made to goe into yᵉ chamber wᵗ an outward door & inward door, & a door into yᵉ chamber, the chimnies alsoe to bee well *slatted.* Three windowes, large & handsome, two below & one above, the timber all to bee such as may be iudged sufficient by workmen wᵗ ground sills & good girts, cross yᵉ house to lay ioice; yᵉ house thorout to bee well and sufficiently braced: this house is to bee done by yᵉ midle of August next ensuing. The town are to provide yᵐ wᵗ nailes and hinges, & also claboard & shingles, & sawn boards for yᵉ inward work; likewise yᵉ town shall cart all yᵉ timber or other stuff needful for yᵉ sayd house. In consideration of yᵉ premises yᵉ town are to give yᵉ sayd Andrew Messenger, & Richard Darling, yᵉ full sum of twentie three pounds, after yᵉ English account to bee payd in wheat & indian corn; wheat at six shillings yᵉ bushel, & indian corn, at three shillings six-pence; to be payd at Christmas next, or as soon as it is merchantable; to bee payd in as many bushells of wheat as indian corn: yᵗ yˢ is our act, we testifie by subscribing our hands yᵉ day & date above written.

       ANDREW MESSENGER,
       RICHARD DARLING.
Subscribed before Daniel Denton. Records I. p. 17.

 May yᵉ 11th, 1662. A town meeting called; agreed upon with Goodman Baylie, & Samuel Smith to get stones for yᵉ minester's house enough to make a back for *the* chimnies & harths & ovens, good & sufficient stone for yᵉ work, as yᵉ place will afford to bee got & brought in place by this time six weeks: they are to have forty shillings for yᵉ sayd work:

 Goodman Messenger & his son Richard Darling are to get *the* shingles for the minesters house and to have half a crown a hundred for yᵉ shingles the shingles to be three foot long & not above six inches broad w^t ye sap hewd out : al ye money above written to bee payd in ye same pay y^t ye carpenters have, or at ye same prices

Records I. p. 18.

August ye 9th.

Henry Whitney and Ric. Everet deputed to lay out some of ye towns money in Mr. Coe's hands and alsoe some in ye sayd everets hands to buy boards for ye minesters house & lime & to hire a mason : if need require.

Records I. p. 18.

They evidently set a high value on the gospel, not delaying until some missionary, by foreign aid, should find his way among them, to labor single-handed, in the midst of the indifferent, or opposers, but preparing the way for a minister, by furnishing the means of giving him a welcome reception. Can we wonder that God has so signally blessed an enterprise which was begun in such a spirit? May such men never want worthy successors, who, when the interests of religion demand it, shall be ready, " every man to pay and bring in what shall come to their shares " of any necessary expense!

December 20th, 1662. The town appointed a committee of five men to " make the rate for the minister's house, and transporting the minister;" from which it appears that a minister had now been engaged to settle at Jamaica. And under date of February 14th, 1663, seven years after the settlement of the town, appears for the first time in the records, the name of the first minister of this place,

ZECHARIAH WALKER.

December ye 20th 1662. A town meeting called:

The town have voted & concluded & agreed upon y[t] these five namely Mr. Coe Goodman Benedick Goodman Smith Goodman Baylie & Daniel Denton shall make y[e] rate for y[e] minesters house, & transporting y[e] minester. Goodman Baylie refusing y[e] town have chose Luke Watson.

Records I. p. 20.

January y[o] 12th, 62.

A town meeting called: voted & agreed upon by y[e] town y[t] y[e] rate for y[e] minesters house shall be leavied upon medows & home lotts.

Records I. p. 20.

January y[e] 29th, 1663.

It is voted by y[e] town y[t] Abraham Smith shall have thirty shillings a year for beating y[e] drum upon Sabbath days & other publike meetings daies, & to have his pay in tobacco pay or wheat at 6s & 8d & indian at 4s.

Records I. p. 26.

February y[e] 14th, 1663. A town meeting called:

Voted & agreed upon by y[e] town y[t] Goodman Benedick and Nathaneel Denton shall be overseers in behalf of y[e] town to supply Mr. Walker's wants w[t] what hee shall stand in need of according as y[e] town shall agree to make a supply: and to appoint men as their turns come to bring in what shall bee needfull in y[e] premises, as need shall require:

Voted by y[e] town at what rate or price Mr. Walkers maintenance shall bee payd in: concluded y[t] hee shall have three score pounds per annum; y[t] it shall bee payd by rate y[e] rates to bee leavied upon lands & estates: that is to bee payd in corn: y[e] wheat to be payd at six shillings a bushell and indean at three shillings six-pence bushell.

Records p. 21.

February 14th, 1663. It is voted by y[e] town y[t] Mr. Coe and Goodman Benedick and Daniel Denton shall make a rate for Mr. Walkers maintenance.

Records I. p. 22.

March y⁰ 2d, 1663. Wee whose names are underwritten doe by these presents give unto Mr. Walker his heirs or Assignes y⁰ house & home lot y' hee lives in w' y⁰ accommodations belonging to it, upon y⁰ previso y' iff hee goe away and leave y⁰ town w' out any just grounds or cause given by y⁰ town y' y" y⁰ town shall have y⁰ reffusall of it paying for such labours as hee hath or shall expend upon it & it shall return again to y⁰ town: but iff y⁰ town shall act soe y' they bee y⁰ cause off his going away y" y⁰ lot to remain as his and his heirs onely y⁰ town to have y⁰ reffusal off it to buy it for what it shall be worth & iff it happen y' y⁰ sayd Mr. Walker should die y" his wife shall let y⁰ town have y⁰ reffusall off it iff she shall sell it.

ROBERT COE,	RODGER LINAS,
JOHN STICLAN,	JOHN HINDS,
THOMAS BENEDICK,	BENIAMIN COE,
ANDREW MESSENGER,	WILLIAM SMITH,
DANIEL DENTON,	JOSEPH THURSTON,
JOHN BAYLIES,	NATHANIELL DENTON,
THOMAS FOSTER,	SAMUELL SMITH,
RICHARD EVERETT,	WILLIAM BRINKLY,
EDWARD ROUSE,	JOHN RODES,
JOHN SKIDMORE,	WILLIAM FOSTER,
HENRY WHITNEY,	GEORG CUMMINS.
ABRAHAM SMITH,	
SAMUELL MATHEWS,	Records I. p. 25.

The above twenty-four names include, it is probable, the whole number of freeholders in the town at the time. From the foregoing extracts it appears that Mr. Walker's salary was £60 per annum, with the use of a house and a home lot, to be his in fee-simple if he remained as minister of the town, or if the town should so act as to be the cause of his going away. In raising this generous support, so much beyond what many infant churches at the present day, especially in new settlements, feel themselves able to do, every inhabitant contributed his due proportion.

Mr. Walker was a young man about twenty-five years of age, and preached at Jamaica as a licentiate. Mr. Wood says he probably came from England, and Mr. Crane, in his MS. history of this church, adds that he probably came from England before he was ordained, but as a licentiate. Mr. Thompson, however, asserts that he was a native of Boston, and was the son of Robert Walker, who was made a freeman at that place in 1634, where Zechariah was born in 1637.

August ye 30th 1663. A town meeting called voted & agreed upon by ye town y^t A meeting house shall bee built twentie-six foot square, & that Mr. Coe & Ralph Keeler shall agree to George Norton for ye building off it.
Records I. p. 27.

December ye 1st 1663 Old Style :
Further voted y^t Francis Finch and Abraham Smith shall bring in an account of men's estates as soon as may bee, y^t a rate may be made for ye minester.
Records I. p. 28.

December ye 3de, '63. Further voted and concluded upon y^t all ye inhabitants of this our town shall pay towards ye maintenance of ye minestry according to what ye possesse.
Records I. p. 29.

Feb. ye 27th '63. Further voted y^t Samuel Mathews & Joseph Smith shall succeed Thomas Benedick & Nath: Denton in gathering up & looking affter to supply Mr. Walker w^t such things as hee shall stand in need off.
Records I. p. 32.

December y⁰ 13th 1664. Joseph Thurstone & John Heins apointed to gather up an acount of men's estates for Mr. Walker's rate:

Thomas Benedick Senior & Daniel Denton shall make a rate for yᵉ minester Records I. p. 32

Att a toune meeting the 4th of September 1665 itt was Agreed that Mr. Walker shall have three score ponds a yeare well & truly payd in corn at prise currant or other pay equivolent and this to be cearfully gathered & payd in to Mr. Zacharah Walker yearly within the moneth of December evary yeare Denring the time of Mr. Walkers aboode & exarcising his giwfts amonngst us as before as likewise for his farther in curidgement the town doth agree to cut & drawe all the wood hee spends to till his ground et harvest his corn, besides the three score ponds Above mentioned .....* it is farther to be understod that Mr. Walker is to take his whete at 5 shilling pr bushells and other pay equifolent, as likewise for the tiladge of his ground it is to be understood that ground only yᵗ Mr. Walker hath now broke up. Records I. p. 40.

March yᵉ 12th 166⅔. At a town meeting fully agreed upon that Mr. Walker shall have in liew off what is above written, sixtie-five pounds p. annum to bee payd as is above writen in wheat at five shillings p. bushell provided Mr. Walker does engage to continue wᵗ us from year to year & also procure an ordination answerable to the yᵉ law whereby hee does not only capacitate himself for yᵉ preaching off yᵉ word but for yᵉ baptizing off infants: & so yᵉ above written order for tilling off land & yᵉ like to bee rendered null:* at a town meeting off yᵉ constable & overseers agreed upon yᵗ Mr. Coe shall have the five pounds mentioned in yᵉ next above written agreement & in lew thereoff shall doe yᵉ work mentioned in yᵉ agree-

---

* What follows is in different ink and hand and at another time.

ment to Mr. Walker uppermost written according as is there exprest. Robart Coe Geo Woolsey William Rescoe Daniel Denton Beniamin Coe Andrew Mesinger John Foster Samuel Smith John Roads Joseph Smith

Records I. p. 40.

This proposal, that he should procure ordination, as it shows a solicitude to enjoy the ordinances of the gospel, and particularly recognizes the duty of dedicating their offspring to God in baptism, speaks volumes in favour of the piety of the first inhabitants. He did not, it would seem, obtain ordination agreeably to the wishes of the town, for he took his departure from Jamaica shortly after, in consequence, as is evident, of the strong desire of the people to have an ordained minister. On the 7th of August, 1668, the town appointed a committee to make a final settlement with him. This committee was directed to pay him for the improvements he had made on the parsonage and glebe, from which it is evident, according to the terms of the agreement made March 2d, 1663, that his departure was not from any occasion given by the people.

He went to Stratford, Conn., where he received ordination, but removed to Woodbury in 1678, of which place he was the first minister, and where he died, January, 1699, aged sixty-two. Robert Walker, who was a Judge of the Superior Court of Connecticut, is said by Thompson to have been his son, and Gen. Joseph Walker, an officer of the Revolution, his grandson.

It is quite certain that there was no church regularly constituted during Mr. Walker's residence in Jamaica.

february 23 Anno 1666 It was agreed that Abraham

Smith shall haufe thirtie schelinges a year for beting of the drum of the Sabbath day this to be paid by the town in generall his time to begin from the date heirof this was agreed upon by a full town meeting.   Records I. p. 42.

the 7 of august 1668 At a tound meeting the tound have chosen John Foster nathaniel Denton mister waters & John Ouldfield & given them full power to agre with Mr Walker consarning the price that the tound shall give mister walker for the land that he has now in posetion or the price onle for the labors that he has bestowed upon the land which they shall judg just & equall & if thes men above mentioned & mister walker can not agre they have liberty to chouse 2 men of another tound mister walker on & thay a nother to judg the price of the land & labors or onle the labors as mister walker & thes four men shall agre

By me John Skidmore Clark

Records I. p. 45.

the 14 of September 1668

At a tound meting the tound have voted & concluded to take the Best & prudents corse as may be for the procuring of a minister as sone as convenient time will permit   Records I. p. 46.

How very humble an aspect this place must have presented two hundred years ago! A cluster of houses in the wilderness, the greater part of them built of logs, and roofed with thatch from the marshes! Let us, in imagination, enter one of them. We find, perhaps, two ceiled or covered rooms below, with lofts above for chambers, and a lean-to kitchen, unceiled and open to the roof. We find in them no luxurious furniture such as fills our dwellings. On their tables are a few pewter dishes and spoons, with wooden bowls and trenchers. For food they do not lack venison and fish, but bread is scarce; even the crusts of their fathers' tables in old England would have been esteemed a luxury. It often consisted of little more than meal and water and salt, boiled to the consistency of pudding. Their dinner was of boiled Indian pudding, boiled Indian corn mixed with beans, with a slice of salted venison, with boiled cabbage, baked or boiled pumpkin, brown bread and cider, or home-brewed beer. At breakfast and supper milk or pea-porridge took the place of tea and coffee. Cooking which required sugar was too expensive for our early ancestors. They felt greatly the want of cattle, swine and sheep. The few they had were by day committed to herdsmen* and nightly brought to strong enclosures of logs within the settlement, and put under the care of watchdogs for security against wild beasts and depredations of the savages that still roamed the forest. They rise early (in the winter before the dawn) and enter on the duties of the day. Family worship and breakfast over they are in summer in the field by six o'clock. A gun is carried along with the implements of husbandry, not so much through fear of the Indians as that they may be prepared, should a wolf, or bear, or deer be discovered while at their toil. Their dress was fitted to their work. The father wore an old three-cornered hat, no cravat, short frock of strongest warp, leather breeches and leggins confined above the knee and tied over the shoe like a buskin. The boys wore close-fit-

---

* Paid 12s. a week.

ting caps of home manufacture, short jackets of the coarsest fabric, with leather breeches and leggins. The duties of the women were more onerous than those of the men. Whether sick or well, the baking, cooking, washing, ironing and clothes making and mending had to be done, and there was no hired help to be had. Their work was unremitting as the morning and evening, summer as well as winter. Many of them had been nurtured amid the luxuries of the best homes of England. "On the unfloored hut, she, who had been nurtured amid the rich carpets and curtains of the mother land, rocked her new-born babe and complained not. She, who in the home of her youth, had arranged the gorgeous shades of embroidery, or, perchance, had compounded the rich venison pastry as her share in the house-keeping, now pounded the coarse Indian corn for her children's bread, and bade them ask God's blessing ere they took their scanty portion. When the snows sifted through their miserable roof trees upon her little ones, she gathered them closer to her bosom; she taught them the Bible and the catechism and the holy hymn, though the war-whoop of the Indian rang through the wild. Amid the untold hardships of colonial life she infused new strength into her husband by her firmness, and solaced his weary hours by her love."* Not a few of the early settlers had been familiar with the comforts and forms of aristocratic life. With all their cares and gravity they had their festive gatherings and social fireside enjoyments.

As the people prospered, and increased their ma-

* Mrs. Sigourney.

terial possessions, they were able to supply themselves with a better class of houses, and more of the comforts of life. A rate list of "the Towne Estate of Jemaica, *anno* 1683," less than thirty years after the settlement was made, has been preserved,* showing the great progress the town had made in population and wealth. The number of "heads," or rateable polls, had become eighty-seven, which, multiplied by five, the usual mode of estimating population, would show that the number of inhabitants had already increased to four hundred and thirty-five. Samuel Smith is put down as having the largest estate. He had fifty acres of land, (*i. e.* probably land under cultivation, the wild lands not entering into the estimate,) twenty cattle, and two horses. Captain Carpenter stands next to Mr. Smith in the amount of his estate. He was captain of a "company of ffuzileers," and we find him ordered with his company, and such volunteers as were willing to serve his Majesty, to Fort James in New York, to defend it against the fleet of the Prince of Orange, which appeared on the coast in July, 1673.† Nicholas Everit, Joseph Smith, in the order of the value of their estates, come next on the list. Then we have William Creed, John & Jos. Ludly, [Ludlam] Thomas Bayles, Edward Higbee, John Rodes, Sen., Nathaniel Denton, Sen., all of them among the most prosperous of the citizens, and all of them still represented by numerous descendants in this congregation. Nathaniel Denton had fifty-five, the largest number of acres under cultivation. Daniel Denton, the Town Clerk, now famous among

---

* Doc. Hist. of N. Y., Vol. II. p. 519. See Addenda, in this Vol.
† Doc. Hist. N. Y. Vol. III. pp. 91-99.

bibliographers and antiquarians as the author of the earliest account or history of New York, appears to have had a much smaller amount of property than any of the foregoing. He is set down as possessed of no land, two horses, three cattle, and an estate of £56. His work was published in 1670, under the title of "A Brief Description of New York, formerly called New Netherlands," etc., and was republished by the Historical Society of Philadelphia, and by Gowans of New York, as late as 1845. He was a son of the Rev. Richard Denton of Hempstead, and was associated with his brother Nathaniel, John Bailey, John Foster, and Luke Watson, in the purchase [1664] of a large tract of land in New Jersey, and in the settlement of Elizabethtown. "The four families found at Elizabethtown by (Gov.) Carteret, were the pioneers of the Jamaica Colony."* But neither of the Dentons became permanent residents of Elizabethtown. Daniel was schoolmaster, doctor, and justice, as well as clerk and author. He probably visited England at the time his work was published. The following somewhat singular minute is in the Records: "June ye 13 [1684] it is voted that Mr. Daniel Denton shall have liberty to come and setell himselfe & his family in this towne. By Ben. Coe, Clark." p. 132. The rate list also shows the number of horses, cattle, and swine, owned among the people at its date. During the seven years preceding 1688, there were in Jamaica twenty-seven marriages, seventy-one baptisms, and twenty-three burials.† The number of baptisms would clearly

---

* Whitehead's E. Jersey under the Proprietors, pp. 38, 39.
† Doc. Hist. N. Y., Vol. III. p. 197. See Addenda, in this Vol.

indicate the continuance of Mr. Denton's Presbyterian practice of baptizing the children of such parents as were not members of the church.*

The labours of the day are over. It is a winter evening. Captain Carpenter, Daniel Denton, Thomas Bayles, and others have come, let us suppose, to spend it at the house of Nicholas Everit. They have nuts and cider or home-brewed beer. The older ones of the party talk of *home*, as they still love to call the country from which they have fled. They describe cities and palaces to the wondering children, born in the wilderness, and who have seen no grander house than that in which the minister lives. Perhaps some one has served in the armies of Cromwell or the King, and tells how battles were fought, and lost or won. Perhaps some one was present, or had seen those who were present when the King was beheaded in front of the banqueting hall of his own palace, and describes the fearful scene. Or they talk of that dreadful plague in London which had just then swept off so many of its inhabitants that grass grew in the streets, and the whole city presented a scene of mournful desolation; or that memorable conflagration, which destroyed more than thirteen thousand houses and eighty-nine churches, making night as clear as day to the distance of miles around, its effect on the sky being perceptible even on the Scottish border. Perhaps some one had heard Baxter preach, and tells of his melting voice and terrible appeals. Or they tell stories of witchcraft, in which delusion they shared with the best and wisest people of their age, Sir Mathew Hale himself not excepted;

* p. 63 seq.

for in 1670 we find the people of Jamaica petitioning the Governor against a certain witch settling here, a woman* from Wethersfield; the poor creature seeking rest found none, as she had been expelled from that place on the same charge. Or they tell stories of fearful encounters with wild beasts, or of successful hunting expeditions. Or they talk of the bloody Indian wars; and some one tells of the seven Indians who were arrested and confined in a cellar at Hempstead on a charge of theft; though it was afterwards discovered that some Englishmen had themselves committed the crime, and how Governor Kieft sent Underhill and Ensign Opdyke, with a band of soldiers, to punish them.† Or they tell how this same Underhill (called by the Dutch annalist, Sergeant Major Van der Hyl) was sent to take vengeance on Pennewitz, a great sachem of the country, and with one hundred and twenty soldiers marched towards Hempstead, and at a place called Matsepe (Massapequa?) about one hundred and twenty of the Indians were slain.‡

Thus passes the evening away. But the company disperses at an early hour, making their way cautiously along the rough and overshadowed paths and roads; for those who did not permit the daylight to find them in their beds, retired early to their rest.

Or, let us try to imagine the scene presented here on a Sabbath morning two hundred years ago. The day is observed with a strictness now unknown in the general community. At the morning family prayer several chapters are read from the Bible. After break-

---

* Catherine Harrison. Mr. Onderdonk's notes.
† See Breeden Raedt, as translated in Doc. Hist. N. Y. Vol. IV. p. 105.
‡ On the bounds of Hempstead and Jamaica is a river then called Massepe.

fast an hour is occupied by the children in learning by heart a portion of Scripture, a psalm from Sternhold and Hopkins, and the catechism. The father hears them say their lessons, and acts as the superintendent of this, the best of Sabbath schools. At eleven o'clock Abraham Smith* beats the drum; for the sound of the church-going bell was as yet unheard among "the valleys and rocks" of this island. The entire population are astir, wending their way towards the house of God. The people of Hempstead passed an order, 1650, in their general court, imposing a fine, which was to be doubled at every repetition of the offence, on every person who "without just and necessary cause" should neglect to attend "public meetings on the Lord's day and public days of fasting and thanksgiving, *both forenoon and afternoon.*"† They are said to have been more rigid in this respect than the people of any other town on the island; but in all of them there appears to have been an enforced pecuniary support of, and attendance on the preaching of the Gospel. In the throng we see going up to the sanctuary, are representatives of every, or nearly every family in the settlement. The dress of those whose pecuniary means afford it, is expensive, elaborate, and ornamental. The men wear broad-brimmed hats, turned up into three corners, with loops at the side; long coats with large pocket folds and cuffs, without collars, having buttons of the size of a half dollar, plated or of pure silver; vests without collars, very long, with graceful lappet-pockets; shirts with ruffled bosoms and wristbands,

---

* Town Records, Jan. 30, 1662, and Jan. 29, 1663.
† Dr. N. S. Prime's Hist. of L. I., p. 280.

3

with gold or silver sleeve buttons; neck cloths of fine linen, or figured or embroidered stuff; small-clothes with silver buckles of liberal size; and shoes ornamented with straps and silver buckles. A finely dressed gentleman wore a chocolate colored coat, buff vest, full bush wig powdered white, and white top boots. The best dress of the rich was a scarlet coat, with full sleeves, and cuffs reaching to the elbows, the wristbands and vest fringed with lace, with gold buttons and sword. The visiting dress of ladies was more costly, complicated, and ornamental than their husbands and brothers wore. Their bonnets were of silk or satin; their gowns rich brocades, extremely long waisted, with long trails and expanded farthingales, ornamented with flounces and spangles. But on the Sabbath their apparel was simple and appropriate; a cheap straw bonnet with a single bow outside, calico dress of sober colors, simple white muslin collar, neat shawl, and a stout pair of shoes.*

The gathering people enter the sanctuary. It is a humble edifice built of logs and thatched. It is without pews or pulpit; benches supply the place of the one, and a table or rude desk that of the other. This, doubtless, was the character of the house, (for precisely such a house was built by the first settlers at Easthampton, and in other places,) which this town voted to build in 1663.

The people are all assigned seats by some one appointed for the purpose, according to their age and

---

* For habits and manners of the colonists, see Hist. of Medford, Mass., by Rev. Charles Brooks; Hist. of Dorchester, to which I am specially indebted; Hollister's Hist. of Conn.; Palfrey's New England, Vol. II.

standing in the community; a tythingman sits among the children. Mr. Denton, or perhaps "Goodman Benedic," lines a psalm out of Sternhold and Hopkins, and the services proceed. Their souls are borne upward by song and prayer, or are melted within them as they hear the young preacher tell of the rest that remaineth in that better land, which they expect to enter, at their next remove. The Scriptures are read and commented upon.* The hour-glass stands by the side of the Bible, and has run out, been turned, and half run out again, when the service closes. The people spend a half hour of intermission around the doors, or under the neighboring trees, when they enter again to sing, and pray, and hear the word. The service closes, at half-past two, and the people go home to partake of a meal, chiefly prepared on the preceding day, in which the dinner and supper of ordinary days are united. The Sabbath day apparel is now taken off and the mother gathers her little ones around her to hear the Catechism, and question them respecting the texts and sermons of the day, and to talk to them as only mothers can, of Christ and heaven. Thus ends our forefathers' sabbath.

Or death enters (for where does death enter not?) the infant settlement,† and they are gathered, to deposit in the newly-cleared soil, one, who came into the wilderness only to die. How many tender memories are awakened in those who have left the graves of their

---

* Reading the Bible without comment was called dumb reading, and an imitation of the hierarchical church. Mr. Onderdonk's MS notes.

† In 1668, great sickness in N.Y. and over the land. Some daily swept away. A day of humiliation ordered by the Governor. Mr. Onderdonk's notes.

kindred, on a far-distant shore. The minister addresses them, or preaches a sermon, and they sing a solemn psalm; perhaps like the Puritans of New England, to avoid the formality of the Anglican Church, prayer is omitted, and no words are pronounced at the grave. But refreshments are provided for all who attend, and presents given to many.

November the 5th, 1668.

At a tound meeting the tound did agre w^t John wascot to fens the burring* plas w^t good sufitient 5 rail fens be the midell of march next insuing he is to fens it 10 rod squar & he is to have 4 pound in corent pay for his pains & labor.   Records I. p. 46.

The 29th of March, 69, it was voted & agreed upon that mister waters should go to greenwiche to give mister Jones a invitation to give us a visit that the toune might have opertunyty to make an agreement with him concarning the work of the ministry.   Records I. p. 48.

Dec. 5, 1670: voted, that William Brinkly shall have a peece of land on the west sid of the buring place leving a soficient high-way between his fence & the Beverpond.   Records I. p. 53.

* There is a possible doubt of this word but it seems confirmed by 2d extract below.

CHAPTER III.

1670–1692.

REV. JOHN PRUDDEN — A CONVENIENT PEW TO PREACH IN — PERMISSION GIVEN TO MR. PRUDDEN TO BUILD ON THE MINISTER'S LOT — THE TOWN "FURTHER THE COMING INTO A CHURCHWAY" — MR. PRUDDEN LEAVES — REV. WM. WOODROP — FORTY ACRES APPROPRIATED FOR THE USE OF THE MINISTER IN 1676 — MR. PRUDDEN RETURNED, AND ARTICLES OF AGREEMENT WITH HIM — "RULES OF THE GOSPEL IN THIS TOWN" — WAS THE CHURCH PRESBYTERIAN OR CONGREGATIONAL ? — REV. RICHARD DENTON — TESTIMONY OF DUTCH MINISTERS THAT HE WAS A PRESBYTERIAN — PRESBYTERIANS AT FLUSHING AND NEWTOWN — DR. WOODBRIDGE'S HISTORICAL DISCOURSE — GOV. STUYVESANT TO THE MAGISTRATES OF HEMPSTEAD — PRESBYTERIANS IN NEW ENGLAND — COTTON MATHER'S ACCOUNT OF MR. DENTON — CHURCH GOVERNMENT ACCORDING TO THE SYNOD OF DORT — MR. PRUDDEN'S PETITION TO THE GOVERNOR TO ALLOW HIM TO BE MINISTER OF CONGREGATIONALISTS — MR. P. BECOMES A PRESBYTERIAN — GEORGE SCOT — ARCHIBALD RIDDELL — THE TOWN VOTES IN FAVOR OF PRESBYTERIAN ORDINATION IN 1700 — REV. GEORGE MCNISH — THE CHURCH FOSTERED BY THE DUTCH PRESBYTERIANS — THE OLDEST CHURCH OF THE PRESBYTERIAN NAME IN AMERICA — VOTE RESPECTING THE ERECTION OF A MEETING HOUSE IN 1689 — MR. PRUDDEN GOES TO NEWARK — HIS DEATH AND EPITAPH.

JOHN PRUDDEN.

NEARLY two years passed away before the town succeeded in obtaining this minister, during which the Rev. Eliphalet Jones, then of Greenwich, Conn., but who settled in Huntington in 1676, was invited to visit the town; but it does not appear that he complied with the request. Mr. Prudden was called in 1670. He was a son of the Rev. Peter Prudden, who came to New Haven in company with the celebrated John Davenport, and had charge of the church in

Wethersfield, Conn., in 1638. John was born at Milford, Conn., November 9th, 1645, to which place his father had removed, with a few of his congregation, in 1640, and begun the settlement of that town.* He graduated at Harvard College† in 1668, and was twenty-five years of age when he came to Jamaica.

At the same town meeting at which Mr. Prudden was called, it was ordered "that a convenient PEW should be made for the minister to preach in," from which it may be inferred that the house of worship, built in 1663, was but a rude edifice.

6th March 1670 At a town meeting it was voted & concluded that whereas the town hath given Mr Prudden a call to be our minester for this present year it was agreed y^t he should have from this towne for his maintenance fourty pounds a yeare for this present yeare in good curant cuntry pay & likewise the use of the house & land & accomadations which Mr walker was in the possession of when he lived amongst us & is commonly called the minesters lott And this to continue unlese thay or he shall see cause to make any othere agreement:

This writen by order of the toun by me Anthony Waters

   Clark of the Sessions   Records I. p. 56.

The same time it was agreed & concluded y^t there should be a convenient pew made for the minester to preach in & one hired to beet the drom to give notice the time when the towne shall com to meetting.

                  Records I. p. 56.

The 1 of Jeneay 1671 At a towne meeting it was voted & the towne did agree that mister Preden shall have forty

---

* Hinman's Cat. of Puritan Names of Conn., 66.   † Trien. Cat.

pound in corent cuntrey pay of the tound & the hous & land that he is in posetion of for this present year acording to the former town order & if the said mister Preden doth lay out any charge upon the said acomidations wharby it is mad beter the tound shall alow him for it if he leve it, at the same townd meeteing it was voted that Nicklas Evrit should beet the drum to give the tound warning to com to meeting on the sabbath & he shall have twenty shilling for his pains.
Records I. p. 70.

at a towne meeteing held the 24 of May Anno 1672 It was voted & agreede upon that George Woolsey & John Oldfielde Samuell Smith & Nathaniell Denton shall in the behalfe of the towne make an agreement with me^r John Preuden upon such conditions as followeth: namely that if me^r John Preuden will ingage to continue amongst us upon the same tearmes for maintenanse as he hath hitherto had of us & not to leave the plase soe longe as the towne contenues paying the same some of mony that they nowe pay & if hee will doe soe then the towne are welling hee should build & when he removes being okeationed soe to doe by the towne then the towne will pay for what the accomadations is bettered by what he hath done.
Records I. p. 69.

May the 27 1672 Wee whose names are heare underwritten being deputed by the towne to agetate & agree with me^r John Prudden for his continuation amongst us as our minester wee have acordingly come to this agreement with him namely that hee is to stay & continue in the minestry amongst us soe long as the towne doth continue paying to him the same som of mony yearely as at present they doe but if in case the towne dose not performe theire parte in paying him his allowed some yearely & soe okeation his removal then the towne shall pay him for what the acomadations is made better by what hee hath done upon the acomadations & further it is agred upon that if me^r prudden dose see caus to remove & giveth satesfactory reasons to the towne for his removall the towne not being neglegent on theire parte in paying him his alowed som then what me^r Prudden makeeth the acomadations better by any laboure hee bestoweth upon it shall be left to the towne free without any consideration for his paynes only this if the towne dose not see cause to pay for the howse that hee is nowe aboute to builde then Me^r Prudden shall have liberty to remove ye howse of from the tounes lot & if in case that Me^r Prudden should stay amongst us dureing his life then the toune shall make good to his wife whatsoever the acomadations is bettered by any thing that hee hath done upon it: & for the confermation of this agreement the town did voluntaroly ingage themselves at a towne meeting held the third of June that they would not obstruct or hinder but rather further the coming into a church way acordeing to ye rules of the gospell in this towne by Me^r Prudden & such as will joyne with him:

JOHN PRUDDEN

Written by me Nathaniell Denton
        Clerke   Records I. p. 71.

May 24th, 1672, it thus appears from the records, that Mr. Prudden desired the town to allow him to build a house on the minister's lot, so called. The town accordingly appointed a committee to make an agreement with him. Three days after, on the 27th of May, this committee, on behalf of the town, entered into a written agreement with Mr. Prudden, to this effect: that his salary, £40 per annum, was to continue as before; that he might proceed to build on the minister's lot; that if he should leave them through their default, they would reimburse him for the expenses incurred; or in case the town should not see fit to pay for the house, then he should have liberty to remove it from their lot. "And for the confirmation of this agreement *the town did voluntarily engage themselves, at a town meeting, held the third of June, that they would not obstruct or hinder, but rather further the coming into a church way, according to the rules of the Gospel in this town, by Mr. Prudden, and such as will join with him.*" The "coming into a church way, according to the rules of the Gospel," is language that cannot be mistaken; it must refer to the organization of a church. It proves that up to the 3d of June, 1672, there had been no regularly constituted church of Christ in this place. The town had now been settled sixteen years, and it was ten years since Mr. Walker began his labors. But the inhabitants, it should be remembered, were few and isolated, and every thing was in an unorganized state, at the time of Mr. Walker's arrival. Mr. W., moreover, was unordained, which fact, as the people earnestly desired to have the sacraments administered, finally led to his removal.

The question now arises, whether a church was organized at, or soon after, the above-mentioned date. This question, I think, is sufficiently answered in the affirmative, from the fact that the vote to further the organization of a church was passed at a town meeting convened to confirm the agreement which their committee had previously entered into with Mr. Prudden; and that he remained, in accordance with the conditions he had entered into with the town.

We pass on to January 13th, 1674, when it appears

from the Records that the town desired "a positive answer" from Mr. Prudden whether he would remain with them as their minister; his answer was "that he was now under an engagement to another people." They proceeded to settle with him, and he took his departure, after having been the minister here about four years. To what people he was under an engagement, I have not been able to ascertain. The town immediately adopted measures of "inquiry after another minister;" and on June 24th, 1675, we find them voting to give Mr.

WILLIAM WOODDROP

or Woodruff, £60 together with the use of the "parsonage," and lands attached, to be their minister. He was one of the ministers ejected by the Act of Uniformity, in 1662, who found refuge in this country. He is mentioned by Cotton Mather, who calls him Woodrop. He remained here but one year, when he removed, as Thompson asserts, to Pennsylvania.

In June, 1676, the town appropriated forty acres of meadow, together with upland, for the use of a minister. It is this land which is referred to in the Act of the town, 21st of April, 1753, and which is there said to have been continued, "for the use of a minister of the Presbyterian denomination, since that time." Under the same date, June 19th, 1676, articles of agreement are recorded, between the town of Jamaica and the Rev. John Prudden, who, it appears, had returned, by which the town agreed to give him, "his heirs or assigns," certain lands provided he should discharge "the work of a minister for ten years; his salary to be forty pounds and his firewood.

at a towne meeteing called the 13th of January Anno Domini 1674

The towne desired a posetive answer of M^{er} John Prudden conserning his staying with us & his answer was that hee was nowe under an ingagement to another people soe that he could not stay with us any longer

at the same towne meeteing he M^{er} Prudden desired a pese of grounde of the towne which he had taken up & fenced & cleared a little way of from the reare of Beniamin Coes lot the which pese of grounde was given to him that is to M^{er} Prudden upon the accounte that there should be noe more satesfaction exspected from the town by M^{er} Prudden for anything that he hath done upon the townse lot the new howse only exsepted.

at the same towne meeteing it was voted & concluded that the constable & overseors should make inquirye after a minister for this towne Records I. p. 73.

March the 6th Anno Domini 1674 or 5

At a towne meeting then called it was there & then voted & concluded on by the towne that the some of fifty pounds should be payed by the towne to any such minister as the towne can procure to come & live amongst them I say fifty pounds a year annually for his incorigement

and to the end that the towne might obtaine a minister they did at the same towne meeting make choise of Jonas holsteade & John Foster to goe to M^{er} Pek* or any other minister that may be procured to come & live amongst us as our minister Records I. p. 73.

Jamaica this 12th of Marche Anno 1674 or 5

The constable & overseers have let to John Skidmore the townes lot that is to say the barne & home lot for the space of one year in consideration where of that is to say for the

---

* Mr. Jeremiah Peck of Elizabethtown?

use of the barne to cure a crop of tobacco in & the land to plant a crop upon & the fruite of yᵉ orcharde he is to repaire the fens about the orcharde forthwith soe as to secure the orchard til this time twelvemonth & for the other fens to secure it soe that he may preserve his crop of corne & alsoe to make & hang a paire of barne doores to the barne & if in case that the towne doth procure a minister that shall come time inough to make use of the frewte of the orcharde then the town shall pay for the barne doores makeing that this is our agreement witness our hands this day and date above written

NATHANIEL DENTON
JOHN SKIDMORE
Records I. p. 103.

Jemaicae June 24th Anno Domini 1675

there being a towne meeteing it was then & there voted concluded & agreed upon by the towne that they would duely & truely pay unto Meʳ William Wooddrop the full & just som of three score pounds per annum to bee our minister in such pay as will pas currently from man to man that is to say if in wheate at five shillings per bushell peise* at foure & rye at foure indeand corne at three shillings per bushell as alsoe the use of the house & orcharde which is commonly calde the towne or Parsonige house with the medowe at present & after the crop is of the grounde to have the benefit of all such lands & houseing as belongs to the saide towne lot that this is the townse acte done the day & date above written by the towne in general teste NATHANIEL DENTON

towne clerk   Records I. p. 74.

Jeneway the 24 1675

At a town metting it is voted & concluded that whereas their was three score pounds a yeer promised to M Wood-

---

* Peas.

rop in county pay it is now concluded that they will alow him the forenamed some of thre score pound in merchants pay to be payd at Yorke only these men under written eare freed from the alteration of the pay

BENIAMIN COE   JONATHAN MILLS
JOHN OLDFIELD

Records I. p. 74.

april the 4th 1676 These presents may witness that the constable and overseers have let out to James heynds the town lot & house w^t the apurtinanes their unto belonging for this yeer insuing upon the conditions folowing first that the sayd Jams shall repayer & make sufisant all the out side fenceing belonging to the sayd lot w^t new posts & rayls where their is nede & to secure the orchard from any damage & to leave the fence sufisant at the end of ye yere & to alow to the towne for the sayed housin & acomidation the full & just (some) of £2 10s for the yere in good pasable pay as it pas between man & man & further it is agreed that if the town shall have a minister at any time before the terme of the yeere be expired then Jams shal returne the hous barne & orchard to the dispose of the toune & shall alow to the toune six shiling an acore for the remainder of the home lot beside the orchard & Jams to be alowed for his labour about the fence but if Jams shall keepe this lot in hands tell mickelhnass that he have takin the crop of the land & if the town have ocation to make use of this acomidation at micklmes then Jams shall resigne it up to the towne the towne abating Jams 20 shiling in witnes of the premises we have set our hands

JAMES HINDES
BENIEMIN COE
in the name of the town

Records I. p. 77.

June yᵉ 19 1676 At a town meeting it is voted & concluded that their shall be 40 acors of medow designd & sett apart for a parsonage lot in the east neck joining to the lots of medow layed out with upland proporsianable to other lots layed out in the towne to continue at the dispose of the towne to a minister when they shall have ocation to make of it

subscribed by me Beniemen Coe
clarke

Records I. p. 94.

June yᵉ 19 1676 Artickels of agreement betweene the towne of Jemaica the on party & Mʳ John Pruddin the other as followeth

that the toune doe fully & freely give unto Mʳ John Pruddin the house land & acomidations in this towne which was designed & set apart for a minister wᵗ all the priviledges & apurtinancis which doe or here after may pertaine unto the sayed acomidations wee say we doe fully & frely give unto the sayed Mʳ John Pruddin to poses & quiatly to injoy for himselfe & his ayers or asigns forever upon the condision following namely that Mʳ John Pruddin doe continew in this toune discharging the worke of a minister for the terme of ten yers insewing if god continew his life & liberty soe longe but if by death he be taken away before the expiration of the ten yeer then notwithstanding the hole acomidations remain sure & firm to his ayers after him But if the sayed John Prudden doe leave the towne before the end of the ten yeere then the acomidations to returne to the towne the towne satisfying him for what he have expended upon the same & further the towne doe hereby promise & ingage to give unto John Pruddin forty pound the yeer & his fire wood free during the time that he shall continew in the town inployed in the worke of the ministry this forenamed forty pound to be dewly & trewly payed annually to him or his order the on halfe in marchants pay delivered at Yorke & the other halfe in country pay in this towne as it pas betwene man & man that this covenant was the truth concerning both the town & Mr Pruddin to the best of my knowledg subscribed by me

BENIEMIN COE
clarke

By order from the constable & overser

Records I. p. 94.

wee whose names are here under written ingage to bring Mr Pruddin a load of woode a pese yearely by subscribing our names.

NATHANIEL DENTON	NEHEMIAH SMITH
GEORGE WOOLSEY	JONAS HOLSTEADE
JOHN EVERET	JOHN SKIDMORE
THOMAS SMITH	SAMUEL SMITH
WILLIAM RUSCOE	JOHN RODES
ABELL GALE	ANTHONY WATERS
HENERY FOSTER	WAIT SMITH
JOSEPH SMITH	SAMUEL MATHEWS
JOHN OLDFIELDE	JOHN CARPENTER
ROGER LYNAS	Records I. p. 115.

ye constable & oversers have & doe give libberty unto Richard Jones to make use of ye meting house for to teach scoule in for ye yere ensuing provided he keep ye windowes from breaking and keep it deasent & clean one Saturday nights against ye Lord's day & seats to be placed in order :—excepting what times ye constable & oversers shall have ocation to make use of it then they to have it at their disposal by order of ye constable & oversers

SAM. RUSCO
clarke

[no date: but Jan 1676-7 precedes & march 1676-7 next follows—all in one hand—viz. Rusco's] Records I. p. 80.

A town Meeting called Aprill ye 3d 1688 the town have agreed w^t John Heins for a piece of eight to goe to Woodbridge & to desire ye minister there to give ye town a visit in order to setling amongst us & the town doe appoint ye clark to write a letter to ye s'd minister & to give him an invitation to come amongst us to dispense ye word of God here : on behalf of the town

Thes men following have payed every one there bit upon ye account above mentioned

CAPT CARPENTER	JOSEPH SMITH
NEHEMIAH SMITH	JOSEPH THURSTONE
JONAS WOOD	JOHN WOOD
NATH DENTON JR	SAMLL SMITH
JOHN LUDLUM	SAMLL MILLS
GEORGE WOOLSEY JR :	DANLL DENTON JR
MR WHITE :	Records I. p. 150.

August ye 3^d 1688 a town meeting called—The town have made choise of theese men following (viz) Mr. Whitehead Capt: Carpenter Mr White Nathaniel Denton Wait Smith Joseph Thurston John Oldfield & Samll Smith to endevour & use meane for ye procuring such a minister as shall sute w^t & bee accepted off by ye town : by order of ye town

DANLL : DENTON clark
Records I. p. 154.

This is the proper place to consider the significance of the noticeable expression *the rules of the Gospel in this town,* or the question, whether the church which was formed in 1672, in accordance with these rules, was Presbyterian or Congregational. Mr. Prudden was undoubtedly a Congregationalist, and this expression was probably intended to guard against the introduction of any thing inconsistent with the settled and well-understood principles of the people of the town. The controversies at Hempstead prove that the distinction between Independency and Presbyterianism was well known to them, and perhaps they had something to do with this cautious manner of expression. Attention is invited to the following facts, as going far to settle the above question.

The Rev. Richard Denton, who was minister at Hempstead at the time Jamaica was settled, and from which town the leading members of the colony came, was beyond all question a Presbyterian. In a Report to the Classis of Amsterdam, made in 1657, by the ministers in charge of the Dutch Church in New York, the Revs. Joh. Megapolensis and Samuel Drisius, we have this significant passage: "At Heemstede, about 7 Dutch miles from here there are some Independants; also many of our pursuasion and Presbyterians. They have also a Presbyterian preacher, named Richard Denton, an honest, pious, and learned man. He hath in all things conformed to our church. The Independants of the place listen attentively to his preaching, but when he began to baptise the children of such parents as are not members of the church, they sometimes burst out of the church."* This extract shows that the writers carefully made the distinction between Independents and Presbyterians, and proves that the line was distinctly drawn between these parties at Hempstead. The writers make the same distinction in other parts of the letter, and state several important facts. Thus, they say: "At Flushing they heretofore had a Pres-

---

* See this letter entire as translated by Rev. Dr. De Witt, Doc. Hist. N. Y., Vol. III., page 103.

byterian preacher, who conformed to our church, but many of them became endowed with divers opinions, and it was with them, *quot homines tot sententiæ*" [as many opinions as there were men]. "At Middeburgh, called alias, Newtown they are mostly Independants, and have a man of the same persuasion there, Johannes Moor, who preaches there well, but administers no sacraments, because (as he says) he was permitted in New England to preach, but not authorized to administer sacraments, and he has thus continued now for many years. In this village are also many other inhabitants Presbyterians, but they are not able to maintain a Presbyterian Preacher, whilst we know not that any of this sect are to be found among the English in N. England, among whom there are preachers." The Rev. Sylvester Woodbridge, Jr., formerly pastor at Hempstead, now Dr. Woodbridge, of California, says in his historical discourse delivered at Hempstead in 1840, "The Rev. Richard Denton was a Presbyterian minister of Coley Chapel, parish of Halifax, in the northern part of England." It appears that at Hempstead he "in all things conformed" to the church of Holland, which can mean nothing less than that he was distinctively Presbyterian; and the Independents exhibited great signs of dissatisfaction. It appears, also, from a letter of Gov. Stuyvesant,[*] addressed "to the Magistraats off Heemstead," that he had visited that place the same year, 1657, for the purpose of "settlingh off mister denton's continuance according to agreement of the tents (tenths) for the present year;" and that Mr.

---

[*] Doc. Hist. N. Y., page 189.

Robert Fordham who had been "sum tymes minister [of] the toun of heemsted," and had left the place, and "the excreys of the ministery" without the Governor's knowledge and permission, had returned, or that a party was labouring to bring him back, in opposition to Mr. Denton. May not the origin of the Jamaica colony, in which were two persons of the name of Denton, sons of the minister at Hempstead, have had some connection with this religious dissension? During the six years after the commencement of the colony, before the organization of a regular congregation, there can be no doubt those among the first settlers who had been in communion with Mr. Denton's church at Hempstead, retained their connection with it, enjoying occasional communion with their brethren, and visits from their pastor. As to that portion of the primitive inhabitants, who it is supposed came from New England, some of them may have been drawn to the English settlements on this end of the island, because there were no churches, distinctively Presbyterian, in New England. Previous to the year 1640, four thousand Presbyterians, it is said, arrived in New England; and of the two thousand ministers ejected by the Act of Uniformity, in 1662, a considerable number, found refuge in this country; one of them, Wm. Woodruff, became minister of this church. For proof of the strong Presbyterian element which pervaded New England, we need nothing better than the Saybrook Platform itself.* Thompson says of Mr. Denton, that he returned to England

---

* Trumbull's Hist. of Conn., Vol. I., page 487.

in 1659, where he died in 1662, at the age of seventy-six. He states this on the authority of the Rev. Mr. Heywood, his successor at Halifax.* In Savage's Genealogical Dictionary, he is said to have died at Hempstead in 1663. After Mr. Denton's departure, a long and angry controversy was carried on between the Independents and Presbyterians.

"Among those clouds," (says Cotton Mather, meaning the ministers who came from England,) "was our pious and learned Mr. Richard Denton, a Yorkshire man, who, having watered Halifax, in England, with his fruitful ministry, was by a tempest there hurried into New England, where first at Weathersfield, and then at Stamford, his doctrine dropped as the rain, his speech distilled as the dew, as the small rain upon the tender herb, and as the showers upon the grass. Though he were a little man, yet he had a great soul; his well accomplished mind, in his lesser body, was an Iliad in a nut-shell. I think he was blind of an eye, yet he was not the least among the *seers* of Israel; he saw a very considerable portion of those things which eye hath not seen. He was far from cloudy in his conceptions and principles of divinity, whereof he wrote a system, entitled *Soliloquia Sacra*, so accurately considering the fourfold state of man, in his created purity, contracted deformity, restored beauty, and celestial glory, that judicious persons, who have seen it, very much lament the churches being deprived of it. At length he got into heaven beyond clouds, and so beyond storms; waiting the return of the Lord Jesus Christ, in the clouds of heaven, when he will have his reward among the saints."

Thompson says that he was educated at the Univer-

---

* Hist. of Long Island, Vol. II., p. 20.

sity of Cambridge, where he graduated in 1623, and was minister of Coley Chapel, Halifax, seven years. He probably arrived in New England with Gov. Winthrop in 1630 (Savage says 1639); went first to Watertown, but in 1635 with others commenced the settlement at Wethersfield. In 1641, he is found among the proprietors of Stamford, where he was owner of a valuable real estate.

Another fact. In 1674, 9th of May, Mr. Prudden having left, two years after the people had given their voice in favor of the organization of a church, we find Mr. Nathaniel Denton addressing a letter to the colonial secretary, regarding the maintenance of the minister of Jamaica, asking an order to compel certain persons in the town to pay their proportion towards the support of the minister, in which he refers to "instructions" that the people were not to maintain "any other way of church government than what is according to the Synod of Dort," and expressly asserts that "our minister" is "noe ways repugnant to that Synod."* By a way of church government which was according to the Synod of Dort, must have been meant the Presbyterian way.

Another fact. In a petition addressed to Gov. Dongan in 1688, by the Rev. John Prudden, in which he styles himself "quondam minister of Jamaica," he states that a considerable part of his salary is withheld, through the refusal of several inhabitants "to pay their proportion levied by yearly rates," and asks, as a lawsuit "would be unpleasant and discommendable on all hands," that an order may be issued by the

* Doc. Hist. N. Y., Vol. III., p. 193.

Governor, enforcing payment. He then goes on to say "Your humble petitioner only requesteth further that if a considerable number OF THE CONGREGATIONALL PROFESSION & PERSWASION should be desirous y^t he would continue to bee their minister, and maintain him at their own cost & charge by a voluntary contribution, your Excellency & the Hon. Council would pleas to give approbation thereunto," etc.* A certificate is added, signed by Nehemiah Smith and John Carpenter, that Mr. Prudden had continued in the town the full term of ten years, (the term agreed upon in articles on record, at the time of his return in 1676, June 19th) "discharging the work of a minister according *to the way of ye churches in New England*." This certificate that he had discharged his work as a minister according to the way of the churches of New England, taken in connection with his petition to the Governor to be permitted to form a Congregational church, or a separate assembly of the Congregational persuasion, doubtless suggests the reason why his salary was not paid, and the people refused to fulfil the contract to give him in fee the land set apart for the use of the minister, provided he should discharge the work of a minister for ten years. This is the land referred to in the Act of the town, 21st April, 1753, there said to have been continued "for the use of a minister of the Presbyterian denomination, since that time" [1676]. Mr. Prudden, in styling himself "quondam minister," would seem to indicate that he ceased to fill the office when the ten years of his engagement expired. In 1689 he was chosen deputy

* Doc. Hist. N. Y. Vol. III. p. 195.

to the Colonial Assembly, by the town. If he resumed charge of the congregation it is probable he concluded to conform to "the rules of the Gospel in this town," and, instead of making the people Congregationalists, himself became a Presbyterian, for in 1692 he was called by the church in Newark, N. J., which, according to Dr. McWhorter* was Presbyterian from the beginning.

In the extracts from the Town Records, on a preceding page, there is one, under date of April the 3d, 1688, of more importance as to the question under consideration, than at first sight would appear. The clerk was appointed to write a letter to the minister of Woodbridge, and "give him an invitation to come amongst us to dispense the word of God;" and money was contributed to meet the expense of sending a messenger to bear the letter, and to invite "the minister there to give the town a visit in order to settling amongst us." Now, who was the minister of Woodbridge? Woodbridge N. J. is undoubtedly meant. The small place in Connecticut, in the vicinity of New Haven, of that name, could not have been settled, or could not have had a population sufficient to form a separate congregation, at this early period. The Rev. Archibald Riddell was the minister of Woodbridge, N. J. from 1686 to 1689.† A large colony of Scotch people settled in and around Perth Amboy as early as 1684–5. Two vessels arrived in 1684, one having one hundred and sixty, the other one hundred

---

* MS. Hist. of Newark, quoted in Dr. Hodges' Hist. of Pres. Church. Vol. I. p. 43.

† Whitehead's Contributions to E. Jersey History, p. 384.

and thirty passengers. In 1685, George Scot of Pitlochie, connected with some of the most distinguished families of Scotland, wrote his "Model of the Government of the Province of East Jersey," the object of which was to encourage emigration, and sailed himself, accompanied by nearly two hundred persons. He says in his "Model, &c." "You see so it is now judged the intercrest of the *Government* altogether to suppress the *Presbyterian Principles;* & that in order thereto the whole force & bensill of the Law of this Kingdom are levelled at the effectual *bearing them down*, that the vigorous putting these *Laws* in execution, hath in great part ruined many of these, who notwithstanding thereof find themselves in conscience obliged to retain these principles; while in the other hand *Episcopacy* is by the same Laws supported and protected." He then goes on to urge those whom he addresses to transport "themselves thither where they are by law allowed *the free exercise of their principles.*"* George Scot was the son of Sir John Scot of Scotstarbet in Edinburghshire. He was fined a thousand pounds for frequenting the conventicles of John Welsh and Samuel Arnot, and was again fined a thousand pounds for "harbouring" John Welsh. He was repeatedly fined, and on one occasion, seven hundred pounds, and as often cast into prison. His wife, Lady Pitlochie, was also fined for attending conventicles. At length he petitioned the Council from the Bass prison for his release, engaging to "go to the plantations," and to

---

* Of the four copies of the original edition of the "Model," known to exist, one is in the possession of Gov. King of Jamaica. It is reprinted in Whitehead's "E. Jersey under the Proprietors."

take with him Archibald Riddell, one of the obnoxious preachers. They set sail September 5th, 1685, in the "Henry & Francis," a ship of three hundred and fifty tons, and twenty great guns, Richard Hutton master. Soon after leaving the harbour of Leith, a fever broke out among those who had been long lying in loathsome prisons, which soon assumed a malignant type. The mortality was dreadful. Seventy died, among them the Laird of Pitlochie, his wife, with her sister-in-law, Lady Aithernie and her two children.

The Rev. Archibald Riddell, a zealous and pious preacher, was the brother of Sir John Riddell. The first serious proceedings of the Government against him appear to have been prompted by his connection in some way with the rising of Bothwell in 1679. He was arrested, and sent first to the tollbooth in Jedburgh, and from thence removed to the prison in Edinburgh. He was summoned before the Committee of public affairs, and although he convinced his examiners of his moderation and loyalty, he would not clear himself from the charge of having preached in the fields, nor promise to refrain from field-preaching in future. "I know not," he said, "but he who has called me to preach this while byegone in houses, may, before I go out of the world, call me to preach upon tops of mountains, yea upon the seas; and I dare not come under any engagements to disobey his calls." He was therefore remanded to prison, and kept there until, on the application of Scot, he was released with the view of emigrating to New Jersey. His wife died on the voyage. He took charge of the Congregation of Woodbridge within a month after his arrival. In

1689, in consequence of the political changes in his native land, he set sail for Scotland, accompanied by a little son ten years of age. The vessel was captured by a French man-of-war, and after being marched in chains from Rochefort to Toulon, he was imprisoned nearly two years, when he was exchanged and allowed to return to Scotland. He settled at Kirkaldie. His daughter, Janet, married James Dundas, son of Sir James Dundas, who was settled at Perth Amboy.*

Thus it appears that the minister of Woodbridge, who was invited to come and settle at Jamaica, to dispense the word of God, was one of the Scotch worthies, a covenanter, who was willing to go to prison or to death rather than renounce his principles. Wodrow refers to the call he received from Long Island, and declined.† The records exhibit a zeal on the part of the people of Jamaica to secure his services, which we scarcely observe in any other instance. The letter contained a formal invitation to him to become the minister. In the next minute, that of August 3d, 1688, a large committee is appointed to secure such a minister "as shall suit with & be accepted of by the town." There seems to have been no doubt that Mr. Riddell would suit the town, as they knew whence he came, and for what.

We come now to a fact which clearly settles, if that has not already been done, what was meant by "the rules of the Gospel in this town." After the Rev. Jeremiah Hobart, who had been minister at Hempstead and succeeded Mr. Prudden here, had supplied the place for a short time, the Rev. John Hubbard became

---

* Whitehead's Contributions, and Wodrow's History.   † IV. 335.

minister; and we have this significant record in regard to him: "At a town meeting held at Jamaica, Nov. 25, 1700, it was agreed by vote that whereas Mr. John Hubbart hath continued here among us, in this town, in the present work of the ministry, some considerable time, the town does show their willingness to continue him still, & to have him ordained accordingly, provided it be *according to the rule and way of the Presbyterian way*, & it is the *unanimous mind* of the town that he be ordained accordingly, & that every man shall pay toward the ordination as much as he shall see cause to pay." Hubbard is always called, in Smith's History of New York, a Presbyterian.

It may be added that on the occurrence of the first vacancy in the pulpit, after the formation of the Presbytery of Philadelphia, the Rev. George McNish, one of the original members of that presbytery, in the spring of 1710, was called to be minister. There have been ruling elders in the congregation from time immemorial. In the earliest records of the church, it is never styled any thing but Presbyterian; there are, however, no records or minutes running past the middle of the last century. On the inside of the cover of the register of the church, the following is written: "This book is the gift of Mr. Daniel Smith, one of the Elders and Deacons of the Presbyterian Church and Congregation of this town of Jamaica in Queen's County, in the Province of New York, for the use of said congregation, in & by his last will & testament, bearing date the 14th day of July, 1753, & who departed this life on the 15th day of October, 1754, being 90 years and 7 months old." The book was bought in

1755, and this inscription appears to have been made by Mr. Hinchman, the purchaser. It appears that Mr. Smith was born some eight or nine years before the formation of the church. He probably acted as an elder from a very early period.

What do these facts indicate as to "the rules of the Gospel in this town," or the form of church government most approved by a majority of the people? Of course, it is not to be presumed that the church was organized, in all respects, or transacted its business always in accordance with Presbyterial rule, before there was a Presbytery to organize and preside over churches, and license and ordain ministers. It is only supposed that they endeavored to act, so far as it was possible in their circumstances, on Presbyterial principles, somewhat, probably, as the Presbyterians of Ireland did, prior to the formation of the first Presbytery in that country, under the jurisdiction of the bishops of the Anglican church; i. e. under the auspices of the Church of Holland, the model of which church was expressly secured to the people, at the time of the surrender of the province to the English, in 1664.* The Dutch ministers who inducted† Mr. Vesey, the first rector of Trinity Church, by order of Gov. Fletcher, may have ordained and installed some of the first pastors of this church. To the Dutch belongs the honor of transplanting Presbyterianism to this continent. We hazard little, therefore, in saying that the church in Jamaica is the oldest Presbyterian church, estab-

---

* Articles of Surrender.
† Dr. Brownlee's Hist. of Ref. D. Ch. in America. Letter of Rev. Dr. De Witt to the author.

lished by the English, in America. It had been in existence some eight or ten years before Francis Makemie, usually styled the father of American Presbyterianism, arrived in Maryland. It is evident from the letters of Gov. Stuyvesant and the New York ministers, that the Dutch had a warm side towards Presbyterians, as being one in faith and order with them, whilst they looked with doubt or suspicion on other denominations, who sought to establish themselves within the province.

A town meeting on the 10th day of June 1689 Mr Prudden & Nathaniel Denton Senior was chosen to go to York to meete with the rest of the deputis of the respective townes for to consider & advise one with another of what shall be for the good welfare & service of the contrey & to act with the rest of the deputies in any thing that may tend therunto & also if they shall see cause to make any aplication to our Sovereign King & Queen for any thing that may tend to the good of the whole Collony to act with them.

By order of the Town per me
NATHANIEL DENTON
Clerk

Jamaica a town meeting called the 19th June 1689 Mr John Prudden and Mr Daniel Whithead was chosen for deputis for this towne of Jamaica to meete with the rest of the deputis of Queens County for the chusing of two committy men out of the County for to go to Yorke to sit as a committy of safety & also together with the rest of the Deputies to give the two men that are chosen by them their instructions & power how far & in what the two

Committee men shall act & do when they come to York by order of the Town

per me NATHANIEL DENTON
Clerk
Records 1. p. 126.

December the 6 Anno 1689 A town meeting called It was there & then voted & concluded that there shall be a meeting house built in this town of Jamaica 60 foot long & 30 foot wide & every way else as shall be convenient & comely for a meeting house.

Jan 9 1689

a town meeting called It was there & then voted & concluded that Danl Whithead William White Joseph Smith & Nathaniel Denton shall be the men to procure & agree with such a workman or workmen as they shall see cause for the building & finishing such a meeting house as is above mentioned for length & width & every thing else that shall be convenient & comely & what these four men above mentioned shall do the town will stand by them & perform what agreements they make in paying according to their abilities or estates proportionably by order of the town

Per me NATHANIEL DENTON
Clerk

A town meeting called the 22d of January 1689 or 90 the town did vote & conclude that Capt John Carpenter & Nehemiah Smith shall be added to the four men before-named for the agreeing with a workman or workmen for the building of a meeting house & what they six men or the major part of them shall do the town to stand by it by order of the town

per me NATANIEL DENTON
Clerk

At a town metting held att Jamaica August y⁰ 21ˢᵗ 1691: It was voated & concluded that upon sum propossalls mad by Mr. John Pruden to yᵉ town about his arrerages & for his inceragement to continue amongst us that six men be chosen to agree dibate & conclude yᵉ matters as well for his arrerages as for his further continuancy in yᵉ ministry & make report to yᵉ town theroff as spedely as possible — —

at yᵉ same town meeting it was voated & concluded yᵗ Capt Whithed Capt Carpenter Joseph Smith Jonas Wood Samuell Denton & Wait Smith are chosen to agree with Mr. John Pruden according to yᵉ above record.

Records I. p. 183.

At a town metting yᵉ 5: day of August 1691 the maior partt of yᵉ people that was then there did Except of Mr. Pruden's proposall to yᵉ metting.   Records, I. p. 164.

At a town metting held yᵉ 2d day of September 1691: it was voted & concluded that the record made yᵉ 19th of June 1676* conserning Mr Pruden should be establisht & confirmd in every poynt exactly

By Saml Ruscoe
Clark
Records I. p. 184.

At a towne meting caled & held the 3d day of September 1691: it was voated & concluded that Mr Pruden shall have three score pounds yᵉ yeare payd him & his feyer-wood free for which Mr Pruden duering the time he stayeth amongst [us] is to perform the office of a minister amongst us

    according to gospel rules   By Sam Ruscoe
town clark
Records I. p. 191.

August 23d, 1692, Mr. Prudden received a call from

* See page 62 of this volume.

the First Presbyterian Church, Newark, N. J., to succeed Mr. Pierson, which he accepted. He continued the minister of that Church till June 9th, 1699, when, for some cause not now known, the pastoral relation was dissolved. He died at Newark, December 11th, 1725. His epitaph is as follows:

> *Here lies the body of the Rev. Mr.*
> *John Prudden, minister of the*
> *Gospel, who departed this life*
> *11 Dec. 1725, aged 80 years.*
>
> NOR GRACE, NOR FAVOUR FILLS MY REINS,
> LO, ROOM FOR THEE REMAINS.

Dr. McWhorter, in a sermon preached January 1st, 1801, says that "he sustained a worthy character, as a man of sense and religion, though he does not appear to have been a popular preacher." His descendants are numerous, and reside chiefly in Morris Co., N. J.; but numerous descendants of his daughters, Joanna, wife of Nathaniel Moore, and Keziah, wife of Elnathan Baldwin, reside in Pennington, and other parts of Mercer Co.*

* See the Rev. George Hale's Letter in the *Addenda*.

CHAPTER IV.

1692—1699.

FIRST MOVEMENT TOWARDS ERECTING THE STONE MEETING HOUSE — APPLICATION TO THE ASSEMBLY — VANE A TARGET TO BRITISH SOLDIERS IN THE REVOLUTION — DATE ON IT — STYLE OF THE BUILDING — JEREMIAH HOBERT — GEORGE PHILLIPS — HIS "DYOTT" PAID FOR — PEOPLE SEND TO THE "MAIN" FOR A MINISTER — MR. JONES, LATE OF DANBURY — SUBSCRIPTION LIST FOR THE SUPPORT OF A MINISTER — VOTES OF THE TOWN RESPECTING MEETING HOUSE AND MR. PHILLIPS — THE GOV. PETITIONED RESPECTING THE SETTLEMENT OF MR. HOBERT — DISPUTE RESPECTING MEETING HOUSE SETTLED — ACCOUNT OF MR. HOBERT — MEETING HOUSE FINISHED.

IT was in December, 1689, as we have already seen, that the initial movement was made by the town, for the erection of the old stone church, which occupies so important a place in the history of this congregation. At another town meeting, held the following month, a committee was appointed to procure and agree with workmen to construct the house. In 1693, the people of Jamaica applied to the Provincial Assembly, for the passage of an act, to enable them to levy or collect money for this purpose.

Mr. Faitoute says that "from the date of the vane which was taken down from the steeple, because very much injured by the musket balls of the British soldiers, who were continually shooting at it as a mark in the time of the late war, it appears to have been completed in 1693 or 1699; two dates are given, as there is some difference in the opinion of those who saw the vane after it was taken down"* The true date probably was 1699. This building stood near the middle of the main street, not far from the head of what is now known as Union Hall street. It was a substantial stone edifice, of a quadrangular form, with a pyramidal roof, and belfry in the centre; and was used for a house of worship until the year 1813, when the present church was erected; that is, for about one hundred and fourteen years. This was the church for the possession of which the Presbyterians contended with Church of England men, for nearly a quarter of a century; a full account of which will be given in the proper place.

October 25th, 1692, a call was given to Rev. Jeremiah Hobart, or Hubbart, minister of Hempstead, but he did not at this time see fit to accept. June 8th, 1693, "It was agreed to endeavour to procure Mr. Jones, late minister of Danbury," to be minister of Jamaica. But the next preacher was Mr.

GEORGE PHILLIPS

who labored here about three years, from 1693 to 1696. He was a licentiate merely, and of course was not pastor of the church; was son of the Rev. Samuel Phillips of Roxbury, Mass., and born in 1664; graduated at Harvard in 1686. He probably left this place on the death of his father in 1696. He subsequently went to Brookhaven, where he was ordained in 1702, and continued pastor to his death, June 17th, 1739. He is said to have been a faithful preacher, and extended his labors to destitute places. The Hon. Silas Wood says

* MS Hist., written in 1793.

of him that "he was distinguished for a peculiar vein of natural wit. His ordinary discourse was tinctured with this peculiarity; and tradition has preserved many of his remarks that exemplify it."

Mr. Phillips was probably a single man at the time he lived in Jamaica, as we find the town agreeing as a part of his salary " to pay for his dyott where he shall be dyated," i. e. to pay for his board. In another minute the word is spelled " diatt."

At a town metting held the 25th of October 1692 it was voated & concluded without any interruption to give unto Mr. Jeremiah Hubbert the sum of sixty pounds yearly to be dewly payed according to ye currant markett prise & every inhabitant within ye s^d township to cut & cart him a waggon load of wood all this to be duly payd & performed yearly during his labour in the ministry amongst us p^r me Saml Rusoe   clark   Records p. 163.

at ye same metting Joseph Smith seanor was appointed & chosen by a generall voat to carry this above written copy out of ye records to Mr. Hubberd & to discourse with him about anything to his further satisfaction

Per me Sam Ruscoe clark

Records I., p. 165.

Att a towne metting held ye 9th day of march 1692 Joseph Smith was choasen to acompany Nehemiah Smith to ye main* in order to ye procurement of a minister according to a former order

pr Samuell Ruscoe clark

Records I. p. 124.

att a toun metting att Jamaica held ye 17 of September 1692 Nehemiah Smith was deputed & chosen by ye persons at s^d metting for to goe to ye main in order to ye procuring

---

* New Jersey or Conn.

of a minister for ye town of Jamaica & to bring him over to us: to give us a vissit in order to a further treatty & in case such a one doth come over & wee doe not agree with him for his continuance amongst us then to satisfy him for his journey in coming to us by ye town

pr SAMUELL RUSCOE
clark
Records I. p. 127.

June ye 8 93 it was agreed upon to indeavor to procure Mr Jones late minister of danbery to be our minister or to give us a vissitt according to ye tenor of this above record.

Records I. p. 127.

At a town metting held ye 3^d day of January 1692 it was voated & concluded that Saml Smith Mr Whithead Nehemiah Smith William Creed Wait Smith Nathaniel Denton John Carpenter Junr are impowered to agre upon procuring a settlement convenient for a parsonag in Jamaica & that they shall have liberty to make sale & dispose of what parsinag land as shall to them seem mett & conveniant for ye procuring thereof

per SAML RUSCOE clark
Records I. p. 185.

at a metting held at Jamaica ye 8 of June 1693 it was votted & agreed that ye mai^n partt of y^e seven above named shall have libberty to procure y^e parsonage house & lot either by exchaing of other land or by giving of money for y^e same John Baylis protests against the giving of any land

SAML RUSCOE
clark
Records I. p. 185.

Att a toune metting held att Jamaica January y^e first 169$\frac{4}{3}$ it was voated & concluded upon that y^e parsonage remaining in yᵉ hands of yᵉ town thay doe engage to give unto Mr Phillipes the money raised by a free giuft & to pay for his dyott wher he shall be dyated the same freely given as above sᵈ being sixty poundes this being for one yeare from yᵉ date hereof   Per SAML RUSCOE clark

Records II. p. 548.

Att yᵉ same mettinge it was voatted that John Oweke & Richard oldfield Samuell Denton & Daniell Smith shall gather the sumes promised to yᵉ minester & to pay it to yᵉ minester quarterly from yᵉ persons hereafter named —

Records II. p. 548.

Capt Whithead	. 02 00	Sam Smith seor	.	. 00 15
Mr Harreson	. 01 10	Joseph Oldfield	.	. 01 00
Ben Thirston	. 01 00	Tho Welling	.	. 00 10
Sam Denton	. 01 00	Ben Coe	.	. 00 06
Nath Denton	. 01 10	John Cokefer	.	. 00 12
Hope Carpenter	. 01 00	David Lues	.	. 00 06
Nehemiah Smith	. 01 10	Will Sallyer	.	. 00 08
Wait Smith	. 01 05	Ben Wiggens	.	. 00 10
Jos Smith senʳ	. 01 00	Sam Mathews	.	. 00 15
Jos Smith J.	. 01 00	Sam Carpenter	.	. 00 15
Cap Carpenter	. 01 10	Ben Smith	.	. 00 15
Dan Sexton	. 00 15	Mr Whitte	.	. 01 00
Tho Smith	. 01 00	Hendrik Arreson		. 00 06
Captⁿ Wollsey [Geo.]	01 10	Jonas Wood	.	. 01 04
Tho Wollsey	. 01 00	Tho Wiggens	.	. 00 12
John Ludley	. 01 00	John Bayles	.	. 01 10
John Smith	. 01 00	Robt Read	.	. 01 00
Sam Milles	. 01 00	Nicoles Everet	.	. 01 00
Will Creed	. 01 00	Natt Higbee	.	. 00 10
John Wollsey	. 01 00	Hend Hegeman		. 00 10
Edward Hare	. 00 15	Joⁿ Roads	.	. 01 00
Nat Smith	. 00 12	Able Galle	.	. 00 10

John Everitt	. 00 15	John Hanson	. 00 12
Sam^ll Ruscoe	. 00 10	Steven Couert	. 00 05
John Gale	. 00 06	John Brewer	. 00 05
Richard Oldfield	. 01 00	Hendrik Lott	. 00 12
Sam Smith	. 01 10	Doros [Polhemus]	. 00 12
Captn Carpenter Jun^or	01 00	John Ouke	. 00 10
Daniell Smith	. 00 15	Dowe Jansen	. 00 06
Peter Whitte	. 00 10	John Lambertts	. 00 06
Joseph Phillipes	. 00 10	Jan Monfort	. 00 07
Jon^than Wood	. 00 10	Garett Lubertson	. 00 08
Antho Watters	. 01 00	Petter Hendrikes	. 00 07
Will Brinkley	. 00 15	Gerret Jansen	. 00 06
Will Ludlum	. 00 10	Jacob Janson	. 00 06
Ralph Hunt	. 00 10	Johanes Williamson	00 04
Edward Higbey	. 01 00	Gerett Classen	. 00 10
Daniel Thirston	. 00 15	Thos Chambers	. 00 10
Edward Burrowes	01 00	Za ry Milles	. 00 10
Gershom Wiggens	. 00 10	Widdow Denton	. 00 06
Jo than Milles	. 00 10	Richard Green	. 00 12
Sam Dein	. 00 10	Alex^ander Smith	. 00 08
Hendrik	. 00 10	Joseph Ludlum	. 00 15
Josias Wiggens	. 00 10	Tho Humphreys	. 00 06
Thos Watters	. 00 12	Eldert Lucas	. 00 12
Timothy Milles	. 00 05	John Snedeker	. 00 05

Records II. p. 549.

Jamaica march ye 8th 9¾ ther was agreed upon betwixt Mr Phillipes & the townsmen of ye above s^d towne that is that Mr Phillipes is to have all ye over plush of ye money freely giuven above ye three score pounds & to take ye parsonage into his own hands & the towne to pay for his diatt for ye first quarter of this present yeare:

   entered per me SAMLL RUSCOE clarke

Records II. p. 523.

at a mettinge held at Jamaica January ye first 169¾ in

order to the building a metting howes for y̆ towne of Jamaica ther was choasen John Owkea Samll Dein Saml Denton Capt^a Carpenter & John Smith which above s^d fivel men are to devid y̆ towne into five squadrans & to see timber & stones & lime all gotten & fitted proportionabley as shall be nessesary for s^d worke   Sam Ruscoe clarke
Records II. p. 523.

att a towne mettinge called by order from y̆ Justices of this County att Jamaica febr y̆ 17 169?, in order to y̆ chois of two vestrymen persuant to an act of Assembley: Nehemiah Smith & William Creed was choasen to be vestrymen for Jamaica & to mett with y̆ rest of y̆ vestrymen from other tounes with full power with y̆ rest to chuse two churchwardens & to ackt as the s^d act of Assembly derickts & to meett on tuesday next from this date
   pr Samll Ruscoe clarke
Records II. p. 523.

At a towne mettinge called accordinge to ordere held at Jamaica; Aprill y̆ 3^d 169 [4] then agreed upon & confirmed by a publique voatt of y̆ inhabitants in generalle: that Mr Phillipes now our present minister continuing his liffetime anongst us in y̆ above toune in ye worke of y̆ ministry & shall dye amongst us that then their shall be paid unto his widow, or relict left amongst us one years sallery y̆ sallery beinge sixty poundes

at the same towne mettinge it was likewise agreed that y̆ agreement made betwixt Mr Phillipes & y̆ townsmen shall stand accordinge as it is entered upon record before this
Records II. p. 494.

The foregoing list* is given in full for several reasons. It probably presents a pretty accurate catalogue of the

   * Page 85.

freeholders of the town at its date. It was the beginning of a new method of supporting the minister; that is to say, by voluntary contributions or subscriptions, rather than by a tax laid on all the inhabitants. It shows also that the Dutch Presbyterians cordially united with the English in sustaining Divine worship. We find Jansen, Hendrikes, Hegeman, Snedeker, uniting with the Dentons, Carpenters, Everitts and Smiths. The record clearly implies that "the sumes promised to ye minester" were quarterly, not annual subscriptions. The appointment of "vestrymen," February 17th, 169¾, was under the law passed by the Assembly, the preceding September, that "would not do well for the Dissenters, and but lamely for the Church."

July 15 1697 att a towne metting it was farly agreed by lott that ye metting howes shall be betwixt ye sessions howes & ye crossway west of s^d sessions howes

Saml Ruscoe clark
Records II. p. 546.

att a towne metting held January the *fuift* 169⅔ it was agreed & concluded by voatt that there shall be a church erected & bult in this towne & to begine s^d worke this nexte spring in march ore soneer & to soe follon s^d worke with all care & dilligence that may be untill it be finishd

Records I. p. 524.

att a towne mettinge october ye 2^d 1697 :—ye west end of ye town dos condescend that ye mettinge howes shall be sett up by or att ye most convenient place nere ye pund ye east end pepeoll procuring as good a bell as flatt bush metting howes bell is [one line illegible]

Saml Ruscoe clark
Jamaica Records, III., 546.

At a towne metting held at Jamaica the 13th of September 1698 ther Joseph Smith and Jonas Wood was choasen & apoynted to treat with his Excelency in & about settlinge & establishinge Mr Hobert amongst us in the worke of yᵉ ministry
Records I. p. 159.

At a toune meetinge held September yᵉ 13 1698 then was deputed [and chosen, erased in original] Captⁿ Carpenter, Captⁿ Wollsey Jonas Wood Benjamin Thurston Capt Whithed Joseph Smith John Smith Edward Burrougs John Hansen to carrye on the worke of a church or mettings house them or the mager partt of them & to see yᵉ same truely caryed out & ended
Pʳ SAML RUSCOE clark
Records I. p. 81.

At a towne metting called according to order at Jamaica aprill the 15 : 1698 the peopell & inhabetants of this towne did publicqly signify their redines & willingenes for the continuinge Mr Hubertt our present minester in the worke of yᵉ minestry amongst us by holding up ther hands in a publicq voat All thes abovesᵈ orders signed & past
SAML RUSCOE clarke
Records II. p. 524.

At a towne mettinge held at Jamaica January yᵉ 4 169⅔ it was agreed by voat that John Oke* Richard Oldfield & Theodorus Polhemus & Daniel Smith senior shall forth [with] take all diligent care in goeinge about amongst the neaibourhod to see what money can be raised by a freewill offeringe for the buildinge of yᵉ church in the towne of Jamaica & to make retorne to yᵉ towne of what sume can be raised
Records II. p. 515.

Whereas ther hath ben severall differances had moven

* Present pastor's name, Okey.

and dependinge within the toune of Jamaica in Queens County & Island of Nassau conserning the buldinge or errectinge a mettinge howes or church within s^d town :: & as alsoe the accountes & demands & charges thereunto &c which with all other controversies had moveing or dependinge or any wais relatinge thereunto being this day mewtually refered by Daniel Whitthead Esq^{er} Joseph Smith Esquier Nicolas Eavrett Esq^{er} Edward Burrowes Jonas Wood: of the one party & Fredrick Hendricksen John Okea Willm Creed Hendrik Lott Doros Polhelmus Elderd Lowkes & Robertt Read of the other parties on behalf of themselves & others conserned have this day referd all the said matter & differance in controversy: unto the finall hering & determination of John Coe Esq^{er} Judg: Samuell Edsall Esq & Content Titus Esq^{er} Justices & we doe for us our heires Exececutores & administratores oblidge ourselves joyntly & severally in the penal sume of one hundred poundes current moneys of New York: unto each other his heirs excecutors or adminestratores to be paid unto the parties observant by the parties defective in the performance of the award of the above s^d parsones as wittnes our hands & seals in Jamaica this 15 of Aprill 1701 & in ye 13th yeare of his majest^s reigne ye 3^d &c:

    DANIEL WHITHEAD WILL^m CREED
    NICOLAS EAVERITT HENDRICK LOTT
    JOSEPH SMITH   ELDERD LUKES
    JONAS WOOD   FREDRIKE HENDRIKES
    JOHN OKE   THEODORUS POLHEMUS

Signed sealed & delivered in
 presence of
JOHN HARRISON
PETER CHACKE [of Newtown]
     a true copy p^r SAMLL RUSCOE Clarke

Records II. p. 360.

Jamaica aprill the 15th 1701 whereas by vertue & power unto us dellivered by the within [above] 'obligation &c to heare arbetratt & determine & finall conclution bringe all & eavery the controverties therein mentioned : & wee havinge dewly & impartially considerd the same: & heringe boath parties &c doe give in this our award as followeth : viz that wee award all thoos at the west of Jamaica that is the Duchmen & William Creed & Robert Read: that hath not perfectly & wholly payed their rattes assessed for the buldinge the church or mettinge howes in Jamaica: shall pay their severall partes unpaid within three weekes after this date then them & their heires to be forever acquitted of any claime or demand whatsover conserninge the buldinge or erectinge s^d church or mettinge howes or any disbursments thereon : & the parties conserned in opposition to each other in s^d controversy : to releas Exoneratt & acquitt each other of all former controverties consernenge s^d church or mettinge howes : desiringe thay may ameeably agree & live in love together & this we give in as our award as under our hands & seales the above s^d date.

JOHN COE
SAMUELL EDSALL
CONTENT TITUS*

a trew copy p^r Sam^ll Ruscoe clarke

Records II. p. 361.

The Mr. Hobert referred to in the record of the 13th of September, 1698, has been supposed to be the Rev.

JEREMIAH HOBART

of Hempstead, to whom an invitation had been presented in 1692. As his name is sometimes written Hubbert in the Records, and Hubart, he has often been confounded with the Rev. John Hubbard, his succes-

---

* Ruling Elder, Newtown.

sor. He was a son of the Rev. Peter Hobart, who came to New England in 1635. The late Rev. J. H. Hobart, D.D., a bishop of the Episcopal Church, is said to have sprung from the same family.

Jeremiah Hobart was but five or six years of age when his father emigrated to this country. He studied at Harvard, where he graduated in 1650. He commenced his labors as a preacher of the Gospel at Topsfield, Mass., and was ordained at that place in 1672. He was called to Hempstead, May 6th, 1682, after that place had been destitute of stated preaching for almost twenty-five years.

In further explanation of this Record, it may be observed that the Governors of the colony, by their interpretation of the act of 1693, claimed that no minister could be settled without their special license. It was this disposition to meddle with ecclesiastical affairs, which led very soon after to such unhappy consequences in Jamaica.

Mr. Hobart's ministry here was short, not continuing over one or two years. He went from this place to Haddam, Conn., where he was installed, Nov. 14th, 1700, and where he died on the Lord's Day, March 17th, 1717, aged 87, having preached on the morning of that day. His daughter, Sarah, was the mother of the celebrated David Brainard.

The extracts from the records which precede also show that the church, the first movement for the erection of which was made in 1689, was not completed until full ten years after; and that the work was accomplished, under no slight embarrassment, which it required much perseverance to overcome. The people were not fully agreed as to the site on which it should stand. All the matters in controversy were at length referred to the Justices, who brought in that "all those at the West of Jamaica, that is Dutchmen & William Creed & Robert Read" should pay their assessments, and be forever acquitted of any other claims. Thus the matter was settled. The stone church was finished and paid for, and the vane*—a rude imitation of the Dove, sacred emblem!—that swung to the winds of a century,—began its silent monitions to the passers and worshippers below.

* This vane was formerly in possession of the late Judge Lamberson's family.

CHAPTER V.
1700–1724.

JOHN HUBBARD — ORDAINED IN THE PRESBYTERIAN WAY — VESTRYMEN AND CHURCHWARDENS ELECTED — SILAS WOOD, ESQ. — REV. MR. THOMAS, HEMPSTEAD — COTTON MATHER ON JAMAICA — CHIEF JUSTICE SMITH ON THE JAMAICA TROUBLES — "WATCH TOWER," LIVINGSTONE, SCOTT AND SMITH — CORNBURY'S ORDERS TO INQUIRE INTO THE RIOT, AND TO MR. HUBBARD TO VACATE THE PARSONAGE — ORDER TO WARDENS AND SHERIFF TO SELL THE CORN — ORDER TO LAY TAX AND FINE THE WARDENS AND VESTRY FOR REFUSING — REV. MR. BARTOW'S ACCOUNT OF THE RIOT — MR. HUBBARD'S DEATH — REV. P. GORDON BURIED UNDER THE CHURCH — REV. W. URQUHART — REV. F. GOODHUE'S CALL AND COMMISSION — HIS EARLY DEATH — ELEGANT LATIN LINES ON HIM — REV. G. M'NISH CALLED — THE CHURCH TAKEN POSSESSION OF BY THE PRESBYTERIANS — ACCOUNT OF MR. M'NISH — THE PERSECUTION CONTINUES — MEMORIAL OF THE PEOPLE TO THE GOVERNOR — S. CLOWES INFORMS OF THE RIOT IN 1710 — ORDERS AND FINES IN RESPECT TO IT — REV. THOS. POYER — MEMORIAL OF THE CLERGY IN RESPECT TO HIM — GOV. HUNTER, COL. MORRIS AND COL. HEATHCOTE ON THE CHURCH DIFFICULTIES — SUBJECT BROUGHT BEFORE THE QUEEN IN PRIVY COUNCIL. — THE LAWSUIT — MR. M'NISH'S CHARACTER AND SERVICES — HIS DEATH — REV. ROBERT CROSS — EJECTMENT SUIT DECIDED AGAINST MR. POYER — GOV. BURNET TO BISHOP OF LONDON — MR. POYER AND MR. CAMPBELL TO SECRETARY — THE CHURCH RECOVERED.

IT was during the ministry of Mr. Hobert's successor, the Rev.

JOHN HUBBARD,

that the memorable controversy for the church property commenced. He was born in Ipswich, Mass., in 1677, and graduated at Cambridge in 1695. In the following minute, referred to on a former page, when considering the Presbyterial character of the church, his name first appears in the records:

at a towne mettinge held at Jamaica Nouember the 25 1700: it was agreed by voatt that whereas Mr John Hobbertt hath continued here amongs us in this towne in the present worke of the minestry sume considerrable time the town dos show ther willingnes to continue him still & to have him ordained acordingly provided it be accordinge to ye Rule & way of the presbetterrine way & it is the unanomoss mind of the towne thot he be ordained Acordingly & that every man shall pay towardes the ordaination as much as he shall see cos to pay.

By SAMUALL RUSCOE clark

Records II. p. 454.

As Mr. Hubbard continued at Jamaica, it is to be presumed he complied with the terms of the above vote, and was ordained "according to the rule and way of the Presbyterian way." It is not improbable he was ordained and "inducted" by the Dutch ministers of New York.

Under the act of 1693, for the settling of the ministry, Queens County was divided into two precincts or parishes. The parish of Jamaica included the towns of Jamaica, Flushing, and Newtown, and was required to raise £60 by a tax on all the freeholders, for the support of the ministry, and to elect churchwardens and vestrymen. Vestrymen were accordingly chosen in Jamaica February 17th, 1693-4, to meet with others to be chosen from the other towns. Nehemiah Smith and William Creed were chosen, but it does not appear that any thing was done by them in this capacity. They were elected, probably, to comply with the terms of the law, but the law itself remained dormant, to all intents and purposes, until the accession of Cornbury to the government. In January, 1702, vestrymen and churchwardens were again chosen (all Presbyterians, of course), and the following month they proceeded, as empowered by the act, to call Mr. Hubbard, who was already their minister, to be the minister of the place. For forty years the people of Jamaica had been of one mind in matters ecclesiastical; and, up to the date just mentioned, it is not probable that a single Episcopalian had settled in the town. "There was not," says the late Silas Wood, Esq.,* "an Episcopalian church or an Episcopal minister in the colony of New York, at the time of the conquest in 1664, and if there were any Episcopalians among the inhabitants, the number must have been very small. The inhabitants belonged either to the Dutch Reformed Church, or were English Non-conformists." The Episcopal population was very much confined, at first, to the city of New York; and the first Episcopal church in the province was erected in that city in 1696. The Rev. Mr. Vesey, the first Episcopal minister, performed divine service, for the first time, in Trinity Church, February 6th, 1697. "Although the statutes of uniformity," continues Wood, "did not extend to the colonies, and although the religious constitution of the colony† was a perfect equality among Protestants of all denominations, yet the colony governors strove to give some legal ascendancy to the Episcopal over other denominations. They incorporated their churches, which they refused to the Presbyterians. They obstructed the Presbyterian ministers who came into the colony, in the exercise of their functions, and, under the pretence of ecclesiastical au-

* Hist. of L. I., p. 41.   † See Charter.

thority, required them to apply to them for license to preach." As late as 1773, according to the same author, not more than one in fifteen of the population of the colony were supposed to be Episcopalians. The people nevertheless were taxed to support the Episcopal ministry, exclusively, under the act of 1693; an act which the Assembly declared was passed for the benefit of the Dutch Reformed and the Presbyterians, equally as for the Episcopalians.

It is admitted that the old stone meeting-house and parsonage were built by the town, and the parsonage lands were given by the town; but this was done when the inhabitants were all of substantially the same religious faith. This property, it may be remarked in passing, was valuable :* according to a letter of Cotton Mather to Messrs. Robinson and Reynolds, of London, the parsonage alone was estimated to be worth fifteen hundred pounds. The valuable glebe attached is, no doubt, to be included in this estimate. There is not the least evidence that there was a single member of the Church of England residing in Jamaica at the time

---

* Extract of a Report on the State of the Church in the Province of New York, Anno 1704, submitted to the Society for Propagating the Gospel in Foreign Parts, by C. Congreve.

"*Queens County:*

"At Jamaica there is a tolerable good church built of stone, a Parsonage house, an orchard and 200 acres of land belonging to it, and £60 per ann. settled by Act of Assembly for maintenance of the minister, who is Mr. William Urquhart, lately arrived. There is in the Church a Common Prayer Book and a cushion, but no vestments nor vessels for the communion table. The churchwardens and vestry are chosen by a majority of the parish, who are chiefly ———— [blank in the MS] and the churchwardens, when chosen, would never qualify themselves according to law, and refuse soon to provide bread and wine for the Holy Sacrament, at which there is now about twenty communicants, in a great measure brought over to an entire conformity by the Rev. Mr. Mott. There is in this parish near 2000 souls."

the church was built; much less when this property was set apart for the support of a minister. The Rev. Mr. Thomas, missionary at Hempstead, thus wrote to the Society for Propagating the Gospel in Foreign Parts, March 1st, 1705: "The people of Hempstead are better disposed to peace and civility than they are at Jamaica, yet my lord's (Cornbury's) countenance, next to the Providence of Heaven, is my chiefest safety. I have scarce a man in the parish, truly steady and real to the interest and promotion of the church, any further than they aim at the favour or dread the displeasure of his lordship." If there was scarce a man at Hempstead favorable to "the Church," where the people were so much better disposed than at Jamaica, it is absurd to maintain that "churchmen," could have had any hand in building the church, or a valid claim to any of the church property in this place. It is not improbable there were some here, as at Hempstead, who, after the strenuous exertions of the missionaries for four or five years, and the violent acts of usurpation on the part of the governor, would, to secure the favour of his lordship, profess to be Episcopalians. The following is an extract of a joint letter, dated July 4th, 1705, of Messrs. Urquhart, of Jamaica, and Thomas, of Hempstead, to the Society: "The ancient settlers have transplanted themselves from New England, and do still keep a close correspondence, and are buoyed up by schismatical instruction* from that interest,

---

* Cotton Mather's Letter to Messrs. Robinson and Reynolds shows that he took a deep interest in the affairs of the church at Jamaica. The following is an extract: "At the same time there is a town called Jamaica, on Long Island, under the government aforesaid; a town consisting of considerably above an hundred families, and exemplary for all Christian know

which occasions all the disturbance and opposition we meet with in both our parishes. They have hitherto been used to a dissenting ministry, and they still support one at Jamaica, which has a most pestilential influence over our people, who, from their cradles were disaffected to conformity." Nothing, therefore, can be more evident than that those who had been trained up under "a dissenting ministry," and who were disaffected to conformity from their cradles, were the men who built the church and gave the property in question. To some account of the controversy which took place respecting this property, and which lasted for twenty-five years, I shall now proceed.

I quote first from the History of New York by Wm. Smith, formerly of New York, and late Chief Justice of Lower Canada.

"The summer following (the arrival of Lord Cornbury, in 1702,) was remarkable for the uncommon mortality which prevailed in the city of New York, and makes a grand epoch among our inhabitants distinguished by the 'time of great sickness.' On this occasion Lord Cornbury

---

ledge and goodness, and a church with a worthy pastor in it. About half a score of families (and of meaner character) in this town declared for the Church of England, and thereupon a minister of their profession was sent to them (one Urquhart), who is maintained by the aforesaid society. But this little company having the advantage (right or wrong) to be uppermost, took away from the dissenters (if it be proper to call such a disproportionate number so) their meeting-house, computed to be worth six hundred pounds, and compelled them to build another. They also seized the Parsonage, which had been until now enjoyed by the town, and is esteemed worth fifteen hundred pounds.—The good people there do adorn the doctrine of God their Saviour by a most laudable silence and wonderful patience under these things. But if such things proceed, that noble Society for the Propagation of Religion in America will greatly wound religion, and their own reputation also, which ought to be for ever venerable." This was dated 14th October, 1706.

had his residence and court at Jamaica, a pleasant village on Long Island, distant about twelve miles from the city.*

" * * * The inhabitants of Jamaica had erected an edifice for the worship of God, and enjoyed a handsome donation of a parsonage-house and glebe, for the use of their minister. After the ministry act was passed by Colonel Fletcher, in 1693, a few Episcopalians crept into the town, and viewed the Presbyterian church with a jealous eye. The town vote, in virtue of which the building had been erected, contained no clause to prevent its being hereafter engrossed by any other sect. The Episcopal party, who knew this, formed a design of seizing the edifice for themselves, which they shortly after carried into execution by entering the church between the morning and evening service, while the Presbyterian minister and his congregation were in perfect security, unsuspicious of the zeal of their adversaries, and a fraudulent ejectment on a day consecrated to sacred rest.

"Great outrage ensued among the people, for the contention being *pro Aris et Focis*, was animating and important. The original proprietors of the house tore up their seats, and afterwards got the key and the possession of the church, which were shortly after again taken from them by force and violence. In these controversies the Governor abetted the Episcopal zealots, and harrassed the others by numberless prosecutions, heavy fines, and long imprisonments, through fear of which many who had been active in the dispute, fled out of the province. Lord Cornbury's noble descent and education should have prevented him from taking part in so ignominious a quarrel; but his

---

* Four horse-carts and sixteen wagons were hired to go from Jamaica to Brooklyn Ferry for Gov. Cornbury's effects, and a horse for the trumpeter. —Mr. Onderdouk's MS Notes.

lordship's sense of honour and justice was as weak and indelicate as his bigotry was rampant and incontrollable; and hence we find him guilty of an act complicated of a number of vices, which no man could have perpetrated without violence to the very slightest remains of generosity and justice. When his excellency retired to Jamaica, Mr. Hubbard, the Presbyterian minister, lived in the best house of the town. His lordship begged the loan of it for the use of his own family, and the clergyman put himself to no small inconvenience to favour the governor's request; but in return for the generous benefaction, his lordship perfidiously delivered the parsonage-house into the hands of the Episcopal party, and encouraged one Cardwell, the sheriff, a mean fellow, who afterwards put an end to his own life, to seize upon the glebe, which he surveyed into lots, and farmed for the benefit of the Episcopal party. These tyrannical measures justly inflamed the indignation of the injured sufferers, and that again the more embittered his lordship against them. They resented, and he prosecuted: nor did he confine his pious rage to the people of Jamaica; he detested all who were of the same denomination; nay, averse to every sect except his own, he insisted that neither the ministers nor schoolmasters of the Dutch, the most numerous persuasion in the province, had a right to preach or instruct without his gubernatorial license; and some of them tamely submitted to his unauthoritative rule."—Vol. I. pp. 169–172.

I quote next from No. 17 of a Series of Articles, under the head of " Watchtower," contained in the New York Mercury for June 2, 1755. These Articles, were written by Wm. Livingstone, J. Morin Scot,* and Wm.

---

* Brig -General in the Revolution, Member of the Continental Congress, of the State Senate, and Secretary of the State, Died September 16th, 1784. Onderdonk's Rev. Incidents, Queens Co. p. 67.

Smith,* who gave £50 a year for the use of the first page of the aforesaid paper.

"Mr. Hubbard, the Presbyterian minister, having preached to his congregation on Sunday morning, dismissed them as usual, altogether unsuspicious of any evil designs against him or his people. In the afternoon he returned to his church, and, to his great surprise and astonishment, found an Episcopal clergyman, a person doubtless of a very pacific spirit, reading the liturgy to a handful of auditors who had devoutly seated themselves in the pews. Mr. Hubbard had not the least intimation of the trick, till he had actually entered the church, and upon the discovery of it left his pious successor to the sole possession of the pulpit, whilst he himself peaceably retired to an orchard, where he preached a sermon to the graver part of his congregation, who followed him. All of them were not such passive, self-denying Christians: a tumult began at the church-door, and many ran in and tore up the seats of their families, for which some were afterwards rigorously prosecuted, and others who escaped underwent a year's banishment.

"Not long after this pious ejectment, the Presbyterians got the key of the church, regained possession, and locked up the doors. But early in the morning on the following Sabbath, several heroic Episcopalians, with proper instruments† for the purpose, forcibly broke open the church-doors, and retained possession till the parson attended the public service. The Presbyterians after this made several fruitless attempts to possess themselves of their church, but the prosecutions which ensued on their endeavors were so heavy that they thought proper to desist from any fur-

* The Historian.
† Mr. Faitoute says in his MS history, written in 1793, he had been informed by an aged gentleman that a crowbar was used.

ther attempts, and the Episcopalians held the possession of it for nineteen or twenty years after, till it was recovered from them, with the parsonage-house and glebe, in a due course of law, about the year 1727.

"His excellency Gov. Morris, was then Chief Judge of the Supreme Court of New York, and sat on the bench at that trial. Such was the resentment of the Church party on the loss of the verdict, that Morris himself did not escape their malignant aspersions, but, so late as 1734, was put to the trouble of refuting the charge of partiality on the trial, contained in a public representation, sent home aginst him while he was in England, soliciting his restoration to the Chief Justice's place, from which Governor Cosby had removed him.

"The parsonage-house and glebe were taken away in a manner not so violent, yet more iniquitous. Lord Cornbury, to flee the dreadful mortality which triumphed in New York City, in 1702, retired to Jamaica, and in a friendly manner entreated Mr. Hubbard for the use of the parsonage-house during his stay in the country. The clergyman generously put himself to inconvenience to oblige him. On his return to New York, Lord Cornbury put the church party in possession of the house.

"Usage so base enkindled resentment in almost every man's breast, and the country was full of strife and contention. Cardwell, the sheriff, under protection of Lord Cornbury, was a great instrument of his arbitrary measures. He seized the glebe, surveyed and divided it into lots, which he leased out for the benefit of the Episcopal denomination. Every attempt to recover their rights plunged the people into new difficulties: they were indicted and informed against, fined and imprisoned; and many, to escape the fury of the Government, fled into the neighbouring colonies.

"Incensed at last by a series of oppressions, the *civil* vestry and church-wardens of Jamaica, who were elected by the major vote of the inhabitants, called Mr. McNish, a Presbyterian clergyman, to be their minister, hoping thereby to exempt themselves from the annual tax, raised by virtue of the Ministry Act, passed March, 1693. The project, for several years, had its expected success. The vestrymen, to avoid the censure of the law, annually raised the salary as had been usual. But Mr. McNish refused to receive it, though far the greatest part was a tax on his own congregation, and as often as it was offered, presented it to the people according to their proportionable assessments. Offended at this stratagem, the Episcopalians contrived to defeat it, and again recover the tax for their own benefit. To that end the justices of Hempstead, who were creatures of the Governor, arbitrarily intruded their votes amongst the vestry of Jamaica, and carried a major voice for appropriating the salary to the church parson. But as their right of sitting there was protested against by the vestry, Lord Cornbury, to secure a major vote for the Episcopal minister, commissioned no less than sixteen Justices of the Peace for the single parish of Jamaica. This artifice was effectual, the number of vestrymen, church-wardens and justices being only twelve. But what right these tools of arbitrary power had by virtue of the Act of Assembly, or any other law, to vote with the vestry for the support of a minister whom they had not called, remains to this day an inexplicable mystery."

ORDER

To the Atorney Gen¹. to enquire into a riot at Jamaica.

At a Council held at ffort Anne this 27th day of July 1703.

Present—His Excell. Edward Viscount Cornbury, &c.,
Rip Van Dam Esqr
John Bridges Do' of Laws
Sa: Sh: Broughton ⎫
William Lawrence ⎬ Esqrs
Gerard Beekman ⎭

His Excell. acquainted this Board with two Letters from Jamaica in Queens County, giving an acco' of a Riott committed there by one Hubbard a Dissenting Minister and others of the inhabitants of the said Town. Ordered that the Attorney Gen" doe enquire into the facts, and as they shall appear to him prosecute the persons according to Law.

By order of his Excell. in Councill,

B. COSENS, Cᵏ Councij

Endorsed, *Order of Councill of the 27th July* 1703
For the Attorney Generall.

LORD CORNBURY'S ORDER

To Rev Mr Hubbard to vacate the Parsonage house.

By his Excellency Edward Viscount Cornbury Capt Genll. and Governour in chief of the Province of New Yorke New Jersey &c., &c.

You are hereby Required to deliver the Possession of the house Lands and p'misses wheron you now dwell and which belongs to the church of Jamaica in Queens County to yᵉ high sherife of the said County after a reasonable time for removing your goods and stock from the p'misses and hereof you are not to fail at your perill. Given under my hand att fort Anne in New Yorke this fourth day of July 1704, CORNBURY.

To Mr John Hubbard

AN ORDER TO THE SHERIFF,

To eject Rev. Mr Hubbard from his house in Jamaica.

By His Excellency Edward Viscount Cornbury Capt Gen^{ll} and Goven^r in Chief of the Province of New Yorke New Jersey &c.

Whereas by my order under my hand dated herewith I have ordered Mr John Hubbard to deliver the possession of the house land p'misses whereon he now dwells and which belongs to the church of Jamaica in Queens County to you after a reasonable time for removing his goods and stock from the p'misses. You are therefore hereby required to deliver the possession of the s^d p'misses after you have received it from the s^d Mr Hubbard to Mr William Urquhart and if it happen that ye s^d Mr Hubbard shall in contempt of my said order refuse to deliver ye possession of the p'misses to you as aff'^d, then and in such case you are hereby required & impowered to enter on ye p'misses, and possession so taken to deliver to the said Mr Urquhart and all Justices of the Peace and others her Majty's officers both civil and military are hereby required to be aiding and assisting unto you at the execution hereof.

Given under my hand att fort Anne in New Yorke this fourth day of July 1704 CORNBURY

To Tho: Cardell Esqr
High Sheriffe of Queens County

Endorsed,
*An order to the
High Sheriffe of Queens County*

AN ORDER

To the Church wardens and sheriff of Jamaica, By his Excell. Edward Viscount Cornbury Capt Gen^{ll} and Govr in Chief of the provinces of New Yorke New Jersey &c.

You and every one of you are hereby required forthwth to sell and dispose for ye best price and advantage that Cann be made and gotten the Corn collected by or delivered to you or any or either of you for the maintenance and benefit of the Minister of Jamaica and ye moneys thereof made to retain in your hands untill you Receive further orders from me for the payment of the same to the uses for wch the s^d corn was delivered to you and hereof you are not to faile att your Perill Given under my hand att fort Anne in New Yorke this 4th day of July 1704

CORNBURY

To the Church Wardens of the Church of Jamaica and to the High Sheriffe of Queens County.

AN ORDER

To the Justices* and Church Wardens of Jamaica By his Excell. Edward Viscount Cornbury Capt Gen^{ll} and Govr in Chief of the Provinces of New Yorke, New Jersey, &c.

You are hereby Required to pay ye moneys made of ye corn collected for the maintenance of a Minister for the town of Jamaica in Queens County and wch remains in your hands to the Rev Mr William Urquahart and for soe doing this shall be your sufficient warrant. Given under my

---

* Cornbury commissioned sixteen Justices for the single parish of Jamaica, who intruded their votes amongst the Vestry, and thus secured a majority for appropriating the salary to the church parson.

hand att ffort Anne in New Yorke this twenty eighth day of August 1704

CORNBURY

To the Justices of the Peace for Queens County
and to the Vestrymen and Church Wardens
of the Church of Jamaica in the said
County.

AN ORDER

To the Justices and Vestrymen to levy a tax for the Minister of Jamaica, By his Excellency Edward Viscount Cornbury Capt Gen^{ll} and Govern^{r} in Chief of ye Provinces of New York New Jersey &c.

You are hereby required forthwith to lay a tax on the Inhabitants of Queens County for raising the maintenance for the Minister of Jamaica in the said County for this present year and the said tax laid to levy and collect or cause to be Levyed and collected pursuant to the act of assembly passed in the sixth Session of Generall Assembly begun the 12th day of September 1693 Entituled an act for settling a Ministry and raising a maintenance for them in the Citty of New York, County of Richmond, Westchester and Queens County and hereof you are not to faile. Given under my hand at ffort Anne in New York this twenty fourth day of August 1704.

To the Justices of the Peace of Queens County
and the Vestrymen of the Church of Ja-
maica in the said County.

ORDER

To Fine the Churchwardens, Etc., For Refusing to Levy said Tax.

[Council Min. IX.]

In Council 31 *March* 1705

The Churchwardens and Vestry of Jamaica being sum-

moned to appear before this Board this day and Robert
Coe one of the Church Wardens & John Talman Henry
Wright Samuel Carpenter Sam¹ Higby Anthony Waters
John Everett John Coe Jonathan Hazard & Daniel Lawrence nine of the Vestry appearing accordingly they were
called in and examined concerning their neglecting or refusing to raise a tax for the maintenance of the Minister of
that place directed to be raised for that purpose by Act of
Gen^{ll} Assembly of this Province and having offered nothing
to this Board in their Justification it is ordered that the
Penaltyes expressed and contained in the said Act be
Levyed pursuant to the directions thereof on every one of
them ye s^d Churchwardens & Vestry so neglecting or refusing to do their duty as aforesaid.

Rev. Mr. Bartow to the Sec. of the Soc. for Propagating the Gospel in Foreign Parts.

W. CHESTER NEW YORK, 1st Dec. 1707.

TO THE SEC.

Sir, after a voyage of 11 weeks we arrived at New York
Sep. 29, 1702, where we found a very mournful town,
nearly 20 persons dying daily, for some months. I went
next day to Col. Graham's, Westchester, and on Monday
returned to New York. Mr. Vesey got me to preach for
him on the appointed fast that week. I preached there or
at Westchester every Sunday till Lord Cornbury returned
from Albany, when I went to Jamaica to wait on his Lordship (who went there by reason of the sickness in New
York) to deliver him my credentials, and receive his commands, which were to continue in Westchester and the
first half year being winter I lodged at a public house
preaching once every Sunday and upon occasion visiting
the sick. After winter was over, I lived at Col. Graham's
six miles from the Church and all the summer preacht

twice every Sunday, sometimes at West Chester and sometimes at Jamaica on Long Island about – miles distant from Mr. Graham's at my own charge, nor have I had any board given me since I came, and once I met with great disturbance at Jamaica. Mr. Hobbart, their Presbyterian minister, having been for some time at Boston returned to Jamaica the Saturday night as I came to it, and sent to me at my lodging (being then in company with our Chief Justice Mr. Mompesson and Mr. Carter her Majesty's Comptroller) to know if I intended to preach on the morrow. I sent him answer that I did intend it.—The next morning the bell rang as usual, but before the last time of ringing Mr. Hobbart was got into the Church, and had begun his service of which notice was given me whereupon I went into the Church and walked straightway to the pew expecting Mr. Hobbart would desist being he knew I had orders from the Government to officiate there, but he persisted and I forbore to make any interruption. In the afternoon I prevented him beginning the service of the Church of England, before he came who was so surprised when after he came to the church door and saw me performing divine service that he suddenly started back and went aside to an orchard hard by, and sent in some to give the word that Mr. Hobbart would preach under a tree, then I perceived a whispering thro' the church and an uneasiness of many people some going out, some seemed amazed not yet determined whether to go or stay. In the mean time some that had gone out returned again for their seats and then we had a shameful disturbance: hauling and tugging of seats, shoving one the other off, carrying them out and returning again for more, so that I was fain to leave off till the disturbance was over, and a separation was made by which time I had but about half of the congregation, the rest remaining devout and attentive the whole time of the service; after which we lock't the church door and committed the key into the hands of the sheriff; we were no sooner got into an adjoining house but some persons came to demand the key of their meeting-house which being denied they went and broke the glass window, and put a boy in to open the door and so put in their seats and took away the pew-cushion saying they would keep that however for their own minister; the scolding and wrangling that ensued are by me ineffable. The next time I saw my Lord Cornbury he thanked me and said he would do the church and me justice, accordingly he summoned Mr. Hobbart and the head of the faction before him and forbad Mr. Hobbart ever more to preach in that Church, for in regard it was built by a public tax it did appertain to the established church (which it has quietly remained ever since and now in possession of our Rev'd Brother, Mr. Urquhart.) My Lord Cornbury threatened them all with the penalty of the statute for disturbing divine service, but upon their submission and promise of future quietness and peace he pardoned the offence."

How the youthful pastor was affected by such troubles as these we are not informed. His conduct, when he so unexpectedly found the Rev. Mr. Bartow reading the liturgy in his pulpit, in retiring to an adjoining orchard, and inviting his people to accompany him, there to worship Him who dwelleth not in temples made with hands, proves him to have been an amiable and discreet man. It is not improbable, however, that the failure of his health had some connection with his peculiar trials. He died at the early age of twenty-eight years. In the Boston "News Letter," No. 79, October 22, 1705, appeared the following:

"Jamaica on Long Island, Oct. 11. On Fryday, the 5th

current, dyed here the Rev. Mr. John Hubbard, Pastor of a Church in this place, aged 28 years 9 months, wanting 4 days."

Thompson says respecting him : " He was one of the most excellent and amiable youths which New England produced, and his death was extensively and deeply lamented." He was the first minister buried in this town. But no monument or headstone marks the spot where his ashes repose.

The Presbyterian congregation, after they had been excluded from their church edifice, worshipped, as Mr. Faitoute says* he had been told by aged people, in a building at the eastern extremity of the village. In 1702, the Rev. Patrick Gordon, the first Episcopalian minister, arrived from England; but he died before he could be inducted, "and was buried," says Dr. Humphreys, Secretary to the Honorable Society, in his History of the Society, "in a MEETING-HOUSE in Jamaica." The Rev. Mr. Bartow, of Westchester, as we have shown, by a letter from his own hand, is undoubtedly entitled to the honour of having figured so conspicuously in the affair of taking possession of Mr. Hubbard's pulpit. After Mr. Gordon's death, Mr. Vesey, the first rector of Trinity Church, N. Y., supplied Jamaica with "constant lectures ;"† and other Episcopal ministers in the province rendered occasional services. A Mr. Honeyman, against whom charges‡ seriously affecting his moral character had been made, and a Mr. Mott, severally preached for a short time, when the Rev. William Urquhart arrived, and was inducted as

---

* MS Hist. † Petition of the clergy to the Bishop of London.
‡ Mr. Urquhart's Letter to the Sec. of the V. S.

rector July 4th, 1704. Mr Hubbard was, at that time, in possession of the parsonage; but he was ordered by Cornbury, "to deliver up the same to Mr. Urquhart, which accordingly was done quietly and peaceably,"* and Mr. Urquhart remained in possession till his death, which took place in August, 1709. The Rev.

FRANCIS GOODHUE

was Mr. Hubbard's successor in the ministry. It would not have been surprising if the congregation, their church and parsonage occupied by others, and their minister in the grave, had remained for some time in a destitute and scattered condition. Such was the effect of similar arbitrary proceedings at Hempstead. Mr. Goodhue was settled the year following Mr. Hubbard's death.† He was a native of the same place, and probably had been a companion of Hubbard in childhood, as he was but one year younger. He was a son

---

* Petition of Epis. Clergy.
† REV'D MR. GOODHUE'S COMMISSION.
As Presbyterian minister of Jamaica L. I.
[Deed Book X.]

By His Excellency Edward Viscount Cornbury Capt Gen¹ & Gov' in Chief of ye Provinces of N York, New Jersey & of all the Territories & Tracts of Land Depending thereon in America & Vice Admiral of the same &c.

To MR. FRANCIS GOODHUE, Greeting:

I do hereby Licence & Tollerate you to be Minist' of the Presbyterian Congregation at Jamaica in Queens County on the Island of Nassau in the s^d Province of New Yorke & to have & Exercise the ffree Liberty & use of yo' Religion pursuant to Her Maty^s pleasure therein signified to me In her Royal Instructions & during so Long Time as to me shall seem meet & all Ministers & others are hereby Required to take notice hereof. Given under my hand and seale at ffort Anne in New York this —— day of this instant January in the ffourth year of Her Maty^s Reign Annoq: Dmi 1705-6

CORNBURY

By His Excys Command
  William Anderson D secy

of Deacon William and Hannah Goodhue, and was born in Chebecca parish, Ipswich, Mass., October 4th, 1678. His grandfather, William, was one of the most influential and respectable men in the colony of Massachusetts, whose "many virtues" are said to have "conferred honour upon his name and family." Francis Goodhue graduated at Harvard in 1699, and was settled at Jamaica in 1706. At the close of the summer of 1707, he went from this place on a journey to New England; little did he or his people think that he was to return no more. He died of fever on his way, at Rehoboth, Mass., near Providence, R. I., where he was buried. Seekonk was the Indian name of the place; and in 1812 its western section was incorporated as a separate town, and is now called by this name.

The ministry of Hubbard, and that of Goodhue, were short, but they were doubtless eminently useful in keeping the congregation together, under its adverse circumstances. It is deeply affecting to contemplate the situation of the congregation called thus to mourn over the early graves of two ministers who, having been pleasant and lovely in their lives, in death were not far divided.

The following elegant lines on Mr. Goodhue are taken from the Boston "News Letter" of February 28, 1723.

> Libertas nomen; bonitas conjuncta colori
>   Cognomen præbent; Insula Longa gregem.
> Nascitur Ipsvici; dissolvitur inter eundum;
>   Seconchæ lecto molliter ossa cubant.

> Doctrina, officium, pietas, adamata juventus,
> Nil contra jussam convaluere necem,
> Pars potior sedes procedit adire beatas
> Gaudens placato semper adesse Deo.

Which may be thus translated:

Liberty [Francis] gives him a name; *good* joined to *hue* a surname; Long Island a flock. Born at Ipswich, he dies whilst travelling. His bones softly repose in their bed at Seekonk. Learning, sacred office, piety, amiable youth could avail nothing against death decreed. The immortal part enters into Paradise, rejoicing to be forever in the presence of God reconciled.

For two or three years the congregation appears to have been vacant, but in the spring* of 1710, the Rev.

GEORGE McNISH

was called to be minister. He was a native of Scotland or Ireland, and came to this country in 1705, with the Rev. Francis Makemie, often styled the father of the Presbyterian Church in this country. The Rev. John Hampton came, at the same time, with Mr. McNish, both of them no doubt induced by Mr. Makemie, who had resided many years in this country, and who visited Europe expressly to prevail on ministers to come and settle here. Messrs. Makemie and Hampton were the two Presbyterian Ministers who were imprisoned and fined by Lord Cornbury in 1706 for preaching without a license from him. Mr. Hampton was arrested at Newtown, where he had preached,

---

* The case of ——, and opinion &c. referred to in Gov. Hunter's Letter, 25th Feb., 1711.

and was brought to Jamaica and imprisoned in the Presbyterian Church over night; and, the next day, marched to New York.

In June, 1706, by order of Gov. Seymour, of Maryland, the Somerset County Court licensed Messrs. McNish and Hampton.

Upon the removal of Col. Ingolsby, who administered the government for a short time after the death of Lord Lovelace in 1709, the Supreme authority devolved on Gerardus Beekman, Esq., President of the Council. He was not under the influence of the bigotry which had actuated the English governors, and the Presbyterians at once availed themselves of the opportunity to take possession of their church. There was no Episcopal incumbent at that time, the place being supplied "every other Sunday by the Rev. Mr. Vesey, Mr. Sharp, and the missionaries in the province of New York,"* Soon after, and before the arrival of an Episcopal minister for the place, the parsonage and glebe also passed into the possession of the Presbyterians, the rightful proprietors, and, notwithstanding the strenuous efforts that were made, never again were wrested from them. Possession was secured in the following manner: the parsonage was tenanted by the widow of Mr. Urquhart; she surrendered it to the representatives of the Presbyterian congregation, but was soon afterwards re-admitted as a tenant to them. Her daughter had married a young student of theology, a Presbyterian, of the name of Wolsey, who resided with her. She remained their tenant until the Presbyterian minister was ready to take possession.

* Mr. Bartow's Letter to the Secretary of the Ven. Society.

It was during the brief occupancy of the church edifice, in the spring of 1710, that the wardens and vestrymen of Jamaica, who were Presbyterians, gave a call to Mr. McNish. This gentleman was one of the original members of the Presbytery of Philadelphia, the first formed in America. He preached first to the people at Monokin and Wicomico, in Maryland, who presented a call to him; but it appears from the minutes of the Presbytery held in 1710, that Mr. McNish had not, at that time, accepted the call. At the meeting of the Presbytery in 1711, the call from Jamaica was put into his hands, and "'twas determined to leave his affair respecting Jamaica and Patuxent to himself, with advice not to delay to fix himself somewhere." This minute makes it quite evident that he never became the settled pastor at Monokin. Some time in 1711, he became the minister of Jamaica; although there can be no doubt he had frequently supplied the place during the preceding year.

The Presbyterians, however, were not long permitted to retain the use of their house of worship. Their adversaries succeeded in ejecting them; and six of their number were arrested and brought before the magistrates. They were, however set at liberty, on their own recognizances to appear at the next sessions. They were fined only three shillings each, and even their fines were remitted by the President and Council. The efforts of the Church of England party to re-possess themselves of the parsonage and glebe were not so successful. They made application to a magistrate for redress, who issued a warrant to the sheriff for apprehending the offenders; but it so happened that this officer was now a Presbyterian, and he replied to the Justice that "it was against his conscience to execute the precept." The sequel will show that their persevering attempts, under the administration of Governor Hunter, were equally unsuccessful, and that the property of the Church, other than the house of worship, was never again in their possession. Mr. McNish, on accepting the call which had been given him, had the parsonage and glebe lands confirmed to him by a vote of the town. One Samuel Clowes entered his protest against this vote of the town; he is said to have been of the heroic party, who, in Mr. Hubbard's time, forcibly broke open the doors of the Presbyterian Church.

the 6th day of february 1709-10.
at a towne meeting held at Jamaica of ye freeholders of ye above s^d towne

Present — Jonathan Whitehead Esq, Robert Read Esq, Sam ll Baylys Esq, Tho: Whitehead Esq — Justices.

voted by ye majority of ye freeholders assembled as above s^d that Justice Jonathan whitehead Jonas Wood anthony waters Nathaniel Denton & John Everit or ye major part of them are hereby authorized & appointed for to take into their hands all ye towns land w^h is called parsonage land housing & medow & to divide all ye medow & upland according to every mans right & ye home lot & house &c for to be hired out at their discretion & ye rent to be disposed of to ye proper owners of ye same in equal proportion according to every mans rights Robert Read Peter white Josiah Wiggins Thomas whitehead and Samuel Clows doth protest ag^t ye above vote as unlawfull voted as afores^d y^t capt George Woolsey Nicolas Everit & Benjamin Thurston are hereby authorized and enjoined for to demand ye Key of ye stone meeting house from ye person w^h is in possession of ye same & keep ye said house for y. use of ye towne

voted as afores^d that all particular surveing made by any person in or upon any part of ye comon or undivided land in ye aboves^d township by any person or persons except such as was chosen by publik vote as town surveiers is & shall be esteemed ilegal & unlawful

entered per Zach Mills clark
Town Records III. 483.

At a town meeting held at Jamaica July ye 25: day: 1712 It is voted & concluded that Mr gorg: magnish is our minister & that ye pos sion given unto the said Mr magnish of ye minister house or passonage & land &c by ye trustess of the town Jonas Wood Nathaniell Denton anthony Watters John Everit is approved of by the town & the town further confirm unto the said Mr magnish the possession of ye s^d house & land whiles he stays & continues our ministar

Mr Samuell Clows protest against ye dismising of ye town meeting   pr: Nehemiah Smith cler
Town Records III. 485.

MEMORIAL OF THE INHABITANTS OF JAMAICA

To his Excell^{cy} Coll Robert Hunter Capt General and Governo^r in Chiefe of her Maj^{ties} Colony of New York &c in America.

The Humble Memoriall of the Inhabitants of Jamaica in Queens County.

May it pleas yor Excell^{cy}

This Towne of Jamaica in the year 1656 was purchased

from the Indian Natives by diverse persons our predecessors and Anncestors Subjects of the Realm of England, Protestant dissenters in the manner of Worship from the fforms used in the Church of England; who settled and Improved the land, Have called a Minister of their owne Profession to Officiate among them who continued so to do during the time of the Dutch Government and afterwards severall others successively until the year of our Lord 1673-4.

In the year 1676 the Townsmen set apart divers Lands for the better Incouragement and support of such a Minister.

In the year 1693 the Inhabitants purchased a house and other conveniences for the accomodation of their Ministers who possessed and Injoyed it accordingly.

That about the year 1699 by Virtue of an act of Generall Assembly for that purpose the Majo^r part of the ffreeholders of the Towne built and erected a Meeting house or public edifice for the Worship and service of God after their way, and peaceably possessed and used it.

That in the year 1703 or 1704 being actually and Quietly possessed of the said House lands and other coveniencyes and of the said meeting house, they were with force & violence without any process, Tryall or Judgment at Law turned out and Dispossessed of the same.

All which they humbly submitt to yor Excellencies consideration, Humbly praying such Reliefe as y^r Excell^{cy} shall Judge consist^g with Equity & Justice

NATHANIEL DENTON
ANTHONY WATERS
DANIEL SMITH
SAMLL BAYLES

A Statement of the Church at Jamaica.

7ber 1693. The act of Assembly for settling ye Ministry was past.

Jany 1702. The first Vestrymen and Churchwardens were chosen at Jamaica.

1702. Mr Hubbard a Dissenting minister was called by the Churchwardens & Vestry.

Augt 1704. Mr Urquhart was Inducted by power from my Lord Cornbury.

1706. An act of Assembly past which confirmed that Induction.

1710 in ye Spring. Mr Macknesh a Dissenting Minister was called by the Churchwardens & vestry who are all Dissenters.

1710 July 18. Mr Poyer was Inducted by power from his Exc^ly Coll Hunter.

I humbly conceive that no person that has ye presentation to a Benefice can do it twice. So that if an unqualified person be presented he that presented him cannot afterwards prefer another. This was the case of Mr Hubbard who being a Dissenter was not qualified to accept for which reason my Lord Cornbury gave Induction to Mr Urquhart & ye Assembly by ye said last act declare it to be valid.

That Mr Macknesh has been lately called by ye Vestry &c but by his being a Dissenter was not qualified to accept and therefore Mr Poyer is Inducted by power from his Exc^ly & being so Inducted is Intituled to everything that belonged to his predecessor Mr Urquhart & consequently to ye Sallary which is now about to be appropriated to a Dissenting Minister. The first act of Setting ye Ministry lay dormant wth us 9 years because we had no Church of England Minister to reap the benefit of it.

6

Its lying dormant so long is a plaine Indication of ye opinion of the Dissenters themselves in favour of the Church. ffor if that act was made for the Dissenters (which they do now against all reason assert) why did they never make use of it in all that time & thereby put an end to the continued & endless contentions they have had with their Ministers many of which are not yet paid by them.

Sam'l Clowes to the President of the Council.

HONBLE SIR   JAMAICA 11 April 1710

I wish your Hon^r a great deal of joy in the Trust the Queen has been pleased to confer on you; and begg leave to acquaint yor Hon^r that ye Dissenters here have this day committed a Riot or forceable Detainer in the Church; I persuade myself your hon^r will suppress with all your might such forceable Ways of proceeding so detremental to the public peace. If they have any Right; (as I think 'tis plaine they have none) the Law is open. I therefore pray yor Hon^r Will please allow all due Encouragement to the Queens officers who have committed them for the ffact; & especially by directing ye Queen's Attorney Gen^{ll} to prosecute the offenders whereby you will add to the Glory of your Government by Defending the cause of Christs Church.

I remane
Yo^r most obedient Servt
S. CLOWES.

To the Honble Coll Beakman
Lievt Governor of the
Province of New York.

Order of Council on the Above.

IN COUNCIL 13th April 1710

The President communicated to this Board a letter from

Mr Samuell Clowes of ye 11th Aprill setting forth that the Dissenters had that day Committed a Riot or forceable Detainer of ye Church at Jamaica And therefore Desired y^t all Due Encouragement might be given to the Queens officers who had committed the persons for that Fact Especially by Directing the Attorney Generall to proceeute the offender.

The President also communicated a Mittimus under the hand and seal of Robert Read Esqr one of Her Majesties Justices for Keeping the Peace in Queens County whereby the High Sheriffe thereof was Directed to take into his Custody Hugh Carpenter George Woolsey Jonas Wood, Richard Oldfield Samuel Mills & Jeramiah Smith who he setts forth are convicted of ye said forceable holding (by his own view) and them to keep in the Common Gaol of said County untill they shall be thence delivered by due Course of Law.

ORDERED that the respective Justices of Queens County or the major part thereof Enquire into the Facts abovementioned and Lay a true Representation thereof before this Board by Thursday next, and that a coppy of this Order be forthwith sent to ye said Justices.

JAMAICA in Queens County
ye 19th of April 1710

Wee underwritten Justices of the peace of our Sovereigne Lady the Queen for Queens County assigned in obedience to an order from the honourable the president & her Maties Council of this province dated the 13th Inst (to us directed) have Inquired upon oath into the matter of the Disturbance in the Church of Jamaica & doe find that Mr Justice Read has proceeded therein according to Law and that the Record he has made is a true Representation thereof

We remain

Yo' Honours most obed' Servants

THO: WILLETT   JOHN MARSTON
JO^n JACKSON   THO: JONES
JOHN TREDWELL   WI: CORNELL
SAM^{ll} MOORE   THO: WHITEHEAD

Endorsed

"A Lett^r from ye Justices of ye Peace for Queens County.

IN COUNCIL 20th April 1710

The Justices of ye Peace for Queens County Layd before the Board according to order a Representation of the Disturbance and forceable Detainer of ye Church of Jamaica by some Dissenters which was a Record made thereof by Robt Read Esqr and Certificate of several of ye Justices that the same is a True Record

Upon consideration of this matter The Board is of opinion That the Law being open they ought not to Encourage or Discourage the said Prosecution

Petition of Geo. Woolsey and Others.

To the Honble Coll Gerardus Beekman President of her Majesty's Councill for the Colony of New York and Councill. The Peticon of George Woolsey Hope Carpenter Jonas Wood Richard Oldfield Samuell Mills & Jeremiah Smith of Jamaica in Queens County.

Most Humbly Sheweth

That yor Peticoners Stand Committed till they pay their ffine and charges upon a supposition of their being guilty of a forceable Detainer grounded on the conviction by the view of Robert Read Justice of the peace for

Queens County whereof they are not concious to themselves of being the least Guilty, and of which they humbly conceive they can give sufficient proofe to any Impartiall Judicature.

They therefore humbly pray that yo' Hon" will give them such Relief as shall appear agreeable to Justice. And they shall as in duty bound

   Ever pray &c

    GEORGE WOOLLSE   JONAS WOOD
    HOPE CARPENTER   JEREMIAH SMITH
    RICHARD OLDFIELD   SAMLL MILLS.

Read the 19th day of May 1710 &
al partys to attend on Monday
& the Justices of the peace to be
served with Copy of this Petition.

     IN COUNCIL, 23 May, 1710

M Regnier council for George Woolsey and others Pet. titioners on the Petition read at this Board the 19th Ins and Mr Bickley Councill for the Queen and the Justices of the Peace of Queens County appearing at this Board and being severally heard

It is ordered that the several and respective fines imposed on the petitioners by the Justices of the Peace in Queens County at the last Court of Sessions be remitted. But the charges which alredy are, or if not shall be taxed within the Bounds of Moderation by the Judge be paid by the said petitioners.

The Rev. Thomas Poyer, who is said to have been a grandson of Col. Poyer, who fell in the defence of Pembroke Castle, in the time of Oliver Cromwell, was the successor of Mr. Urquhart. He arrived in the colony in the summer of 1710, and was inducted (as the phrase was) by power from Col. Hunter, July 18th of that year. The Governor claimed the authority of putting Mr. Poyer in possession of the church in disregard of the rights of those whose property it was, but he refused to assume the responsibility of ejecting tenants *a la Cornbury*, by his gubernatorial mandate. And in this determination he was sustained by the Chief Justice Mompesson, who gave his opinion in writing that it would be "a high crime and a misdemeanour," to put Mr. Poyer in possession of the parsonage and lands otherwise than by due course of law. But this part of the history will be best related in the very language of the documents from which it is derived. These documents will disclose the fact that whilst Gov. Hunter was as devoted a member of the Church of England as any of the early Governors, Mr. Poyer and many of the Episcopal missionaries were not a little disappointed that he refused to adopt the peremptory and highhanded measures of Lord Cornbury towards the Presbyterians.

Mr. Poyer to the Secretary of the V. S.
[EXTRACT.]
JAMAICA, ON L'G ISLAND, 5th Oct. 1710.

Honoured Sir,——My predecessor's Widow has not dealt kindly by me, for the day that I was expected in this town she delivered up the parsonage house to the Dissenters.

From the same to the same.
[EXTRACT.]
JAMAICA, L'G ISLAND, 3d May, 1711.

Honoured Sir,——I have great hopes that there will more come over to our Church notwithstanding the many enemies and discouragements I daily meet withall, of which I have in a former hinted to you, but wrote more fully to the Right Honorable and Right Reverend Bishop of London who has a perfect and true state of the case which I hope when duly considered will induce the Honourable Society to assert the right of the Church here; that I may be supported with my salary, due here by an act of the country, one penny of which has not hitherto been paid to me but on the contrary raised and given to one Mr. George McNish an Independent North Britain preacher who has had the assurance, in the face of the country, to aver that the Bishop of London has no power here.

The foregoing extract proves that Mr. McNish had been employed to supply the pulpit in Jamaica previous to May, 1711, although it is evident he was not installed as pastor till after the meeting of Presbytery in September of that year.

Memorial of the Clergy, &c., relating to Mr. Poyer and the Church of Jamaica.

[EXTRACT.]

To the Right Honourable and Right Reverend Father in God, Henry, Lord Bishop of London. The memorial of the Clergy of the Colonies of New-York, New Jersey and Philadelphia, in America,

Humbly Sheweth——Conformable to instructions from his late majesty King William, to the then Governor for the encouragement of Religion in General and the Established Church in particular, and to settle parishes within the said province (New-York) in the year 1693 an act of General Assembly passed whereby it was enacted that in the several cities and counties therein mentioned there should be called and Inducted and Established a sufficient protestant ministry amongst which one was to be for Jamaica, and the two adjacent towns, and another for Hempstead and its adjacent towns, but so unhappy was this province as to remain *a scattered people without any true Shepherd till the year* 1697, *when the Rev. Mr. Vesey came to the city of New-York.*

————Nevertheless it is confessed that they have made use of independent and sometimes itinerant preachers in no wise ordained, out of pure necessity for want of Orthodox preachers, &c.

In the year 1702 came from England the Reverend Patrick Gordon to the Church at Jamaica, who, before he could be inducted was snatched away by death from those people to their unspeakable loss, which, by a petition signed by upwards of fifty inhabitants to his then Excellency, Lord Cornbury, (that noble patron of the Church here) they did sufficiently express, and pray his Lordship to give such directions to the Rev. Mr. . . . Vesey that they might have constant lectures amongst them until that loss shall be made up to them, by her Majesty, which would tend to the advancement of true religion and the best of Churches, and the reconciling their unhappy differences, the which Mr. Vesey willingly and faithfully performed, till the year 1704, when the Rev. Mr. Urquhart was established and inducted in the said Church, by the then Governor, Lord Cornbury. *But one Mr. Hubbard, an independent minister, being then in possession of the parsonage house, his Lordship ordered him to deliver up the same to Mr. Urquhart, which accordingly was done, quietly and peaceably, without any force, and was enjoyed peaceably by the said Mr. Urquhart, for several years,* and the Independents themselves seemed to rest satisfied so far that they unanimously, at their own expense, built themselves a Meeting House in the same town which they now use and enjoy.

It is a noteworthy reason that is here given in proof that the Presbyterians (the appellation "Independents" is used in the reports and letters of the Episcopal missionaries, long after Mr. McNish was settled,) were satisfied to see their minister turned out of the Parsonage, that they unanimously, and, "at their own expense," too, went and built themselves a meeting house. But the memorial proceeds:

After the death of Mr. Urquhart there was nothing but great threatenings thundered against the church and parsonage, but Colonel Ingolsby, then Lieutenant Governor of this Colony recommended to the adjacent ministers to serve the cure alternately, during the vacancy, which they all did willingly at their own expense, and in the meantime the widow of the deceased Mr. Urquhart was suffered to live and enjoy the benefit of the parsonage house and glebe.

No sooner was her Majesty pleased to remove Colonel Ingolsby from the Government whereby the same devolved on Colonel Gerhardus Beckman as President of the Council, but the very next day being the 11th of April 1710, several of the more violent of that sect took possession of the church and forcibly detained the same against a Justice of the peace who came pursuant to the laws in that case made and provided, and recorded the story as in his view and committed the offenders who afterwards were set at liberty upon their own recognizances to appear at the next Sessions at which time they appeared and were by the Court fined so very small that though there were six offenders all their fines amounted to no more than Eighteen shillings, which was put upon them not as a punishment, but rather a cautionary admonition, not to attempt any thing of the like nature for the future, which mild dealing was so far from having any effect upon the Criminals, that they put in a petition to the President and Council concerning what they had judicially done in their fall sessions, and the criminals were so far encouraged as to have their several fines remitted them, and the Justices dismissed from their further attendance as having acted according to law.

After this usage of the Justices so contrary to Law and after such countenance to the criminals shown by the President and Council, it may easily be concluded the Church could not be very secure from the further attempts of such bitter enemies, and accordingly after the arrival of Mr. Poyer, the present minister, but before his actually coming to the place, they entered into the parsonage house upon the possession of the Widow of Mr. Urquhart, who lived in it and kept the Widow out of it by force, though she and her husband had been in possession of the same about six years; (though we have since very great reason to believe that she connived at their entry, for she was soon afterwards readmitted as a tenant to them, with one Wolsey an Independent student and approbationer, who has married the Daughter of the said Widow Urquhart) and after Mr. Poyer was inducted into the Church, the Justice repaired upon complaint to the parsonage house, but got no admittance, whereupon a second record of forcible detainer was made by the Justice, on his own view, and warrant issued by the Sheriff to apprehend the offenders, and to keep them till they should be delivered by due course of law, but the Sheriff who had been lately appointed by the President and Council, in the room of the former deceased, being a strong Independent, told the Justices his conscience would not let him do it, by which means the offenders have as yet escaped punishment, and Mr. Poyer kept out of his possession of the parsonage and glebe.

In a short time after the death of Mr. Urquhart the Church wardens and Vestry (tho' new ones, yet all Independents) called one Mr. George McNish, a dissenting itinerant preacher, who being as much if not more unqualified to accept or officiate than Mr. Hubbard, the present Governor, Mr. Hunter, ordered Mr. Poyer to be inducted into the said church and its appurtenances, which was accordingly done by the Rev'd Mr. Sharp, Chaplain of the forces here on the 18th of July, 1710.

Tho' Mr. Poyer has duly officiated there for the space of one year and a half, and after a very tedious and expensive voyage with his family in a merchant ship, and being cast ashore with his ship above one hundred miles from his parish, he has not received one penny of his salary there since his arrival; but on the contrary, they paid £16 certain (and we believe more that we know not of) of the money raised by the act to the said Mr. McNish.

And now because that upon so firm a foundation it may be expected that Mr. Poyer, the present worthy incumbent of this unhappy place, should by law endeavour to obtain his salary, together with the parsonage house and lands detained from him by the Independents to which method his Excellency Colonel Hunter has encouraged him, by promising him to be at the expense of the suit— We humbly crave leave to offer that we cannot at this juncture, think it at all advisable for him because we are humbly of opinion that a matter of that consequence ought not to be in such a manner undertaken without the express directions of your Lordship and the Honourable Society, and also because such suit must be commenced before Judges who are professed, implacable enemies of the Established Church, *Judges who are advanced in the room of others who were men of character, and true friends of the Church, at an unlucky time, when they were actually doing justice to the Church in this particular; and we could heartily have wished that his Excellency would have been pleased to have favoured Mr. Poyer's petition* by writing to those new officers to enforce them in their duty, and hope that such admonitions would have had a good influence on them; tho' indeed justice from these new judges may scarcely be expected after the acting of three of them, who upon Mr. Poyer's complaint against the Church wardens for the non-payment of his first quarter's salary gave judgment against him, and ordered him to pay costs; in which trial they denied all authority from England in spiritual matters. Neither is it possible to get an impartial Jury in that county, where all are concerned in the event, and the greater number of them stiff independents.

The reasons, may it please your Lordship that induced us to send this representation are drawn from the certain ruin that the loss of this cause will inevitably bring on the Established Church in the whole government of New-York, and which cannot want its bad influence upon the Church in all the adjacent Colonies, especially the Jerseys and Pennsylvania; for if upon the death of Mr. Urquhart who was so firmly established by two acts of General Assembly, and after about six years quiet possession, the salary and parsonage may immediately be seized with impunity and enjoyed as they are by these Independents, why may not the rest of the places in the said provinces (WHICH DO ALL STAND UPON THE SAME FOOT) on the death or avoidance of the present incumbents be in like manner invaded by them, &c.

We beg your Lordship to believe that nothing herein contained is designed as the least reflection upon any person it being only the true plain matter of fact, and which we could not out of a due regard to the interests of the Church, and to your Lordship's omit the transmitting to your Lordship that if the sad effect we justly fear should be the consequence of these things, We may clear ourselves before God and man as having done what was possible for us to prevent it.

All which is humbly submitted to your Lordship's prudent consideration, by, may it please your Lordship, your Lordship's most dutiful, obedient sons and humble servants,

THOS. POYER,
Rector of the Parish of Jamaica and precinct.

WM. VESEY,
Rector of the Parish of New York.

JNO. BARTOW,
Rector of the Parish and Precinct of Westchester.

EVAN EVANS,
Rector of Philadelphia.

JOHN TALBOT,
Of Burlington.

ÆNEAS McKENSIE,
Of Staten Island.

JACOB HENDERSON,
Minister of Dover Hundred.

JOHN THOMAS,
Rector of Hempstead.

New York, 13th November, 1711.

Notwithstanding the declaration in the last paragraph of the foregoing memorial, that nothing it contained was designed to reflect in the least upon any person, the paper clearly contains the insinuation that the Governor had displaced certain officers, who were men of character, and decided friends of the Established Church, and appointed others who were its implacable enemies, and therefore not disposed to do Mr. Poyer justice. The memorial makes another thing plain, viz., that there were other places in the colonies, where property was held, or claimed by the Episcopalians, on the same ground precisely as the property in dispute in Jamaica. In regard to the other point—the relation between Gov. Hunter and the Clergy—the following will show that there was far from being a good understanding between these parties.

Gov. Hunter to the Secretary.
(EXTRACT.)

NEW YORK, Feb. 25th, 1711.

SIR,—Col. Heathcote told me that he was privately informed that there had been a representation against me carried about to some of the clergy for subscriptions. I could not believe it being conscious to myself of nothing that I had done, left undone, or intended, with relation to the Church's interest, that the most consummate malice could ground a representation upon. That worthy gentleman was of the same opinion, but positive that there was such a representation; for which reason, he, in conjunction with Col. Morris, as members of the Society thought fit to write a letter to Mr. Vesey, and Mr. Henderson, in whose hands they understood this paper to be, and who were the principal contrivers and promoters of it, signifying that they had been made acquainted with the designs, and desired to know the meaning of it; that if any thing were wanting for the Church's interest they might join with them in proper measures to procure it, and redress what was amiss. All the effect that this letter had upon these two gentlemen was a deep concern for the discovery, and some sharp reproaches on one another as the discoverers. Neither could the Rev. Mr. Sharp obtain a sight of it tho' he solemnly promised to join with them in repressing any thing for the Church's Interest, provided it did not contain unjust or groundless reflections on the Governor. That gentleman has given an account to the Lord Bishop of London, how he was used by them &c. &c.

Being to guess at the particular facts of which I stand accused, I can think of none that can so much as afford a pretence for such a representation, unless it be the affairs of Jamaica Church here, and that must only be in the opinions of such as think that all laws, human and divine, are to be set aside when they come in competition with what they conceive to be the secular Interest of the Church.

Mr. Poyer having the Society's Mission, and my Lord Bishop of London's recommendation to that Church, I, upon his first application, granted him induction. The Dissenters were in possession of the Manse house by contrivance of the Widow of Mr. Urquhart, the former Incumbent, whose daughter was married to a Dissenting minister there. I consulted the Chief Justice Mompesson how far I might proceed towards putting Mr. Poyer in possession, who gave his opinion in writing, that it could not be done otherwise than by due course of law, without a high crime and misdemeanour. This opinion I sent to Mr. Poyer, and begged him to commence a suit at my cost, but heard nothing from him, until some time after he came to me to complain that the Justices of that County had not done him right, when required in procuring him his Quarter's Stipend, upon which I sent for the Justice he named, * * * * * and in the presence of Col. Morris and Mr. Regnier of this place, told him that I would forthwith give directions that Mr. Poyer should commence a suit against him, and that they should not flatter themselves that it might be dropped through Mr. Poyer's present wants, for he should not want wherewithall to carry it on through all the lengths so just a cause required, and accordingly wrote to Mr. Poyer to that purpose. Mr. Coe, the justice mentioned, told me that all this was the practice (work) of one Clows, a most vicious wretch into whose hands Mr. Poyer unfortunately fell, at his first setting out, and lodg'd in his house, led by his pretended zeal for the Church; but as he himself has since owned to Mr. Sharp, he was soon obliged to change his lodgings, few of his own Communion desiring to come near him, whilst he was in so bad company.

Extract of a Letter from Col. Morris to the Secretary.

NEW YORK, 20th Feb. 1711.

In Col. Fletcher's time, one party of the Dissenters in the County where Jamaica is, resolved to build a Church, and in order to it got subscriptions and materials enough to build it about three feet from the ground, but finding themselves unable to perfect it without the assistance of the rest, which could not be got by persuasion, they resolved to attempt the getting an Act of Assembly in their favour. Col. Fletcher who was then Governor, and James Grahame, Esq., who was then Speaker of the Assembly, perceiving the Assembly inclined to raise money for the building of that Church, and settling a maintenance for ministers, thought it a fit opportunity to do something in favour of the Church, before the zealous fit left them. Accordingly Grahame who had the drawing of their Bills, prescribed a method of Induction, and so managed it that it would not do well for the Dissenters, and but lamely for the Church, though 'twould do with the help of the Governor, and that was all; but 'twas the most that could be got at that time, *for had more been attempted the Assembly had seen through the artifice,* the most of them being Dissenters, and all had been lost. By virtue of this act, the Church was built, and a dissenting minister called. * * * The Church and parsonage house continued in the possession of the Dissenters till some time after the arrival of Mr. Urquhart, when a representation was made to my Lord Cornbury, that the Church and house being built by public Act, could belong to none but the Church of England. My Lord upon this gives his warrant to dispossess the Dissenters, which immediately by force was done, without any procedure at law, and Mr. Urquhart put into possession of them. This short method might be of some service to the minister, but was very far from being of any to the Church, as no such unaccountable steps can ever be. Mr. Urquhart kept the possession during his life, and though he gained not many converts, yet his conduct was so good that I don't think he lost any. After Mr. Urquhart's death, his widow's daughter married a dissenting minister, and she put the parsonage house into his possession, in which it continues until now. This happened much about the time of Col. Hunter's arrival. Whether application was made to him or no I can't tell, but some changes in the magistracy being made, and by a mistake one or two put in that were patrons of the Dissenters, Mr. Poyer and his friends chose to apply to those they were sure would refuse them, and not to those in place who were firm to their interest, and being refused, complained to the Governor, who immediately sent for the person and ordered him to be prosecuted that it might appear whether he had failed in his duty or not. Whether the prosecution was confirmed or not I cannot tell, but I happened to be in the Governor's chamber when this Judge and a Dissenting minister came in and this matter was talked of. He said that the intention of the Legislature at that time was to raise a maintenance for a Dissenting minister, all the Assembly but one being Dissenters, and knowing nothing of the Church; but that being the intention of the law makers was the meaning of the law, and he hoped the Dissenters might enjoy what was so justly their due, or at least not be deprived of it without due course of law, as they formerly had been. I told him the Legislature did not consist of the Assembly only, but of the Governor and Council joined with them, &c. The Governor joined in the argument, and argued with a great deal of force in favor of the Church, who, he said, he could not help thinking was in the right, with respect to their claims—that they might be sure that matters of property should be determined, by the ordinary course of the law, by which perhaps, they, being numerous might weary Mr. Poyer, being a poor man, but that Mr. Poyer should have his purse for the carrying on that suit. A day or two afterwards he told Mr. Poyer so himself. Some time after that he wrote to him giving the Gentleman who carried the letter in charge, to tell him he still continued in the same mind. The Governor being at Jamaica, repeated the offer of bearing the whole charge of the suit, and pressed Mr. Poyer to undertake it. Col. Heathcote also pressed him to undertake it, giving him the same assurance from the Governor, and Poyer promised to do it, but has been prevailed on to decline that method (as he says) till their representation reach England; and I believe the poor man and his friends are weak enough to believe that their superiors there will enter into measures to displace the Governor for not Dragooning in their favor as his predecessor did, &c.

The act to settle the Church is very loosely worded; which, as things stood then, when it was made, could not be avoided—the Dissenters claiming the benefit of it as well as we. And the act without such resting (wresting?) will admit a construction in their favour as well as ours. They think it was intended for them, and that they only have a right to it.

There is no comparison in our numbers; and they can on the death of the Incumbents call persons of their own persuasion in every place but the city of New York. * * * I believe at this day, the Church had been in a much better condition had there been no Act in her favour; for in the Jersies and Pennsylvania, where there is no act in her favour there is four times the number of Churchmen that there are in this province of New York, and they are so most of them upon principle. Whereas nine parts in ten of ours will add no great credit to whatsoever Church they are of, &c.

Mr. Vesey, who had and still makes a tool of that weak man Poyer, with him prevailed upon Mr. Evans of Philadelphia and Mr. Talbot, as I am told by some, to sign a representation in direct terms against the Governor, &c. &c.

What ground Mr. Poyer had for the apprehension that justice would not be done him by the Judges before whom his cause would be tried, appears from the following:

Extract of a letter from Col. Heathcote to the Secretary.

NEW YORK, Feb. 11, 1711.

SIR,—The Ships being still detained by the Ice gives me an opportunity of saying something more* concerning the affairs of the Church at Jamaica. And I am not a little surprised that the Church's misfortune there is wholly charged on account of the alterations of some of the officers there, and that they dare not go to law for that

---

* Col. Heathcote had addressed the Secretary before, under date of Jan. 5th and Jan. 30th, 1711, giving the same version of Mr. Poyer's difficulty with the Governor as that contained in Col. Lewis Morris's letter. Both were members of the Society.

reason: which is a very great mistake because no officers are wanting to do Mr. Poyer justice there either in respect of his salary or otherwise but a Sheriff, that he might be safe as to his Juries, for as his actions will be above £20 in value, so must be tried by the Chief Justice, Mr. Mompesson, who never professed any other religion but that of the Church of England—and the present Sheriff, who had the charge of that County for above a year, is a member of the Church at Jamaica, and was put in that post by Col. Hunter at the request of Mr. Poyer's friends. And altho' the removal which was made among the officers was what I would not have advised the Gov'r to, yet the mistake was not so great as represented; for some time after those changes were made, blaming one of the gentlemen of the Council, who advised the Governor to it, his answer was that the cry of the people was so loud against several of the officers then in place that it was absolutely necessary; and as for those whom he and his friends had recommended, the most of 'em were dissenters, they were on all other accounts much fitter for it: nor were all the old officers turned out, nor all in the new commission dissenters, as I had been told, for that several of the Church were still in place and many who had been in before were continued—it being their design to cast out ill men and not the Church. Now altho' I was not of his mind, yet there was truth in some things he offered; for indeed many of the instruments made use of to settle the Church at Jamaica, in its infancy, were of such warm tempers, and if report is true so indifferent in their morals, that, from the first beginning, I never expected it would be settled with much peace or reputation. For instead of taking an effectual care upon its first settling that none were employed therein but the best and soberest men, and those of the fairest character and best reputation among the people, and caressing and making use of such to help settle it, one Mr. Cardell,* a transient person, and of very indifferent reputation, was recommended, and made High Sheriff of that County; and the settling of the Church was left in a great measure to his care and conduct. By these imprudent measures the leading men were disobliged which soon chased away most of the good and sober people and left her only a very thin congregation.

The following is the record of the Court in the suit of Mr. Poyer for his first quarter's stipend, to which there are so many allusions in the preceding papers. Samuel Coe and Daniel Smith were the Church-wardens.

QUEENS COUNTY, *Ss.*

At a Special Court, held at Jamaica, the 27th day of October, in the 9th year of the reign of our Sovereign Lady Anne, Anno Dom. 1710—Present, JOHN COE, *Judge;* SAMUEL BAYLEY, RICHARD OLDFIELD, *Justices:*

Mr. Thos. Poyer per Mr. Clows complains that the Church Wardens do refuse to pay the one quarter's salary.

Court considered of the compl't and find for the def'ts with costs of suit.

The reasons of the Church Wardens against the compl't of Mr. Thos. Poyer. Qui tam, &c.

1st. Because we had no money.

---

* "He seized upon the church land, divided it into lots, and leased them out for the benefit of his own party. This man, it seems, sustained a despicable character, and being afterwards apprehended for some offence, and thrown into prison, hanged himself in despair."—Thomp. II. 107.

2dly. We had no orders from the Justices and Vestry, according to an Act of Assembly to pay any.

3dly. Because we thought Mr. Thos. Poyer not qualified, according to the Act of Assembly of this Province as Minister or Incumbent of Jamaica, to demand the whole, or any part of the said salary.

True Copy,   Joseph Smith, *Clerk.*

Mr. Poyer to the Secretary.
[EXTRACT.]
Jamaica, L. Island, March 7, 1712.

By the advice of Counsel I have lately served the Dissenter who is in possession of the Parsonage house and Glebe with a lease of Ejectment for continuing the claim but with no design of prosecuting to effect, for in that I shall not presume to do anything till I receive the express commands of the Venerable Society.

In 1712 the Society for the Propagation of the Gospel in Foreign Parts laid the difficulties of Mr. Poyer before the Queen's most Excellent Majesty, and petitioned "that in causes relating immediately to the Church an appeal may lie to your Governor and Council there, and to your Majesty and Privy Council here, without any restriction or limitation of the value or sum appealed for."

Order of Council relating to appeals concerning the Church at New York.
[EXTRACT.]

At the Court of St. James the 8th of January 1712. Present,—the Queen's most Excellent Majesty in Council.

Upon reading this day at the Board a report from the

Lord's Commissioners of Trade and Plantations in the words following, viz. (the report after reciting the hardships of Mr. Thos. Poyer, Clerk, agreeable to the representations of the Society aforesaid, that he was "wrongfully kept out of the parsonage house and glebe by the violence of some sectaries disaffected to the Church," concludes as follows.) This being the state of the case we are humbly of opinion that in cases where the Church is immediately concerned, as in the present case, your Majesty be graciously pleased to allow the Clergy liberty of appealing, from the Inferior Courts to the Governor and Council, only without limitation of any sum, which is humbly submitted.

     Ph: MEADOWS, F. FFOLEY,
     R. MONCKTON, J. A. COTTON.
Whitehall, 25th Novem. 1712.

Her Majesty in her Privy Council taking the same into consideration was graciously pleased to approve the said report, and to order, as it is hereby ordered, that in cases where the Church is immediately concerned, (as in this case) liberty be given to the Clergy to appeal from the inferior Courts to the Governor and Council only without limitation of any sum; and her Majesty is graciously pleased to order that as well in this, as in other like cases liberty be given to the Clergy to appeal from the Governor and Council to her Majesty in Privy Council, without limitation as aforesaid &c.

   (Signed)   EDWARD SOUTHWELL.

Letter from the Bishop of London to Mr. Poyer.

SIR—I do not in the least believe it was in your thoughts to give any uneasiness to the Church or Government; but I must think that your indiscretion hath been the cause of it; of which I should have warned you could I have had the opportunity to do it; and must now entreat you for the future to have a care of foolish and unwary Advisers. Pray therefore think your Governors to be wiser than yourself, and if you miscarry under that conduct, you will come off with reputation, let the event prove what it will: for I must tell you that your application over into England hath done you and the rest of our Brethren no great Service, by referring your case to people at such a distance, as neither do or can know any thing of the merits of the cause. Be wiser therefore for the time to come, and believe me that I shall be always ready to approve myself,

Your most assured Friend and Brother,

H: LONDON.

Fulham, May 21, 1712.

At length an order was passed by the Society for the Propagation of the Gospel for defraying the expenses Mr. Poyer might incur in recovering his salary by due course of law; and in 1716 he commenced his suit, and at length recovered £16 11s. from the Churchwardens. This strife continued from year to year, and "proceeded," says Dr. Elihu Spencer, "to such lengths that many of the principal inhabitants were harassed with severe persecutions, heavy fines, and long imprisonments, for assuming their just rights, and others fled out of the Province to avoid the rage of Episcopal cruelty." As we have seen, the power of the throne itself was invoked in this controversy. That the Presbyterians should have held out, or that they ever succeeded in recovering their just rights against such odds, is truly matter of astonishment. Let the present and future generations never forget that eternal vigilance was the price their ancestors paid for the success with which their exertions were crowned. From such men it is an honour to have descended, and their memory should be held in grateful remembrance.

Mr. Poyer to the Secretary.
[EXTRACT.]
JAMAICA, Nov. 4th, 1718.

HON'D SIR,—The people of this place are encouraged in their obstinacy by their minister, a very designing man and who persuades them to what he will, even not to obey the Lawful commands of the magistrates, and they stick not to say that tho' there is a Law for £60 per ann. to be yearly collected for the minister of this Parish, and tho' Coll. Lewis Morris, the Chief Justice of this Province, has ordered a Writ of Mandamus for collecting the arrearages of the Minister's salary—Notwithstanding these orders, they say, if the Constables offer to collect it upon the Warrants the Justices have given, pursuant to the Writ aforesaid, they will scald them, they will stone them, they will go to Club Law with them, and I know not what.

The minister who in the above letter is represented as exerting such an influence over his people, was the Rev. George McNish. He was settled, as stated already, in 1711, although it is highly probable he had preached here, more or less, for a year and a half before. In 1710 Mr. McNish was the Moderator of the Presbytery. Through his influence the Rev. Mr. Pumry of Newtown united with the Presbytery of Philadelphia; and in 1717 the Presbytery of Long Island was formed. Mr. McNish may therefore be regarded as the father of the Presbyterian Church on Long Island. The Presbytery of Long Island was the first presbytery formed in the Province of New York, and for many years, the Presbyterian Churches in the city of New York and the county of Westchester were subject to its jurisdiction; he may, therefore, with equal propriety, be regarded as the father of Presbyterianism, in its distinctive form, in the State of New York. In 1716, he was again Moderator of the Presbytery of Philadelphia, and consequently preached the Synodical sermon at the first meeting of the Synod of Philadelphia in 1717. His text was John xxi. 17, *Lovest thou me?* The same year (as he appears to have contemplated making a visit to Great Britain) he was deputed by the Synod to act as its representative abroad, for the promotion of religion in this country. This visit, however, he did not make; but the appointment, and other important services assigned him, prove that he was a leading and influential minister, and enjoyed, in no small degree, the confidence of his brethren.

Mr. McNish is said to have possessed about 1000 acres of land at Wallkill, Orange Co. He left but one child, a son named George, who married a daughter of Joseph Smith of Jamaica, and settled in New Jersey.* In the records of the Synod for 1723 there is the following entry:

"Upon reading the list of ministers the Synod found to their great grief that Mr. McNish was dead."

In the Church Register of Newtown it is stated that

---

* He was licensed to preach, but whether ordained is not known. He preached at Newtown between 1744 and 1746. He died at Wallkill in 1779, aged 65.— *Webster's Hist. of Presb. Ch.*

he died March 10th, 1722.* Mrs. Elizabeth Everitt, who died in 1840, at the advanced age of ninety-five, said that she had often seen his headstone in our burying-ground. He was consequently the third minister this church had lost by death, and the second buried in this town.

Although Mr. McNish was minister of this congregation ten or eleven years, it is probable he never preached in the house of worship belonging to it after his installation, as it was not restored until several years after his death. Tradition says that he preached in a building at the eastern end of the village, which was the "Meeting House," undoubtedly, which the Presbyterians are represented to have built in the Memorial which the Episcopal missionaries sent home to the Bishop of London.

Jamaica Apprill y^e $\frac{2}{3}$ 1723

At a town meeting held at Jamaica at y^e time aforesaid it was voted by y^e majority of y^e freeholders then & there assembled

Voted at y^e same meeting that Just Oldfield Sam^{ll} Smith & Jonathan Watters are to take in their possession the parsonage house & home lot for to take care of y^e same untill such time as ye town shall recall it out of their hands

Just Beats protest against the above said vote

Mr Clows protest against the above said vote as unnesary Incertain unreasonable & illeagull

at a town meeting ordered by Just Whithead & Just Messenger   Entered by me Nehemiah Smith
Clerk
Records III. p. 475.

---

* Mr. Pumry, minister of Newtown, appears to have appreciated more than many, the importance of *memoranda* of this sort.

THE REV. ROBERT CROSS

was the next pastor. He was a native of Ireland, in which country he received his education. He was born near Bally Kelley, *anno* 1689. On the 19th of September, 1717, at the first meeting of the Synod of Philadelphia, he presented his testimonials as a probationer, lately come from Ireland, which were approved, and he was recommended to the Presbytery of Newcastle. He was ordained and settled at Newcastle, March 17th, 1719, as the successor of the Rev. James Anderson, transported by the Synod to New York. From the records of the Presbytery of Newcastle, it appears that he received the call of this congregation September 18th, 1723; and between that date and the 16th of October, he left Newcastle and came to Jamaica. He was minister at the time the people here recovered their property, and had the satisfaction of gathering the flock once more beneath their own vine and fig-tree, and of witnessing the joy of men who had become venerable for years, since the period of exile from their house of worship. He married Mary Oldfield, a daughter of Mr. Justice Oldfield. Rev. Mr. Poyer married Sarah, another daughter of said Oldfield.

In the year 1724, ejectment suits were brought by Mr. Poyer, in the Supreme Court of New York, against several tenants in possession of the parsonage lands. Judgment, as the Town Records show, went against Mr. Poyer.* At length, in the year 1727, the Pres-

---

* Jamaica Jenewary ye 20^d 1724-5

att a town meeting held at Jamaica at the time aforesaid voted whereas lately at the Supream Cort of ye city of New York Ejectments was broght by Mr thomas poyer a church of Enland minister against sewerall Ten^{ts} in byterians, after great expense, by a due course of law recovered their church, and had their title to the parsonage and glebe lands confirmed to them. Lewis Morris, afterwards Governor of New Jersey, was, at that time, Chief Justice, and presided at the trial. He encountered no little obloquy; his character was aspersed; and, not long after the trial, he was suspended from the office of Chief Justice by Governor Cosby. Judge Morris wrote to the Board of Trade, showing that the resentment of the Governor was causeless; and he thought it necessary, on soliciting that his office might be restored, to publish the grounds of his decision in the above case.

Fulham Manuscripts.
[EXTRACT.]

NEW YORK, July 14, 1727.

MY LORD:—I have been informed by Mr. Poyer that there is an Action commenced by the Presbyterians of

possesion of the parsonage lands viz homestead & out lands in this town formerly sett apart for the use of a minister & whereas judgement went against the said Mr. Poyer as may appear : now according to the town vote made June y⁰ 19 :—1676 which is that there shall be forty acres of medow designed & sett apart for a parsonage lot in yᵉ east neck joyning to the lotts of meadows laid out with upland proporsionable to other lots laid out in yᵉ town to continue at yᵉ disspose of the town to a minisster when they have occasion to make use of it wee doe vote & agree that Mr Robᵗ Crose minister of yᵉ said town shall have the use benefit & possession of yᵉ said homstead meadows & upland laid out & appropriated for the use abovesaid there being need & occasion for it to be & remaine to him & his assigns duering he shall continue our minister

voted at yᵉ same town meeting that Jonᵗʰ Watters & Samˡˡ Smith doe immediately put Mr Robᵗ Cross minister in possesion of yᵉ abovesaid lands & meadows wherein he is not allready possesioned

Samuell Clowes enter his protest against yᵉ two last votes affirming it not to be in yᵉ power of yᵉ whole township much less of yᵉ major part of this town meeting to make such votes

Entered by me NEHEMIAH SMITH Clerk
Records III., 476-7.

Jamaica in Long Island, for the English Church which they pretend was built by, and was taken by violence from them, by my Lord Cornbury.

I know nothing certain about their claims, but if they take the course of law, I cannot help it; but they having committed a riot in taking possession of the church, the Attorney General here has entered an information against them, and refused them a noli prosequi upon their application, *that their rashness may be attended with charge and trouble at least, if not punishment, which may perhaps discourage them in their suit, or make them willing to compromise it.*

My Lord, &c.,

W. BURNETT.

Governor Burnett was the son of the Bishop of Sarum, and was the Governor of New York from 1720 to 1728.

Revd. Mr. Poyer to the Secretary.

REV SIR   JAMAICA June 16th 1731

By this opportunity I beg leave humbly to represent to my Honb^{le} Patrons the Venerable Society for Propagating the Gospel in Foreign Parts that I have been their Missionary here 21 years & may without incurring the imputation of boasting say that my diligence in the discharge of my functions has been little inferior to any I pray God to give a blessing to the seed sown but so it is that besides the great and almost continual contentions that I have struggled withal amongst the Independents in this Parish having had several law suites with them before I could have the Salary which the Country has settled upon the minister of the Church of England several other law suits for Glebe lands which we have lost and at last even the Church itself of which we had the possession 25 years is taken from us by a trial at law (with what justice I cant pretend to say) tho' I say I have endeavoured as patiently as I could to bear up under all these trials besides the loss of two Wives and Several children yet the infirmities of old age bear very hard upon me insomuch that I find myself almost unable to officiate at the three towns of Jamaica Newtown and Flushing as I have hitherto done and which is absolutely necessary for the Minister of the Parish to do.

The intent of these are therefore to beg that my distressed state and condition may be laid before the Vener^{ble} Society and that they may be pleased to permit me to quit my Mission and to return to great Britain as being for the reasons aforegiven not capable of bearing such fatigues and discharging my duty as I have done for so many years in this place. I humbly beg of my most honored patrons to consider my case & circumstances & I remain &c

Thos Poyer

Revd. Mr. Campbell to the Secretary.

New York November 3^d 1731

Rev Sir

* * * Mr Poyer is a much better man and Christian than himself [Mr Vesey is referred to] whom he endeavors to remove from his Mission in Jamaica, he is a Grandson of Coll Poyer who died in the gallant defence of Pembroke Castle in the time of Oliver Cromwell which alone I hope will recommend him to the favour and protection of the sensible and generous Dr Humphreys; he is a good natured honest man and is beneficent to his neighbors, which I take to be qualities superior to any Mr Vesey is possessed of; He has prevailed with Mr Poyer to send a letter home desiring to be recalled which would infallibly ruin the poor Gentleman and his numerous family;

Therefore I entreat you to take care that the Society's answer may entirely leave it at his own choice; whether to go home or not; this I write at the desire of his best friends.

The secret of this is that Mr Vesey wants to get quit of Mr Colgan and send him to Jamaica tho he must needs be sensible that Mr Poyer will be ruined if he goes home or leaves his Mission * * * * *

Mr. Campbell to the Secretary.
[EXTRACT.]

NEW YORK, Jan. 25, 1732.

SIR:—The Presbyterians by the sly tricks and quirks of the common law, got the church, the parsonage house, and lands into their possession, and now they are resolved to deprive the next missionary of £60 currency settled as a yearly salary, by an Act of Assembly. The next missionary may depend upon it, he must either engage in a Lawsuit against the Dissenters, or throw up the salary abovementioned.

Mr. Colgan to the Secretary.
[EXTRACT.]

JAMAICA, June 14th, 1734.

REV'D SIR: ——— Upon my first coming into the parish, I found the Church in a declining condition. The Quakers and Independents have been very busy to subvert, and by many studied arts and rules, utterly to destroy it— I may say the Christian religion here. One of their stratagems was to sue for an edifice wherein divine service was performed by Ministers of the Church of England for near 30 years, by pretence that they had better right in it than the Church members. And this met with not a little success, for in suing Mr. Poyer, my predecessor, who being defendant in the case, they, upon a very odd turn in the trial, cast him. I am informed that in this suit, the Counsel upon the part of the Church always designed to put the matter upon some points of law which are clearly in the Church's favour, and accordingly at the time of trial offered to demur in law, but was diverted therefrom by the late Chief Justice, Lewis Morris, Esq., (before whom the trial was,) who told them that he would recommend it to the Jury to find a special Verdict, and if they did not, but found generally and against the Church, he would then allow a new trial—which, after the Jury had found a general verdict against the Church, he absolutely refused, when the Counsel for the Church laid claim to his promise, and strongly insisted upon the benefit thereof. I have been told by some of the Counsel for the Church that the only seeming reason he gave for his denial was that a bad promise was better broken than kept, and thus an end was put to the controversy.

The town having recovered their house of worship, Mr. Cross, the Presbyterian minister, was immediately put in possession of it, and his successors enjoyed the undisturbed possession of it as long as that venerable edifice remained. Still, however, the Episcopal clergy continued to be supported by a tax on the inhabitants, Presbyterians, Dutch Reformed, and others, from which they were not relieved until the Revolution of 1776. But to this subject I shall have occasion to refer again.

CHAPTER VI.

1724–1774.

A FREE SCHOOL — THE TOWN TAKE POSSESSION OF THE CHURCH — MR. CROSS CALLED TO PHILADELPHIA — THE PEOPLE STRENUOUSLY OPPOSE HIS REMOVAL — HIS REMOVAL — HIS EPITAPH — WALTER WILMOT — PUT IN POSSESSION OF THE PARSONAGE — MRS. WILMOT — HER DEATH — MR. WHITEFIELD VISITS THE PLACE — HIS PREACHING ON REGENERATION TROUBLES MR. COLGAN — EFFECT — MR. WILMOT'S DEATH — EPITAPH — MR. COLGAN REJOICES — DAVID BOSTWICK — TOWN FORMALLY SURRENDERS CHURCH PROPERTY TO THE PRESBYTERIANS — THE RECORD — MR. BOSTWICK CALLED TO NEW YORK — COMMITTEE OF SYNOD MEET AT JAMAICA ON HIS REMOVAL — MR. BOSTWICK APPOINTED TO SUPPLY NEW YORK — COMMITTEE OF SYNOD MEET AT PRINCETON — VOTE FOR HIS REMOVAL — HIS MINISTRY IN NEW YORK — HIS PUBLICATIONS, CHARACTER AND DEATH — ELIHU SPENCER — ORDAINED AS A MISSIONARY TO THE INDIANS — HIS KNOWLEDGE OF THE INDIAN LANGUAGES — SETTLES AT ELIZABETHTOWN — REMOVES TO JAMAICA — CHAPLAIN IN THE FRENCH AND INDIAN WAR — SETTLES AT ST. GEORGE'S DEL. — REMOVES TO TRENTON, N. J. — HIS READY TALENT — EPITAPH — HIS DESCENDANTS — B. BRADNER — WM. MILLS — NUMBER IN COMMUNION — REVIVAL OF RELIGION — EFFECT OF AN ACCOUNT OF THE REVIVAL AT EASTHAMPTON — MR. WHITEFIELD VISITS JAMAICA, THE SECOND TIME — PREACHES IN AN ORCHARD — A TRACT BY MR. MILLS — MR. SEABURY VS. MR. WHITEFIELD — MR. MILLS DECLINES A CALL TO PHILADELPHIA — HIS DEATH — HIS DISEASE — HIS CHILDREN — HIS MSS. — PEOPLE STILL RESIST THE TAX TO SUPPORT THE EPISCOPAL MINISTRY — MR. BLOOMER ON THE POLITICAL TROUBLES OF 1776 — SHUTS HIS CHURCH FOR FIVE SUNDAYS UNTIL THE KING'S TROOPS ARRIVE.

JAMAICA May the forth 1726 at a town meeting held at Jamaica at the time aforesaid it was voted by ye majority of the freeholders then & there assembled

voted that Mr. Pier [Poyer] Mr Cross Just Betts Just Messinger Just Smith & Clerk Smith are appointed and chosen to see what people are willing to agree to doe or subscribe toward yᵉ incorrigement of a free scoule in yᵉ town entered by me neheᵐ Smith clerk

Records III. p. 478.

Jamaica febrewary the 21ᵈ 1726–7

At a town meeting held at Janaica at yᵉ time aforesaid it was voted & concluded by yᵉ majority of yᵉ freeholders then & there assembled

that yᵉ ground whereon yᵉ stone building or meeting house now stands in Jamaica with yᵉ said building itselfe which are situate near yᵉ middle of the maine street in Jamaica abovesaid near where yᵉ old pound lately stood & in yᵉ occupation of Mr Thomas Poyer shall be granted & assigned unto John carpenter Jonas Wood and Benjamin Thurstone, sume of yᵉ surviving trusteese by whome it was built & it is hereby granted and assigned unto yᵉ said John Carpenter Jonas wood & Benjamin Thurstone to have and to hold the lands in trust for yᵉ town & to be disposed of by them in trust for yᵉ town according to yᵉ first intention of yᵉ builders

Just Beets Mr Poyer Just oldfield & Richard Comes enter their protest against yᵉ abovesaid vote & Mr clows alsoe protest against yᵉ same vote

Entered by me Nehemiah Smith clerk
Records III. p. 478.

In 1734, it appears that the First Presbyterian Church in Philadelphia had given Mr. Cross a call, as the matter of his removal was before the Synod to be there determined. The Commissioners from Jamaica and Philadelphia were heard at length, "and after the most critical examination of the affair, and the solemn imploring the divine assistance, the matter was put to vote and carried against Mr. Cross's transportation." The Church at Philadelphia was divided; there being a considerable party opposed to Mr. Cross. The next year that part of the congregation in favour of Mr. Cross, petitioned the Synod to be erected into a new congregation. The petition was granted by a large majority. In 1736, a call was presented to him from the new congregation, formed agreeably to the permission of Synod given the year before, "and his sentiments concerning it desired by the Synod." In answer, Mr. Cross declared that he thought the Synod could not determine this matter until his people had been duly apprized of it, and that as things now appeared it was "his duty to stay with the people of Jamaica." "After much and long debating about this affair," the Synod at length adopted an overture that judgment should be deferred concerning it until the next meeting of Synod, that the people of Jamaica might be apprized of the business, and have an opportunity to bring in their objections against Mr. Cross's removal.* In the mean time, Mr. Cross was appointed to supply the new congregation in Philadelphia, for two months, before the next meeting of the Synod; and provision was, at the same time, made for supplying the people of Jamaica, during Mr. Cross's absence. The next year, May 27th, 1737, the subject of Mr. Cross's removal to Philadelphia came again before the Synod; the people of Jamaica presented their

---

* Elizabeth Ashbridge, a celebrated quakeress of that day, has left this record: "His people almost adored him, and impoverished themselves to equal the sum offered him in the city; but failing in this they lost him."—*Sprague's Annals.*

reasons why he should not be removed, and the representatives of the newly erected congregation at Philadelphia "put in a supplication" designed to invalidate "the supplication from Jamaica." Mr. Cross submitted himself wholly to the judgment of the Synod. "The Synod entered upon a very serious debate about this whole affair, in which considerable time being spent, at last, after solemn calling upon God for light and direction in such a momentous matter, it was put to the vote, Transport Mr. Cross from Jamaica to Philadelphia or not; and it was carried in the affirmative, *nemine contradicente*. The Synod appointed Messrs. Thompson and Anderson to prepare a suitable letter to the congregation of Jamaica, signifying what was done in said affair." This was ordered at the request of Mr. Cross. In the minutes of Synod for 1738, there is the following entry: "It is reported that Mr. Robert Cross was installed, since our last, according to the Synod's appointment, and that the two congregations in Philadelphia were since united." He remained pastor of the First Presbyterian Church, Philadelphia, till his death, which took place in August, 1766. He was buried in the cemetery of the First Presbyterian Church, Philadelphia. The following is the inscription on his tomb:

"Under this marble are deposited the bodies of Rev. Mr. ROBERT CROSS, who was born near Bally Kally in Ireland anno 1689, and died anno 1766, and of MARY, his wife, who was born in New York anno 1688, and died anno 1766.

"He was removed from a pastoral charge in Long Island to be one of the ministers of the First Presbyterian

Church, in this city, anno 1737. He excelled in prudence and gravity, and a general deportment, was esteemed for his learned acquaintance with the Holy Scriptures, and long accounted one of the most respectable ministers in this province.

"Reader, imitate his virtues and prepare for Death."

In 1735, Mr. Cross published a sermon, preached before the commission of Synod at Philadelphia, which he affectionately dedicated to his people at Jamaica. In the dedication he says: "It is now (my friends) almost twelve years since you called me to the delightful work of the ministry among you." He remained pastor of this church almost fourteen years, and it is evident was very highly esteemed in Jamaica. There is tradition of a revival of religion in the congregation during his ministry, as the fruit of which a considerable number joined the church. It is certain that he was one of the most prominent and influential ministers of the day in which he lived.

at a town meeting att Jamaica 5th aprill 1737

voted by ye majority of the freeholders then and there assembled that Nathan Smith & Hendrick Elderd are chosen assessors for the insuing year & they are obliged to take a new assessment & deliver a coppey of ye same to the vestrymen in order for their making the Parish Rate

Records III. p. 467.

The Rev.
WALTER WILMOT
was ordained here by the Presbytery of New York,

April 12th, 1738,* Mr. Pemberton of New York preaching on the occasion, from Col. i. 7. He was born at Southampton, on this island, in 1709; was educated at Yale, where he graduated in 1735. He married a daughter of Jotham Townsend, of Oyster Bay, a member of the Society of Friends. Mrs. Wilmot was a woman eminent for piety, but she died at the early age of twenty-three years. The sermon preached at her funeral in Oyster Bay, where she was interred, is in my possession. It was preached by the Rev. Ebenezer Prime, of Huntington, from Ezek. xxiv. 16. I have also a copy of the Journal kept by Mrs. Wilmot, which

---

* Fryday 21 aprill 1738 at a publick town meeting of yͤ inhabitants & freeholders of Jamaica at yͤ County Hall Voted ordered & concluded that the parsonage house & homestead together with all & singular the outlands meadow tenements & hereditaments thereunto belonging shall be abide remain & continue in the peaceable occupation & use of Mr Walter Wilmot the present presbeterian minister of the said town for during & so long as he shall remain & continue our minister (at yͤ same town meeting) voted yͭ capt Increas Carpenter Just Henry Ludlum & Just Richard Everit are appointed to put Mr Walter Wilmot in possession of yͤ parsonage house & land & meadow as above exprest　　　pr Samll Smith Junͬ clerk
　　　　　　　　　　　　　　　　　　　　Records III. p. 466.

Whereas at a publick town meeting at Jamaica in Queens County, the freeholders of the said town being duly called & did meet at the County Hall on friday the 21ˢ day of aprill anno: 1738 it was then & there voted by the majority of the said freeholders that Increase Carpenter Just Henry Ludlum & Just Richard Everit should put the Revᵈ Mr Walter Wilmot the present Presbyterian minester of the congregation of Jamaica above said in possession of the parsonage house homestead and all other the land meadow tenements & hereditements there unto belonging We did there fore persuent to the above power on the 26th day of april anno: 1738 take the above premises into our possession & the same did deliver into the peaceable possession & seisin of the said Mr. Walter Wilmot during so long as he shall continue minister of the said congregation as followeth the house & homestead we put into his peaceable possession in presence of James Cebra & Elijah Barton: the outlands & meadow in presence of Benjamin Smith junͬ & James Cebra, as evidences we took with us for that purpose　　　　　　　entered per Samll Smith Junͬ clk
　　　　　　　　　　　　　　　　　　　　Records III. p. 465 & 6.

was published by her husband, after her death. In the dedication "to Mr. Jotham Townsend, father of the deceased, Mr. Wilmot says: "In the latter part of her life, she scarcely seemed to be an inhabitant of this world; for as she had frequently intimations of her departure, so she kept death in view, and made it her grand concern to be found ready. Her time, her powers, her soul, her body, in a word her all, for some months before she left us, seemed devoted to the service and glory of her dear Redeemer." "'Tis with pleasure I can observe your daughter was generally beloved and honoured whilst she lived amongst us. I believe I shall not easily forget you nor your family, out of which I have had so desireable a companion. Her stay with me indeed was short; but it was pleasant and very agreeable: I may say without vanity, we lived together in perfect harmony, and knew no other strife betwixt us, but that of making each other happy: in this we strove to excel; and in this, no doubt, she had the pre-eminence. Let us join to remember the dear infant, the little image of herself, she has left behind her; 'tis the only remaining part of an obedient daughter and tender wife." The affecting little volume closes with this passage from her private papers: "O how many fears attend me! O that I knew how it must be with my soul when I depart this life! I shall within a few days pass through a scene of darkness; and I know not but it will be the dark valley of the shadow of death; and then except the Lord support me I shall fall. O my soul, meditate on the season. Make haste and not delay to be found crying for a sealed pardon from the great Judge of Heaven; that when death approaches, thou mayest be found ready to depart: O Lord, be my helper. Grant that whether I live or die, I may be the Lord's. Be with me this night for the sake of Christ, AMEN. This day sweet advice from a near friend, to trust only in God." On the above her husband remarks: "This perhaps was the last passage she ever wrote. She lived without any remarkable alteration till the Friday following; was taken amiss that evening, was soon speechless, and in a great measure senseless. On Saturday about three of the clock fell asleep ('tis hopeful) in the Lord Jesus Christ. On the next Monday following, she was interred at Oyster Bay, the place of her nativity; and has left me to bewail an unspeakable loss. When I returned home and looked amongst her papers, the following lines to me (which must have been written near two months before her death) lay first in sight, and came first to hand:

> ' Dear partner of my earthly love,
> I quickly from you shall remove;
> My soul will take her hasty flight,
> To everlasting shades of night,
> Or to the endless realms of light.' "

Mr. Wilmot was evidently a man distinguished for spirituality of mind and ardor of piety; and although he died young, it cannot be doubted that his ministry here was crowned with the happiest results; but what those results actually were, from the paucity of our records and the failure of tradition, cannot now certainly be known. In 1740 it is evident Mr. Whitefield visited this place, and that his labours, as elsewhere, were greatly blessed to the awakening of numbers to attend to the salvation of their souls. The effect of his labours may be judged of by the following extracts from letters of Mr. Colgan, the Episcopal missionary here, at that time, to the Secretary of the Society for the Propagation of Religion in Foreign Parts:

JAMAICA, Nov. 22d, 1740.

Some enthusiastical itinerant teachers have of late been preaching upon this Island, the notorious Mr. Whitfield being at the head of them, and among other pernicious tenets have broached such false and erroneous opinions concerning the doctrine of Regeneration as tend to the destruction of true religion and of a holy and virtuous life; and therefore I take this opportunity to beg that the Society would be pleased to bestow upon the people of this Parish a few of Dr. Waterland's pieces on that subject, and of his Lordship, the Bishop of London's Pastoral Letters upon lukewarmness and enthusiasm.

The opinions of Mr. Whitefield on the doctrine of regeneration are perfectly well known; he hardly preached a sermon without insisting upon it; "and one, and perhaps the best of his discourses," says the Rev. Joseph Smith, who published a discourse on his character and preaching, "was *ex professo* on this subject."

It was in 1739 that Mr. Whitefield sailed the second time for America. He arrived in Philadelphia in November of that year, and from thence was invited to New York, where he preached in the open air in the day time, and in the Rev. Mr. Pemberton's Church in the evening, for above a week. It was at this time, probably, he visited Jamaica; and, wherever he preached, thousands were gathered from various parts.

"It was no less pleasing than strange to him to see such gatherings in a foreign land; ministers and people shedding tears; sinners struck with awe; and serious persons who had been much run down and despised, filled with joy."* The Messrs. Tennents, Blair, Rowland, and Mr. Frelinghuysen, a Dutch minister, received him gladly; and these devoted men, or some of them, were doubtless the "enthusiastical itinerant teachers," referred to in Mr. Colgan's epistle, associated with Mr. Whitefield. It is gratifying to contemplate Mr. Wilmot as a man of kindred spirit with these eminently holy and useful men. A work of grace, under their combined labours, evidently took place here, and in the surrounding region, which continued for a considerable period, as appears from the following:

Mr. Colgan to the Secretary.

[EXTRACT.]

JAMAICA, March 23d, 1743.

REV'D SIR,—Our Church here is in a flourishing condition; her being depressed of late by those clouds of error and enthusiasm, which hung so heavily about her, has in effect tended to her greater illustration and glory. If the Society would be pleased to order me some small tracts, such as the Trial of Mr. Whitfield's Spirit, An Englishman directed in the choice of his Religion, Bishop Stillingfleet's Unreasonableness of Separation, &c. [In a previous letter dated Dec. 15th, 1741, from Mr. C. to the Secretary this sentence occurs: "Enthusiasm has of late been very predominant amongst us"—language which

* Gillie's Memoirs of Whitefield, chap. v.

refers to a state of things which we have no difficulty in understanding.]

Mr. Wilmot was of a delicate constitution, and soon followed his wife to the grave. She died in February, and he died on the 6th of the following August, 1744. The following entry is found in the records of the church at Newtown: "The Rev. Mr. Walter Wilmot was taken sick the 15th day of July, 1744, in the evening. Departed this life the 6th day of August following, about two of the clock in the afternoon, and was interred on the 7th inst., and has left his honored mother and people to bewail an unspeakable loss."

Mr. Wilmot was greatly beloved by his people, and his death was sincerely regretted. Many children received the name of Walter, or Walter Wilmot, in memory of him. He was the fourth minister who died pastor of this church, and the third buried in this town. His grave-stone still stands in the burying-ground belonging to the congregation—the inscription on which is as follows:

Here lyes
the Rev. Walter Wilmot,
Dec'd Aug. ye 6th, 1744,
Ætatis 35.

No more from sacred desk I preach,
  You hear my voice no more,
Yet, from the dead my dust shall teach
  The same I taught before.

Be ready for this dark abode,
  That when our bodies rise,
We meet with joy the Son of God,
  Descending from the skies.

Rev'd Mr. Colgan to the Secretary.

JAMAICA, SEPT. 29, 1744.

REV'D SIR,—The several Churches belonging to my Cure (as those of Jamaica, Newtown & Flushing) are in a very peaceable and growing state, whilst other separate Assemblies in this Parish are in the utmost confusion* & this I can write with a great deal of truth that Independency which has been triumphant in this town for the 40 years last past is now in the providence of God in a very faint & declining condition which gives us hopes that better Principles than such as issue out thence will generally prevail amongst us & that we shall be better united than heretofore   Rev'd Sir &c &c

THOS COLGAN.

The Rev.

DAVID BOSTWICK

was ordained here October 9th, 1745, on which occasion President Burr preached from 2 Tim. ii. 15: *Study to show thyself approved of God.* The sermon was published. The Rev. Mr. Pemberton, then minister of New York, delivered the charges, or "an exhortation," as it was called, to the minister and people.

Mr. Bostwick was a native of New Milford, Ct., born January 8th, 1721, and is said to have been of Scotch descent. He was educated at New Haven, and after instructing an academy at Newark, N. J., for a short time, became minister here, at the age of twenty-four. "He continued here ten years, enjoying the respect and affection not only of his own people, but also of his brethren in the ministry." He married Miss Hinman of Woodbury, Ct.

* He refers to dissensions in the Dutch Churches of Newtown and Jamaica in regard to Rev. J. H. Goetschius.

In 1754 he was appointed by the Synod of New York, with others, to visit the destitute parts of Virginia and North Carolina to perform missionary labour. His pulpit was ordered to be supplied, during his absence, by Messrs. Cumming, Horton, Dagget and Park.

At a general town meeting, held on the 21st of April, 1753, the town, by a unanimous vote, three persons only dissenting, viz., Samuel Clowes, Jr., Robert Denton and Joseph Oldfield, gave the meadow and upland which in 1676 had been "set apart for the use of a minister of the Presbyterian denomination," to the elders and deacons of that congregation, to be sold, to have and to hold the money arising from the sale—the interest to be devoted to the support of a Presbyterian minister forever. Daniel Smith, Elias Baylis, Increase Carpenter and Nehemiah Smith, are the persons named as the elders and deacons at that time.

Queens County *ss:* you are hereby required to give warning to all the freeholders of the town of Jamaica to meet at the County Hall of the said County in Jamaica aforesaid on Saturday the 21st instant at two of the clock in the afternoon of the same day to consult upon some proper meathods for disposing of the Parsonage outlands & meadows, for the support of the ministry: agreeable to the true intent & meaning of a voate of the said town made at a towne meeting of the said town on the ninth day of June anno Dom 1676 : & hereof you are not to fail   Given under our hands & seals this 16th day of april anno 1753.   SAMLL SMITH   } Justices
                                              JAMES DENTON }

To the Constable of Jamaica   These   Records IV. p. 6.

At a general town meeting held at the County Hall in Jamaica on Saturday the 21st day of april anno Domini 1753

   Present Sam'l Smith
      Jas Denton Esqs } Justisses
      Abm Polhemus

It was voted by the majority of the freeholders then & there assembled that whereas at a town meeting on the 9th of June 1676 it was voted and concluded that there should be forty acres of meadow designed & set apart for a Parsonage Lott in the east neck joining to the lotts of meadow layd out with upland proportionable to other lotts laid out in the town to continue at the dispose of the town to a minister when they shall have occasion to make use of it & whereas the town hath continued the said meadows & upland set apart therewith for the use of a minister of ye Presbyterian denomination since that time & now find that the land is not of so much use for the support of the present minister who is the Reverend Mr. David Bostwick nor likely to be of such use to his successors in the ministry of the said town as if the same was sold and disposed of & the money arising by the sale thereof put out to intrest; it is now therefore voted & concluded by the town at their meeting on this 21st day of april 1753 that the said meadow & lands set apart therewith be given and granted by the town, & they are hereby accordingly given & granted to Daniel Smith Elias Bayles Increas Carpenter & Nehemiah Smith the present elders & deacons of the Presbyterian church & congregation in the towne *To have & to hold* the same to them their heirs & assigns for ever in trust nevertheless that the said Daniel Smith Elias Bayles Increas Carpenter & Nehemiah Smith or the major part of them & the survivors of them or the major part of such survivors & the last survivor of them do grant bargain & sell the premises in fee simple to the best advantage that they can & that they & the major part of them & the survivors and major part of such survivors & survivor of them do put out the money arising by the sale of the premises to interest upon land security for ye use & benefit of the said town in their maintenance & support of a Presbyterian minister for the use of the said town & it is hereby further voted & concluded that so often as new securities from time to time shall be taken that the same be to the elders of the said Presbyterian church & congregation in said town of Jamaica for the time being & that the interest of the said money arising from the said sale be for the maintenance & use of such Presbyterian minister as shall be chosen by the said town for ever.

The above vote clear only Sam'l Clows Jr. Robert Denton & Joseph Oldfield protest against the above vote.

Enterd p Samll Smith clk

Records IV. p. 5.

In 1755, Mr. Bostwick was invited to take the pastoral charge of the First Presbyterian Church, in the city of New York. The Presbytery of New York referred the call to the Synod, which body appointed Messrs. Gilbert Tennent, Prime, William Tennent, Burr, Treat, Davenport, John Smith of Rye, McCrea, Beatty, Hunter, Allen, Read, Buel, Sacket, Brown, Lewis and Rodgers, to be their committee, to meet at Jamaica on the 29th of October, 1755, "to determine that affair, and any other matters relative to it, that may come before them."

At the meeting of Synod in 1756, "the committee appointed to meet at Jamaica on the affair of Mr.

Bostwick's removal, laid the minutes of their proceeding before the Synod, which were approved, and are as follows:

"At a meeting of the committee of the Synod of New York at Jamaica, October 29, 1755, according to appointment; Present, Messrs. President Burr, Samuel Sacket, Samuel Buel, Israel Read, James Brown, Timothy Allen.

"*Post preces, sederunt qui supra.*

"The committee was opened by a sermon preached by Mr. Buel, from Job xiv. (xv?) 8.

"Mr. Burr chosen moderator, Mr. Allen, clerk.

"The affair of Mr. Bostwick's removal came under consideration. The committee having heard all the several parties concerned in that affair had to offer, after much deliberation, adjourned the further consideration of it till to-morrow, half an hour past eight in the morning, to which time the committee is adjourned. Concluded with prayer.

"30*th day. The committee met according to adjournment. Ubi post preces sederunt.*

"The committee proceeded to a long deliberation on the affair of Mr. Bostwick's removal.

"*Eodem die, (same day,) seven of the clock, P. M.*

"Messrs. Gilbert Tennent, William Tennent, James McCrea, Charles Beatty, Andrew Hunter, and John Rogers, came, being prevented attending the preceding *sederunts* (sessions) by the tempestuousness of the weather.

"The affair of Mr. Bostwick's removal from Jamaica

to New York, reconsidered; and after much consultation, concluded to defer the further consideration of it till to-morrow morning, at eight of the clock, to which time the committee is adjourned. Concluded with prayer.

"31st day. *The committee met according to adjournment. Ubi post preces sederunt.*

"The affair of Mr. Bostwick's removal, &c., reässumed.

"The committee not having sufficient light to come to a full determination of that affair at this time, conclude that it be referred to the standing commission of the Synod of New York, to be convened by the moderator, at Princeton, on the second Wednesday of April next, at eleven of the clock, A. M.; and that Mr. Bostwick be appointed to supply at New York, the whole months of December and January, and the first two Sabbaths of February next; and that the Presbytery of New York provide a constant supply for Jamaica, during Mr. Bostwick's absence. And this committee recommends it to the people of Jamaica to make the necessary winter provisions for Mr. Bostwick's family as usual. Concluded with prayer."

"The commission of the Synod made report to the Synod, that they met on the affair of Mr. Bostwick's removal referred unto them by the committee. The minutes of their proceedings are as follows:

"The commission of the Synod of New York, regularly called, met at

"*Princeton, April* 14*th*, 1756.

"*Present:* Messrs. the Moderator, Aaron Burr, John

Pierson, William Tennent, Richard Treat, James Davenport, John Rogers, Azariah Horton.

"*Absent:* Messrs. Elihu Spencer, David Bostwick, Gilbert Tennent, Charles Tennent, Ebenezer Prime, James Brown, Samuel Finley.

"*Correspondents:* Messrs. Timothy Jones, Timothy Allen, Charles McKnight, John Brainerd, Charles Beatty, David Lawrence, Caleb Smith.

"*Post preces, sederunt.*

"Mr. Caleb Smith was chosen clerk.

"The commission was opened by a sermon, preached by the moderator, from John xviii. 36.

"The Rev. Mr. Johannes Light, a minister of the Reformed Dutch Church, was desired to sit as a correspondent.

"The affair of Mr. Bostwick's removal from Jamaica to New York, was brought before the commission, by a letter from the elders and deacons of the Presbyterian congregation in New York, representing their continued unanimity for Mr. Bostwick, and that the reasons for his removal to them are very much strengthened and increased by his labours among them the last winter, which appeared more fully by their commissioners, who were sent for that purpose. The moderator also reported that he had accidentally left at home, a letter he had received from Mr. Bostwick, representing his low state of health, and fear that he could not attend the commission, and in case he did not, that he would acquiesce in their judgment, about his removal to New York.

"The commission having read the papers containing a representation of the state of the Presbyterian congregation at Jamaica, and their reasons against Mr. Bostwick's removal: after much deliberate consideration of the important affair, and earnest prayer to God for direction in it, adjourned the further consideration of it till to-morrow morning at eight of the clock. Concluded with prayer."

"15*th day. At eight of the clock, A. M., the commission met. Post preces, sederunt qui supra.*

"The Rev. Mr. David Cowel was desired to sit as a correspondent.

"The affair of Mr. Bostwick's removal reässumed. The commission having weighed the reasons for and against it with deep concern, and great deliberation, considering the peculiar circumstances and great importance of the New York congregation, how long they have been destitute; how many fruitless attempts have been made to re-settle the Gospel among them; the little hopes of their being so well united in any other person; and especially the desirable prospect that appears of Mr. Bostwick's great usefulness in that place; cannot but judge it to be his duty to remove; and his pastoral relation to the church and congregation at Jamaica is dissolved for that purpose. But as the commission have a tender concern for the congregation of Jamaica, a great sense of their importance and how their case calls for special regard, they desire the moderator, in his journey to Boston, to look out for a candidate to be sent among them, and appoint the said moderator to supply them one Sabbath on his return; and Messrs. Simon Horton, Ebenezer Prime, and Benjamin Talmage, are appointed to supply at Jamaica the three Sabbaths immediately succeeding Mr. Bostwick's departure, of which Mr. Bostwick is appointed to give them notice. And the Presbyteries of New York and Suffolk are ordered to take special care that they be constantly supplied till next Synod. *The commission also considering that the congregation of Jamaica will necessarily be put to charge in obtaining a re-settlement of the Gospel ministry, do earnestly recommend to the Presbyterian church in New York, to exercise a Christian generosity toward the people of Jamaica, that they may be better enabled to settle another minister.*"

This account of Mr. Bostwick's removal is instructive, as it illustrates the importance which was attached, by the fathers of the Presbyterian Church, to the pastoral relation. The same caution was evinced when Mr. Cross was removed to Philadelphia.

Mr. Bostwick remained pastor of the old Wall-street Church for about seven years. He died after a few days' illness, November 12th, 1763, in the 44th year of his age.* Smith, in his History of New York (see Appendix, p. 307), gives this portrait of Mr. Bostwick: "He is a gentleman of a mild, catholic disposition; and being a man of piety, prudence and zeal, confines himself entirely to the proper business of his function. In the art of preaching he is one of the most distinguished clergymen in these parts. His discourses are methodi-

---

* In the cemetery at Newark, N. J., there is a monument to his widow with this epitaph:

"In memory of Mrs. Mary Bostwick, relict of the Rev. David Bostwick, late pastor of the Presbyterian Church in New York, who departed this life 22 September 1778, aged 57 years."

They had ten children. One son Andrew was a colonel in the Revolutionary Army. One of his daughters married General McDougall, and another General Roberdeau, of the Continental Congress.

cal, sound, and pathetick, in sentiment, and in point of diction singularly ornamented. He delivers himself without notes, and yet with great ease and fluency of expression; and performs every part of divine worship with a striking solemnity."

A treatise from his pen, entitled "A Fair and Rational Vindication of the Right of Infants to the Ordinance of Baptism" was published in 1764, and reprinted in London the following year. This work was republished in New York in 1837. It has a brief memoir of the author prefixed, from which the following passages are taken:

"He was remarkably supported under his last illness, and died in the faith and hope of the Gospel.

"As a preacher Mr. Bostwick was uncommonly popular. His gifts and qualifications for the pulpit were of a high order. His appearance and deportment were peculiarly venerable; possessing a clear understanding, a warm heart, a quick apprehension, a lively imagination, a solid judgment and a strong voice; he spoke in a distinct, deliberate, and impressive manner, and with a commanding eloquence.

"He dealt faithfully with his hearers—declaring to them the whole counsel of God—showing them their danger and their remedy; speaking with the solemnity becoming the importance of the subject, and in language pure and elegant, yet plain and affectionate: never below the dignity of the pulpit, nor above the capacity of any in his auditory."

Mr. Bostwick was the author of a memoir of Pres. Davies, prefixed to his sermon on the death of George II.

After his removal from Jamaica, the Rev. Simon Horton, of Newtown was called to be the minister of the place, as appears from the following passage in Dr. Berrian's late history of Trinity Church, New York:

"In the beginning of the year 1756, the Rev. Mr. Barclay acquainted the Society that the Church had suffered a great loss, by the death of Mr. Colgan, formerly a catechist in this parish, but, for many years, a laborious and worthy minister at Jamaica Town in L. I.; and that the churches under his care were very apprehensive of great difficulties in obtaining a Clergyman of the Church of England to succeed him, because the dissenters were a majority in the vestry of that parish. It too soon appeared that their apprehensions were not without good reason, for the dissenters prevailed by their majority in the vestry to present one Simon Horton, a dissenting teacher, to Sir Charles Hardy, the Governor, for induction into the Parish, but the Governor would not admit him into that cure. After more than six months his excellency was pleased to collate to the cure of the Church, the Rev. Samuel Seabury, Jr."—P. 118.

Mr. Bostwick was succeeded in this place by the Rev.

ELIHU SPENCER, D. D.

He was a descendant of Jared Spencer, one of five brothers, who emigrated from England to Massachusetts early in the seventeenth century. His parents were Isaac and Mary Spencer, and he was born at East Haddam, Conn., February 12th, 1721. He entered Yale College in 1742, and was graduated in 1746. He was ordained to the work of the ministry in Boston,

September, 1748, with a special view to a mission among the Indians. "A better testimony to the piety of the Rev. Dr. Spencer cannot be offered than by stating that he was particularly recommended to the commissioners at Boston, by David Brainerd, who was one of the best of men, as a suitable character for the missionary service among the aborigines."* He was also recommended by Jonathan Edwards. He entered on the study of the languages of the Indian tribes, and could speak several of them with great ease and fluency.†

But the Presbyterian Church at Elizabethtown, N. J. becoming vacant by the death of that great and good man, President Dickinson, the preaching of Mr. Spencer proved so acceptable to that congregation, that a call was presented him to become their pastor. The leadings of Providence were such that he felt it his duty to accept, and was installed there February 7th, 1750. Soon after, he married Joanna, daughter of John Eaton, Esq., of Shrewsbury. In 1753, he was invited by Gov. Belcher to become Chaplain of the New Jersey Regiment, engaged in the French and Indian war, which he does not appear to have accepted. In 1752 he was appointed a Trustee of the College of New Jersey, and held this office as long as he lived.

"In 1756," says Dr. Miller, "he left Elizabethtown, and accepted a call to the pastoral charge of the Presbyterian Church at Jamaica, L. I." He labored here either as pastor, or stated supply, from May 22d, 1758, to May, 1760. He was then appointed by Gov. De Lancey, of New York, a chaplain to the New York

---

* Alden's Epitaphs, p. 104. † Dr. Miller.

forces, about to march to the French and Indian war, which was still raging. Tradition says that the congregation consented to part with him thinking they could entrust their children, who had enlisted in the army, to his care. The following is found in the printed minutes of the Synod of New York, p. 283: "In case Mr. Spencer shall go out as chaplain with the New York forces, the Synod appoints Mr. Simon Horton to supply Jamaica three sabbaths, and Mr. John Smith two sabbaths, and that the Presbytery of Suffolk supply seven-eighths of the remaining time of his absence." Whilst at Jamaica he prepared for the press his Letter to President Styles on "The Dissenting Interest in the Middle Colonies of America," which attracted no small share of public attention. He was likewise author of a pamphlet on the origin and growth of Episcopacy.

On his return from the army he laboured in the congregations of Shrewsbury, Middletown Point, and Amboy; and in 1764, was sent by the Synod of New York and Philadelphia, in company with Dr. M'Whorter, of Newark, to the Southern Churches, especially in North Carolina, on an important service.

After Dr. Rodgers' removal from St. George's, Delaware, to the city of New York, he succeeded him in that pastoral charge, where he remained five years. He removed to Trenton, N. J., in 1770, and continued to be the pastor of that church until December, 1784, when he died. He is said to have been a man of prompt, popular, excellent talents; of highly respectable literary character; one of the most ready extempore preachers of his day, and eminent for his zeal and

8*

usefulness. "Whenever, at the meeting of any judicatory, the ministers were at a loss about a preacher, and he appeared, the remark was—Here comes ready-money Spencer; now we shall have a sermon."

The following is the inscription on his gravestone:

"Beneath this stone lies the body of the Rev. Elihu Spencer, D. D., pastor of the Presbyterian Church of Trenton and one of the Trustees of the College of New Jersey: who departed this life on the 27th of December, 1784, in the 64th year of his age. Possessed of fine genius, of great vivacity, of eminent, active piety, his merits as a minister and a man stand above the reach of flattery. Having long edified the Church by his talents and example, and finished his course with joy, he fell asleep full of faith, and waiting for the hope of all saints."

Dr. Spencer left a numerous family. Only one son, John Spencer, Esq., a lawyer, reached adult age. His third daughter, Margaret, married Jonathan Dickinson Sergeant, Esq., a distinguished member of the Philadelphia Bar, and member of Congress. The Hon. John Sergeant, and the Hon. Thomas Sergeant, eminent jurists, and the late Mrs. Sarah Miller, of Princeton, wife of Rev. Dr. Miller, were their children.[*] The Rev.

BENONI BRADNER

preached here, after Dr. Spencer, from 1760 to 1761. He was son of the Rev. John Bradner, the first minister of Goshen, in this State, and was born in 1734. He graduated at Nassau Hall in 1755. It is not certain whether he was installed as pastor, or preached

---

[*] Dr. Miller, in Sprague's Annals, pp. 165-169.

here merely as a candidate: tradition says that he was installed. He married, in Jamaica, Miss Rebecca Bridges. He is said to have been troubled with shortness of breath, and to have been of a consumptive habit. He left about June 22, 1761, on account of a division in the congregation, although the greater part are said to have liked him. He is never mentioned as a member of Synod; but his name appears as a corresponding member, in 1764. Mr. Bradner became minister of Blooming Grove Church, in Orange Co., in June, 1786. In 1802, he ceased from the labors of the pulpit. He died after a long and distressing illness, January 29th, 1804, in the seventy-first year of his age. The Rev.

WILLIAM MILLS,

a native of Smithtown, on this Island, was the next pastor. His father's name was Isaac, who with two brothers settled at Mills' Pond. He was born March 13th, 1739, was a graduate of Nassau Hall in 1756, studied theology at Neshaminy, was licensed by the Presbytery of New Brunswick in March, 1760, was ordained at Flemington, N. J., April 21st, 1762, and was installed here soon after, having begun to preach as a candidate on the first Sabbath in July, 1761. He married Mary, the daughter of John Reading, Esq., acting Governor of New Jersey in 1747, and again in 1757.

At the time of his settlement here, there were but twelve persons, members in full communion of the church. There were no records to be found belonging to the church. In a book of minutes which he began to keep August 30th, 1767, he says, "When I settled in this place, which was in the year 1762, I found no records belonging to the church, no, not so much as a Register of the names of such as were in full communion. And as the congregation were unacquainted with the business of church sessions, the business of the church which we had to transact was done without strictly attending to the forms of Presbyterianism. Another reason why no minutes have been kept of our proceedings is, that we have been happy enough to have little or none of that business to do which church sessions are very generally employed about, in their meetings. There have, it is true, been a very considerable number added to the church in this time, who have ordinarily been examined by the church sessions, or in their presence, whose names are preserved in a Register kept for that purpose. But notwithstanding all this, I wish, I heartily wish, that minutes had been kept both before, and since my settlement in this church, of its proceedings." The names of ruling elders given are Joseph Skidmore, Esq., Daniel Baylis, Elias Baylis, and Increase Carpenter. At the meeting of the session, June 21, 1770, Nicholas Smith and Samuel Denton, are stated to be present as Elders.

Mr. Mills appears to have been highly esteemed by his people as an exemplary Christian, and faithful minister of the Gospel. During his ministry there occurred a revival of religion, probably in 1764, by which a considerable number were added to the Church. The last of the fruits of that gracious work, Mrs. Elizdeath Everitt, who was born May 4, 1745, left this world in 1840, at the advanced age of 95, having been a communicant nearly 75 years. It appears to have commenced at a time when Mr. Mills was absent from home, and the people were assembled on the Lord's day to attend upon such services as the Elders are in the habit of conducting in the absence of the minister. Among other things, a letter was read from Dr. Buel, the minister at Easthampton, giving an account of a remarkable revival among his people. In the narrative of this revival, which Dr. Buel published, he says, "Some past accounts of this work have been owned of God; which gives ground to hope that a more particular account may have a happy effect, by the divine blessing, for the revival of religion in other places." The effect, when his letter was read at Jamaica, was surprising. The Spirit of God seemed at once to fill the place where they were sitting, the whole congregation was melted to tenderness. An aged member of the church, who deceased several years ago, informed the writer, that she well remembered, though she was but a small child at the time, the very solemn appearance of the family, and their serious conversation, on their return from the house of God. On Mr. Mills's arrival, he found a gracious work had commenced; and, subsequently, a goodly number were received into the communion of the church as the fruit of it.

It was during the summer of 1764, that Mr. Whitefield visited Jamaica, the second time, when such crowds flocked to hear him that he preached in the open air, standing, it is said, under an apple tree, not far from the spot on which Union Hall Academy is now located. In a letter written at this time, he says: "At present my health is better than usual, and as yet I have felt no inconvenience from the summer's heat. I have preached twice lately in the fields, and we sat under the blessed Redeemer's shadow with great delight. My late excursions upon Long Island, I trust, have been blessed. It would surprise you to see above one hundred carriages at every sermon in the new world." There are still remaining a few who remember the interest and gratitude with which they often heard their pious parents refer to this season of heavenly refreshing.

One of the methods which Mr. Mills adopted for doing good was the writing and distribution of small tracts. By the kindness of Mr. Thomas Baylis, an elder of the Second Presbyterian Church, Brooklyn, and a descendant of one of the former elders at Jamaica, I am enabled to present one of these tracts distributed by Mr. Mills, and preserved in Mr. B.'s family.

The Happy Man's Pedigree.

The HAPPY MAN, was born in the City of Regeneration—in the parish of Repentance unto Life: he was educated at the School of Obedience, and lives now in Perseverance: he works at the trade of Diligence, notwithstanding he has a large estate in the county of Christian Contentment; and many times does jobs of Self-Denial; he wears the plain garment of Humility, and has a better suit to put on when he goes to Court, called the Robe of Christ's Righteousness; he often walks in the valley of Self-Abasement, and sometimes climbs the mountain of Spiritual-Mindedness; he breakfasts every morning upon Spiritual Prayer, and sups every evening on the same; he has Meat to eat that the world knows not of, and his Drink is the sincere Milk of the Word:—Thus, happy he lives, and happy he dies. Happy is he who has Gospel Submission in his will—due order in his affection—sound peace in his conscience—

Sanctifying Grace in his soul—real Divinity in his breast—true Humility in his heart—the Redeemer's yoke on his neck—a vain world under his feet—and a crown of Glory over his head. Happy is the life of such an one:—In order to attain which—Pray frequently—Believe firmly—wait patiently—work abundantly—live Holily—die daily—watch your hearts—guide your senses—redeem your time—love Christ—and long for Glory.

The following is an extract of a letter from Mr. Seabury to the Secretary of the Society for the Propagation of Religion in Foreign Parts, referring to Mr. Whitefield's visit to Jamaica:

JAMAICA, October 6th, 1764.

REV'D SIR,—Since my last letter to the Honored Society we have had a long visit from Mr. Whitefield in this Colony, where he has preached frequently, especially in the city of New York, and in this Island; and I am sorry to say I think he has had more influence than formerly, and I fear has done a great deal of mischief. His tenets and method of preaching have been adopted by many of the Dissenting Teachers, and this town in particular has a *continual*, I had almost said, a daily succession of Strolling Preachers and Exhorters, &c.

In 1767, Mr. Mills received an urgent call to the Second Presbyterian Church in Philadelphia, but the Presbytery decided against it. An appeal was taken by the commissioners to the Synod, which was answered by a long remonstrance from the congregation of Jamaica, an address from the Presbytery, and a letter from the Rev. Ebenezer Prime, of Huntington. Mr. Mills also declared that he esteemed it his duty to remain in Jamaica. After a full hearing of the case, the Synod confirmed the judgment of the Presbytery, that it would not be for the edification of the Church to remove him.

This excellent minister died in the 36th year of his age. He had repaired to New York for medical aid, being affected with a chronic disease, and there he ended his days, March 18th, 1774. His remains were brought to Jamaica, and interred under the communion table in the old Stone Church. The following notice of his death appeared in Rivington's Gazette for March 24th, 1774.

On Friday last, died in this city, in the 36th year of his age, the Rev. William Mills, minister of the Presbyterian Church at Jamaica, L. I. His amiable disposition, his peaceful and prudent conduct, his unaffected piety, and rational devotion, remarkably endeared him to those acquainted with him; and as his life was a bright example of the Christian virtues he inculcated on others, so in the prospect of dissolution, he enjoyed that calm serenity of soul, and that good hope which are the peculiar blessings of the righteous. "Mark the perfect man and behold the upright, for the end of that man is peace."

His remains were interred on Monday last at Jamaica; a large number of the most respectable inhabitants of that town and the country adjacent, attended at the funeral, when a sermon well adapted to the occasion was preached by the Rev. Dr. Rodgers, from Matt. xxv. 21.

In a letter of Mrs. Eliz. Hackett, a sister of Mrs. Mills, and residing in her family, dated December 21st, 1773, addressed to her niece, Mrs. Mary Green, of Deerfield, N. J., it is stated that Mr. Mills had been in a very poor state of health since the preceding March, that he had consulted physicians both at New York and Philadelphia, whose opinions were that he was past the power of medicine. They called his disease an induration of the pancreas. "We have but little encouragement that ever he will be a well man again. He has not preached since the first of April, and I have no hopes that ever he will again." It appears that he was sick about one year.

He left six children, of whom several emigrated to the West. William settled at Cincinnati, and Isaac at Elizabethtown, Ohio, which town he named after Elizabethtown, N. J., to which place Mrs. Mills went to reside after her husband's decease. Before his death, Mr. Mills requested his sermons, of which he is said to have had a great number, and his writings to be destroyed; but at the solicitation of the Rev. Mr. Woodhull, of Newtown, who was his nephew, they were given to him. Mr. Woodhull was a son of his sister, Joanna, who married Nathan Woodhull, of Setauket. A considerable amount of property appears to have been left by Mr. Mills, as three improved farms, belonging to his estate, were advertised in Rivington's Gazette, to be sold shortly after his death.

During Mr. Mills's ministry the people again refused to raise by tax the £60 which were appropriated to the support of an Episcopal missionary. This tax, as was stated at the close of a former chapter, was laid upon the people of all denominations. In 1769 the people of Jamaica refused to pay the stipend to the Episcopal minister, and at length made an appeal to the Court of Chancery, to be relieved from the burden. Mr. Bloomer the missionary, who addressed the Secretary in the following, was inducted, on the 28d of May, 1769.

Mr. Bloomer to the Secretary.
(EXTRACT.)

JAMAICA, Feb. 15th, 1770.

REV. SIR,—I am sorry to acquaint the Society that my happiness is much obstructed on account of a troublesome lawsuit I am under the obligation of commencing against the Parish for a salary of £60 a year allowed by an act of the Province to the minister who is legally inducted by the Governor. The law for raising this sum obliges the people of the Parish, consisting of all denominations, annually to elect ten Vestrymen and two Churchwardens who are to call within one year after a vacancy, a sufficient Protestant Minister of the Gospel, whom they are to present to the Governor, or Commander in Chief for induction. And as dissenters compose a great majority of the Parish, they are careful to admit none into these offices but such as are opposed to calling and presenting a minister of the Church of England. And in order to evade paying the salary (which being raised by tax, they complain of as a burden) and at the same time comply with the law, they some years ago called and presented to the Governor, a minister of the Presbyterian persuasion, but he was refused induction:—and as the act only specifies that he who is called shall be a sufficient Protestant Minister of the Gospel, without confining them to any particular denomination, they imagine that the law has been complied with on their parts, and absolutely refuse paying me any money raised by virtue of that act, notwithstanding my being inducted by authority from his Excellency, the Governor, as I am destitute of a call from them, who being dissenters, and chiefly Presbyterians, are averse to the supporting of the Church of England.

The Court decreed in favour of Mr. Bloomer, and it does not appear that the people obtained any redress until the Revolution relieved them. That event put an end to the controversy which had continued in this place, between the Presbyterians and Episcopalians, for three quarters of a century.

REV. MR. BLOOMER TO THE SECRETARY.

Jamaica, February 7th, 1776.

REVD. SIR,

* * * The state of my mission is much the same as I informed you in my last only greatly troubled on account of their political sentiments which are strictly loyal & peaceable. Last week a number of Troops by order of the Continental Congress disarmed this Township & Hempstead & carried off about twenty of the principal persons of Mr. Cutting's & my congregation prisoners to Philadelphia they being accused of opposing the present measures.

I am Revd. Sir &c. &c.

JOSHUA BLOOMER.

REV. MR. BLOOMER TO THE SECRETARY.

Jamaica, April 9th, 1777.

REVD. SIR,

* * * I feel myself happy in having it in my power at this time to write to you from a land restored from anarchy & confusion to the blessings of Order and Good Government. The arrival of the Kings troops & their success on this Island has rendered every loyal subject, of which there are a great number here, happy; previous to that event the Rebel Army which were quartered at

New York had assumed the whole power and their Government was in the highest degree arbitrary and tyrannical; loyalty to our Sovereign was in their judgment the worst of crimes and was frequently punished with great severity. The principal members of my congregation who conscientiously refused to join in their measures, excited their highest resentment, their houses were plundered, their persons seized, some were committed to prison & others sent under a strong guard to the distant parts of Conn' where they were detained as prisoners for several months 'til after repeated solicitations to the Governor & Assembly of that Province they were permitted to return to their Families. The service of the church also gave great offence, the Prayers for the King and Royal Family being directly repugnant to their independent Scheme, they bitterly inveighed & frequently by threats endeavored to intimidate the ministers and cause them to omit those parts of the Liturgy. When Independence was declared by Congress they grew more violent, and I received a letter from one of the committee of New York informing me that my persisting in praying for the King gave great offence & conjuring me as I regarded my personal safety to omit it for the future. Upon consulting my Churchwardens & vestry what measure it was most prudent for me to pursue at this critical juncture ——— they unanimously advised me, that as the Kings Army lay at Staten Island & was daily expected to march into my Parish from whom I should obtain relief, to shut up my church. I agreed with them in opinion as if I did not take that measure I was persuaded that I should be sent to some remote part of New England from whence perhaps it would be a long time before I could be relieved. My Church was accordingly shut up for five Sundays when the Kings troops landed whose success has restored us to those religious principles of which we were deprived by tyranny & persecution. I hope my conduct in this as well as in all other matters will gain the approbation of the Venerable Society as their displeasure would give me the greatest pain; their approbation the highest satisfaction. The Church in this Province has suffered greatly by the death of its Ministers viz: Dr Auchmuty at New York Mr Avery at Rye & Mr Babcock at Phillipsburgh.

I am Revd Sir &c
JOSHUA BLOOMER.

CHAPTER VII.

1775–1815.

MATTHIAS BURNET ORDAINED — MARRIES IN JAMAICA — THE REVOLUTION — PRESBYTERIAN MINISTERS SUPPORT THE CONTINENTAL CONGRESS — REVOLUTIONARY INCIDENTS — MR. BURNET HAS INFLUENCE WITH THE LOYALISTS — SAVES THE PRESBYTERIAN CHURCH FROM DESTRUCTION — HIGHLANDERS ATTEND HIS PREACHING — THE SCOTCH WOMAN AND HER BOTTLE OF WATER — MR. ONDERDONK'S REVOLUTIONARY INCIDENTS — ELIAS BAYLIS ARRESTED — SENT TO THE PROVOST — SINGS IN PRISON — HIS DEATH — OTHER WHIGS SEIZED — WHIGS RETURN AT THE CLOSE OF THE WAR — MR. BURNET LEAVES, AND SETTLES AT NORWALK — DEATH — GEORGE FAITOUTE INSTALLED — ONE OF THE ORIGINAL TRUSTEES OF U. H. ACADEMY — THE OLD STONE CHURCH TAKEN DOWN, AND A NEW ONE BUILT — MR. FAITOUTE'S DEATH.

THE REV. MATTHIAS BURNET, D. D., received the call of this church in the fall of 1774, and was ordained by the Presbytery of New York, and installed as pastor in April, 1775. He was born at Bottle Hill, N. J., January 24th, 1749, and graduated at Princeton in 1769. His first wife was Miss Ann Combs of Jamaica, an Episcopalian; he afterwards married a daughter of Rev. Mr. Roe, of Woodbridge, N. J., who survived him, and died but a few years since in the city of New York.

Mr. Burnet came here just at the breaking out of the Revolutionary war, and continued here till its close. It must be owned that he was one of the very few, if not the only one of the Presbyterian Clergy, who did not openly espouse the cause of civil liberty. Witherspoon, Rodgers, Duffield, Spencer, and the whole Synod, in its official capacity, without a dissenting voice, threw their influence on the side of the Colonies, against the usurpations of the government. In a pastoral letter, adopted May 22d, 1775, the Synod exhorted the people to endeavor to maintain union, to treat with respect, and encourage the Continental Congress, then sitting at Philadelphia, by letting it be seen that "the whole strength of this vast country" can be brought out to carry their resolutions into execution. At the same meeting, the Synod earnestly recommended it to all the congregations under their care to spend the afternoon of the last Thursday in every month in public solemn prayer to God, during the continuance of the struggle.

A large majority of the people of Queen's County were decided loyalists. Jamaica declined to send a deputy to the Provincial Congress, at a town meeting held March 31st, 1775, by a vote of 94 to 83. At a town meeting held on the 6th of the preceding December patriotic resolutions had been passed, and a Committee of correspondence and observation appointed of which the Rev. Abraham Keteltas was chairman. A protest against the resolutions and committee was put forth in January following, signed by 136 persons, 91 of them freeholders. Joseph Robinson of Jamaica, was deputy chairman of the county committee; and Elias Baylis (chairman), Joseph Robinson, Amos Denton, John Thurston, Noah Smith, and Nathaniel Tuthill, were the sub-committee of Jamaica appointed under a recommendation of Congress, May 29th, 1775, all of them, presumed from the names, to be members of the Presbyterian congregation. Elias Baylis was an elder. Congress ordered all persons in Queens County supposed to be unfriendly to the American cause to be disarmed; and Col. Heard, of Woodbridge, N. J. with a force of near 900 marched to Jamaica in January, 1776, and took into custody certain leaders among the disaffected, and disarmed all who could be found who voted against delegates to Congress; and then proceeded on the same errand to other towns. The patriots or defenders of American liberty formed themselves into a company of minute men, and elected John Skidmore, Esq., Captain. Another company was formed who elected Ephraim Baylis, Captain. At the battle of Long Island, a Jamaica company, Captain Jacob Wright, was in Colonel Lasher's 1st New York battalion, in Scott's brigade, and on the day of battle was in Cobble Hill Fort. The day after the battle a detachment of the 17th Light Dragoons were seen dashing through Jamaica, during a severe thunderstorm, in pursuit of General Woodhull. They overtook him two miles east of the town, where, after he had delivered up his sword, they "showered their sabre blows on his devoted head."

The tables were now turned; the Loyalists were protected and the Whigs seized. As fast as they were arrested they were put into the Presbyterian church and guarded until a sufficient number were collected to send to the prison ship. As they were marched off, some, it is said, gazed on them with a fiendish smile of triumph. Some escaped; Rev. Mr. Keteltas got across the sound to Connecticut; J. J. Skidmore went up the North River. The houses, fences, and farms, of the refugees were laid waste; it was a dark day indeed, for the little band who had declared for American Independence.

"Jamaica was occupied by soldiers during the whole war, especially in winter, when the soldiers cantoned here after their summer expeditions. On the side-hill, north of the village, were several rows of huts, extending a mile or so to the east and west, with streets between. The huts were partly sunk in the earth, with a rude stone fireplace and chimney of sticks and mortar, covered with thatch, sedge, reeds, or sods, laid over boards. Boards were in such demand that the old county hall and other buildings, were torn down for building materials. * * * The parade was between the huts and the village. The hospital at one time was in the huts. Here, great mortality prevailed, and the dead were interred so carelessly that after the peace, their bones were seen above ground, and were again covered." Benedict Arnold's Legion, lay near Black Stump. Rev. Sam'l Seabury was chaplain of the "King's American Regiment," Colonel Edmund Fanning. A sermon on "St. Peter's exhortation to fear God and honor the King" preached by him, before his Majesty's provincial troops, was published by order of Governor Tryon.*

During the occupation of Jamaica by the British army, Mr. Burnet was permitted to preach undisturbed, and by his influence with the loyalists, preserved the

---

* For the above resumé and extracts, see Onderdonk's Revolutionary Incidents of Queens County.

Presbyterian Church from destruction. Mr. Onderdonk has preserved many interesting facts relating to this period. To his work I am indebted for the following:

Soon after the British were established in Jamaica, a parcel of loyalists perched themselves in the belfry of the Presbyterian Church, and commenced sawing off the steeple. Word was brought to the pastor, the Rev. Mr. Burnet. Whitehead Hicks, Mayor of New York, happened to be at his house, and as Burnet was a loyalist, soon put a stop to the outrage.

Mr. Burnet, (who had married an Episcopalian,) was the only Presbyterian minister in the county[*] reputed to be a friend of the government, and was therefore allowed to preach here during the whole war. Although he saved the church from desecration, yet after the peace, party spirit ran so high that he was forced to leave.

The Highlanders attended his church, and sat by themselves in the galleries. Some had their wives with them, and several children were baptized. Once when the sexton had neglected to provide water, and was about to go for it, the thoughtful mother called him back, and drew a bottle of it from her pocket.—Pp. 151, 152.

The Church Register shows that a considerable number of infants of soldiers belonging to the 71st, 74th and 80th Regiments were baptized by Mr. Burnet. Mr. Onderdonk also states that General Oliver Delancy, who had been appointed by Howe to induce the loyalists to join the king's troops, had his quarters at Jamaica for some time, at the parsonage-house of the Rev. Mr. Burnet.

But if the minister was a friend of the government,

[*] If Mr. O. had said country, so far as I know, it would have been true.

or concealed his real principles, his people did not generally take him for an example in that respect. I cannot forbear, in this connection, to give from the same interesting volume, the account of Elias Baylis, an elder of this church, whose descendants are numerous in this congregation, two of his grand-children being ruling elders at this time, and whose daughter, Mrs. Abigail Carpenter, was the oldest communicant at the time the first edition of this history was issued, having made a profession of religion nearly sixty years before:

The day after Gen. Woodhull's capture, (August 28th, 1776,) Elias Baylis, Chairman of the Jamaica Committee, was walking over to Nicholas Smith's, at the One-Mile Mill, to hear the news, when he was arrested by a neighbour, who wished to do something to ingratiate himself with the British.

When the venerable man, blind as he was, was brought before the British officer at Jamaica, he exclaimed in surprise, "Why do you bring this man here? He's blind: he can do no harm." The unfeeling wretch who had informed against him, replied: "He's blind, but he can talk." Baylis did not attempt to conciliate the officer, but unfortunately dropped a few words in vindication of the American cause. This was enough. He was shut up in the Presbyterian church that night, and the next day carried to the prison at New Utrecht.* He was subsequently removed to the Provost in New York.

---

* Daniel Duryee, (afterwards assemblyman,) Wm. Furman, Wm. Creed, and two others were put in one pew in New Utrecht church. Baylis wanted them to get the Bible out of the pulpit and read to him. They feared to do it, but led the blind man to the pulpit steps. As he returned with it, a British guard met him, beat him violently, and took away the book. They were three weeks at New Utrecht, and then marched down to the prison-ship.

Elias Baylis was an elder of the Presbyterian church, and stood high in the community for uprightness and ability. He had a sweet voice, and could sing whole psalms and hymns from memory: it will not be surprising, then, to find him beguiling his dreary imprisonment in singing, among others, the 142d Psalm:

> Lord, I am brought exceeding low,
>   Now let thine ear attend,
> And make my foes, who vex me, know
>   I've an Almighty Friend.
>
> From my sad prison set me free,
>   Then I shall praise thy name;
> And holy men shall join with me
>   Thy kindness to proclaim.

The aged man was visited in prison by his wife and daughter. After a confinement of about two months, at the intercession of his friends, he was released, barely in time to breathe his last without a prison's walls. He died in crossing the ferry with his daughter, and his mortal remains now repose, without a stone to mark the spot, or commemorate his worth.

The heartless wretch who arrested him fled, on the return of peace, to Nova Scotia, dreading the vengeance of his fellow-citizens; but after two years' exile, he ventured to return, but looked so poor and forlorn, that he was never molested.

Many other Whigs were seized and sent off to the prison-ship, and among them John Thurston, Robert Hinchman, and David Lamberson, who were Presbyterians. Daniel Smith was confined in the church about a week, with old Daniel Baylis. The officer in charge said to Baylis, "You'll see England." Baylis replied, " 'T will be a sight—won't it?" Increase Carpenter was a commissary to the American army; John J. Skidmore, who went away for safety, did not return until after peace had been declared.

The glorious event of peace was celebrated, by the Whig inhabitants of Queens County, at Jamaica on the Monday preceding December 13th, 1783. At sunrise a volley was fired by the Continental troops, a liberty pole was erected, and the thirteen stripes displayed from it. In the afternoon, officers of the army and a number of gentlemen of the County dined, attended by the music of an excellent band, formerly belonging to the Line of this State. In May, 1784, the courts, which had been closed, were re-opened, and were held, until the new court-house was built, in the Presbyterian Church.*

But to return to Mr. Burnet. At the close of the war, the influential men of his congregation, who had been scattered in various directions, came back to their homes; and, as may well be supposed, were not altogether satisfied with the course their minister had taken. He still, however, had many warmly-attached friends, who argued that it was through his instrumentality the church had been saved from desolation, and it would be ungrateful to turn him away.† But Mr. Burnet found it necessary to resign his charge.

---

* Revolutionary Incidents, pp. 256 and 258.

† I have been informed, by an intelligent aged person, who was intimate in Mr. Burnet's family, that he never spoke either in favour of, or against the British government, and that some supposed he was at heart a sincere Whig.

At the close of his farewell service, he gave out the 120th Psalm, which will afford an idea of the state of feeling on both sides:

> Hard lot of mine! my days are cast
>   Among the sons of strife,
> Whose never-ceasing quarrels waste
>   My golden hours of life.
>
> O! might I fly to change my place,
>   How would I choose to dwell
> In some wide, lonesome wilderness,
>   And leave these gates of hell.
>
> Peace is the blessing that I seek,
>   How lovely are its charms!
> I am for peace; but when I speak,
>   They all declare for arms.

In Mr. Faitoute's "Brief History" of the Church, he thus speaks of Mr. Burnet: "For the greater part of the time Mr. Burnet was with this people, it was a time peculiarly distressing. Being seated near the ocean, and possession being soon after gained by the British troops, after their taking the city of New York, a number of the Whigs made their escape from them, leaving their possessions, and many friends still on the Island. I have been told an attempt was made to destroy the Presbyterian Church, or at least to render it unfit for holding worship in it, which Mr. B. by his influence prevented; and that he saved the woodland from being entirely cut off by the enemy. After the evacuation of New York, and the return of those members of the Society who had fled, some disagreement arose between Mr. B. and his people, which occasioned a desire in him to be liberated from his charge, and he was accordingly liberated by the Presbytery of New

York in May, 1785." He received a call from Norwalk, Connecticut, where he settled November 2, 1785, as pastor of the First Congregational Church. He annually visited Jamaica, and in 1790, being invited, he preached to an overflowing assembly, in the Presbyterian Church, from John iv. 35–38. *Say not ye there are yet four months*, &c. His sermon was published in the American Preacher, Vol. II., and is entitled "Moral Reflections upon the Season of Harvest." In its conclusion he addressed first the minister and then the people. In his address to Mr. Faitoute, he thus alluded to his connection with the congregation during the war: "In the days of my youth I was by the laying on of hands, and particular designation of the Presbytery, placed in this part of the great field of Christ's Church, where numbers of faithful laborers had been before, with a solemn charge to labour in it, and watch over it. For several years I devoted myself to this charge; and though with many imperfections, I acknowledge I did it, yet never with a dishonest heart. In troublous and perilous times I kept it, laboured in it, and watched over it, readily contributing both by word and deed, whatever was in my power for its protection, cultivation, and growth, in the fruits of truth and righteousness."

Mr. Burnet continued at Norwalk until his death, which took place June 30, 1806. The Rev. Dr. Prime, in his history of Long Island, says that he remembers this event with solemn interest. He preached for Dr. Burnet on the preceding day, and parted from him on Monday morning, about two hours before his sudden exit.

The Rev. James Glassbrook was received as an ordained minister from England by the New York Presbytery, in 1786, and began to preach here March 11th, 1786. He so far gained upon the regards of the people as to have a call put into his hands; but some difficulties arose, and the prospect of settlement failed. He continued here till November, 1787, and was for a time stated supply at Pittsgrove (formerly Pilesgrove), Cumberland County, New Jersey. In 1790, he was dismissed from the Presbytery of New York to join the Presbytery of Baltimore. Rev. Asa Hillyer, D. D., afterwards of Orange, New Jersey, preached for about six months, in the year 1788. Messrs. Thompson, Templeton, Tate, Close, Roe, Brush, White, Woodhull, and Hart preached here during the rest of that year, and the former part of 1789. Mr. White preached as a candidate for several months, and many were pleased with him; but the Rev.

GEORGE FAITOUTE

was the next pastor. He was of Huguenot descent, born in the city of New York in 1750; and during his early years attended the Episcopal Church. He graduated at the College of New Jersey in 1774, and was ordained by New Brunswick Presbytery, pastor of Allentown, New Jersey, in 1779, where he remained till April, 1782, when he was installed at Greenwich, in Cohanzy, by the Presbytery of Philadelphia. In May, 1789, a call was put into his hands from Jamaica. "This call," he says in his "Brief History," written in 1793, "after duly weighing and considering of it, I conceived it my duty to accept, and accordingly declared my ready acceptance of it, at a meeting of the Presbytery of Philadelphia, held at Philadelphia, June 16, 1789, as may be seen in the records of the Presbytery. In the month of July following, I arrived at Jamaica with my family, and entered the parsonage house without those difficulties which some of my predecessors had experienced from the zeal of a few bigoted Episcopalians, who were not original proprietors in this place. Since the Revolution, some time in the year 1784, this Church obtained a Charter, which has secured to them their church property, and troubles of this nature we hope will no more arise."

"A dispute had subsisted for some time whether this Church belonged to and was under the care of the Presbytery of Suffolk, which then existed, and was afterwards dissolved by an Act of the Synod of New York and New Jersey. But upon the application of the congregation to the Synod, by their commissioners, after I had come among them, the Synod, at their meeting in Elizabethtown, October, 1789, did agree to annex this congregation to the Presbytery of New York, with which they so much desired to be connected, and with which they believed themselves to have been always connected, notwithstanding the claims of the Suffolk Presbytery. In consequence of this Act of Synod I took my dismission from said Presbytery, and was received by that of New York, who appointed a commission to attend at Jamaica, and proceed to my installation. The commission were Rev. Dr. Rodgers and Dr. McKnight, who attended at the time appointed—15th December, 1789. Dr. McKnight preached the installation sermon, and Dr. Rodgers gave the charge and made the exhortation to the people."

in 1813, and a portion of the stones of which it was composed was used in laying the foundations of the new edifice, which was solemnly dedicated to the service of God, on the 18th day of January, A. D. 1814. The service was as follows:

 Introductory Prayer by Dr. Milldoler.
 Read 2 Chron. 6th Chapter.
 Sung Psalm 132—tune New Salem.
 Dedicatory Prayer by Dr. Milldoler.
 Sung Psalm 84—tune Coronation.
 Sermon by Dr. Milldoler from John ii. 17.
 Concluding Prayer by Dr. Basset of Bushwick.
 Sung Hymn 128, Second Book—tune Mount Olive.
 Benediction by Mr. Faitoute.

Mr. Faitoute lived to preach in this house about one year and a half; and but one of the building committee, Mr. James Herriman, survives. The house was completed with a steeple, which was 102 feet high, and was much admired for its symmetry; but it was taken down a number of years since, on account of an injury which it was supposed to have received in the great September gale. In the spring of 1846 this house was enlarged by the addition of 13½ feet, making it 90 feet in length. It is about 46 feet wide, and contains 144 pews. At the time the lot on which it stands was purchased, the old parsonage, which was the house adjoining the premises of the late Judge Lamberson, near the corner of Fulton and Beaver streets, and the glebe which extended south, along the Beaver Pond, toward Mr. G. Phraner's, were sold, and the place where the minister now lives purchased. The present glebe includes about nine acres of valuable land. There is also a wood-lot of considerable extent in Springfield, belonging to the congregation, besides other property to a considerable amount.

The venerable Dr. Shelton has favoured the compiler with the following interesting description of the Church and Congregation, more than fifty years ago:

"I came to Jamaica in the fall of 1806, and commenced the practice of medicine in connection with Dr. Minema, who had been a surgeon in the American army during the war of the Revolution, and who was at that time somewhat advanced in years. I was at that time just twenty-two years of age, and was actively engaged in the practice of my profession until my son succeeded me in the year 1840, when I began gradually to withdraw from the more arduous duties of general practice, although I have continued to do more or less even up to this day.

"When I came to the village, Mr. Faitoute was the minister of the Presbyterian church, and was even then an old man and very feeble. The parsonage in which he lived was an old revolutionary building, fronting upon what is now called Beaver street, and was but very recently pulled down. Mr. Faitoute continued to preach up to the period of his death, which occurred some ten years after my coming to the village. He lived to preach but about two years in the church now standing, when he died very suddenly. In person, Mr. Faitoute was small of stature and lame, but very gray and venerable in appearance. His disposition and manner, both in his intercourse with his people and in the pulpit was tender, fatherly, and affectionate. In preaching, he was earnest and manifested his sincerity and interest for the spiritual welfare of his charge, by weeping often profusely. His salary was three hundred dollars per annum, and was obtained, not as now by taxing the pews, but by voluntary subscription. This small sum being insufficient for a comfortable support, was aided (eked out) by an annual visitation of his people, at that time denominated "a spinning party." This term, I suppose, was derived from the fact that among other contributions brought by the congregation, consisting of such articles as butter, cheese, wood, etc., were also wool and flax to be spun for the clothing of the family; cotton as an article of domestic economy being at that time unknown. Mr. Faitoute still further added to his means of support by teaching a small classical school.

"The church in which he preached was a square edifice of stone, directly in the street, and about the centre of the village. In dimensions it was exactly forty feet square, with a broad aisle running east and west through its middle, with a door at either extremity. The pulpit was a very small structure, with a sounding board over it, as was customary in those times. A smaller aisle extended from the larger one at right angles, opposite the pulpit to the south wall of the church. Directly in front of the pulpit was a long table, in a line with the smaller narrow aisle just mentioned. The pews, on either side of the pulpit, were placed parallel with this table and extending from the middle aisle up to the north wall. Around this table sat the elders and deacons every Sabbath. It is to be presumed that this table was intended primarily for, and was used at communion services, the communicants sitting around it; but as my knowledge on that point is not sufficiently accurate, I cannot state this as a positive fact. At the head of this table, and directly under the pulpit, sat Mr. Thomas Baylis, one of the elders, who acted as precentor. He had a fine voice, and was a good singer. In the broad central aisle was a row of chairs, the high-backed chairs of those days, extending from one end of it to the other, each numbered and occupied on the Sabbath by its own proprietor. The farmers came to church in their farm wagons; all of which, with one exception, were in their every day working trim. The one which constituted the exception alluded to, had a pair of sides, somewhat better painted and kept in reserve, probably for Sundays. This wagon had the letters D. L., Daniel Ludlum, very prominently painted on the side, to mark it, doubtless, as belonging to a patrician family. They had no tops, were very long-bodied, and on Sundays had two or three rows of the straight-backed, rush-bottomed chairs placed two abreast; over them, by way of cushions, were spread the counterpanes or bed-spreads of the family, neatly folded. Mr. James Herriman, who was, at the time alluded to, a lad of about twelve years, has told me that his father's house being directly opposite the church, was the rendezvous of the congregation previous to service on the Sabbath; the only object of this gathering being, in the winter season, of course, to warm themselves and fill the small foot-stoves which the women all carried, with hickory coals. The church was never warmed in winter in those days. To accommodate the people, Mr. Herriman, senior, was always in the habit, on Sabbath mornings, of building an immense fire of good dry hickory wood. The people would come in; sit around it, until sufficiently warm, fill their pans and retire. My friend, Mr. James Herriman, tells me he can never forget the impression produced upon his youthful mind, by the profound silence of these venerable worshippers of the early times, as they sat, for a few brief moments, around the blazing fire. There was no chatting, nor gossipping, but profound stillness; scarce a word was uttered. The vestibule and outer porch of the sanctuary was not in those days an exchange, where the price of commodities, or the current news of the day, or local gossip could be discussed and opinions ventilated. Two services were held on Sabbath, morning and afternoon, with an interval of one hour between. During this interval the people dispersed themselves around among the houses in the neighbourhood, (Mr. Herriman always entertaining the larger share,) partaking of some slight refreshments brought with them. The foot-stoves were again replenished. The venerable old stone edifice was never desecrated by stoves or furnaces, foot-stoves alone excepted; our pious progenitors seemingly not being conscious of any inconsistency in the idea of striking a balance between the propriety of warming their feet while the total corpus beside went uncared for. No living soul in those days would have had the hardihood and courage to hint at the idea of diffusing warmth more generally and genially through the whole building; but when the old edifice had at length yielded, like all mundane structures, to the progress of time and ruthless innovation, and a new church building had been erected, and men had grown more bold and daring, it was ventured to suggest that God could be worshipped quite as well and devoutly in a warm building as in a cold one. Great was the tumult occasioned. But the innovators triumphed. Mr. Herriman tells me, as undoubtedly genuine, the following story, (doubtless often elsewhere revamped and related,) which I cannot forbear, even at the expense of time and space, of relating. On the first Sunday after the stoves, then known as Shoemakers' stoves, were introduced (with pipes protruding through the windows) no fires were kindled, it being thought advisable, as I suppose, to accustom the congregation to an innovation so bold and shocking. On coming out of the church, Mr. Herriman, who belonged to the reforming party, accosted an old lady—one Mrs. Kettletas, with, 'Well, Mrs. K., how did you like the stoves?' 'Ah, just as I said, and knew it would be; they made me so faint, I thought I should have had to leave the church.'

"You requested some information about the general appearance of the congregation, on the Sabbath, in that venerable old building. The men in those times, those at least who could afford it, wore small clothes, buttoned or tied at the knee, with ribbons, and shoes with large buckles, or high topped boots; the hair powdered and tied up behind in a queue. This was my own dress at that day. The poorer class wore trousers as now. The women wore bodices high or short waisted, with very long, narrow skirts, and long protruding bonnets. In winter, they wore cloaks, precisely like those of the Quaker ladies at the present day, only of red colour. This was then the universally prevailing style, and gave a gay, lively, picturesque aspect to the congregation, which contrasted strangely with the devout solemnity and awful stillness which pervaded the assembly. I have stated above, that a row of chairs, numbered and owned like pews, extended through the broad middle aisle. These being always occupied on the Sabbath, and facing the pulpit, added materially to the grotesqueness and singularity of the *tout ensemble*, as seen retrospectively with more modern eyes. The story of a wild young blood, who, one Sabbath morning in summer, when the doors, at either end of the aisle were wide open, dashed through on horseback, at full gallop, to the great alarm and peril of these women, and the consternation and disturbance of the whole congregation, you already know; and I need only add, that story, though of little consequence, is yet authentic and undoubtedly true. I must add, moreover, that the good people of the congregation felt the insult that had been offered to them so keenly, that they came out of the church, got into their wagons and chased the offender some four miles, but being well mounted on a fleet horse, he effected his escape, and immediately afterwards went into New Jersey, where he remained six months, before he ventured to return.

"The Rev. Mr. Weed succeeded Mr. Faitoute, and came to this place fresh from Princeton Seminary, being of the very first class which graduated at that institution. He came highly recommended by Drs. Alexander and Miller. He was a man of the first order of talent, and as a preacher was extremely eloquent and powerful, chaining the attention of his auditory from the first words which dropped from his lips, with a power that was irresistible. He remained with this people six years, and his ministry was remarkably successful. During the first year of it, there was a powerful revival of religion, in which a large number was gathered into the church; and his labours continued to be blessed, with numerous additions to the church, throughout the whole period of his ministry. As a controversialist, his powers were eminent and remarkable, and he grappled with the prevalent errors of his day, with a boldness and success that marked him as no ordinary man, and inspired even his opponents with respect and fear. During the period of his ministry in this place, the celebrated Quaker preacher, Elias Hicks, the founder of the party in the denomination of the Friends, known from his name as Hicksites—came to Jamaica, and preached at Mr. Hewlett Creed's Hotel, on a week day. Mr., now Dr. Weed was among the number of his hearers; and on the following Sabbath, before commencing his discourse, he apologized to his people for having been seen, during the previous week, among those who had been attracted to listen to the preaching of a man known to be of such loose and infidel sentiments as the celebrated Quaker. He said that he had felt it his duty to do so, in order that having heard with his own ears, he might the better be enabled to judge of the man and his teachings, and so to warn his flock of the danger to which they were exposed, by exposing the unscriptural and pernicious character of his preaching. He then proceeded in a most powerful discourse to refute the errors of Hicks, to point out their dangerous tendency, and with great boldness and ability, to warn his flock to beware of the wolf that was prowling about the sheep-cote.

"Dr. Weed was succeeded by the Rev. Elias W. Crane, who was introduced to the people by the Rev. Dr. Nettleton, and who received a unanimous call. He was a man of excellent natural abilities, and good learning. As a preacher he was earnest and faithful, —the whole burden and theme of his discourses being repentance and life eternal. As a pastor, he was the most beloved of men, and his memory is still fragrant and fresh in the hearts of those who knew him only to love him; and who have taught their children upon whose heads his hands were placed in baptism, to revere the very mention of his name. He was abundant in labours, never tiring in the performance of duty. He had a pleasant smile and a kind and tender word for every one he met. None were beneath his notice. As a friend he was tender, kind-hearted, warm and affectionate to a degree seldom equalled and never surpassed, among the sons of men. His ministry was most abundantly blessed, from its commencement to its termination, with large accessions to the church. Mr. Crane was in every sense and point of view, a boon to humanity, claiming most eminent gratitude to God. It is indeed delightful to think of such a man."

CHAPTER VIII.

1815–1862.

H. R. WEED — REMOVES TO ALBANY — S. P. FUNCK — DISSENSION — REV. A. NETTLETON — GREAT REVIVAL — DISSENSION HEALED — MR. NETTLETON'S METHOD — E. W. CRANE — HIS USEFUL MINISTRY — DR. MURRAY'S SKETCH OF HIM — HIS DEATH — J. M. MACDONALD — THE NEW ERA IN THE HISTORY OF THE CHURCH UNDER MR. WEED'S MINISTRY — THE HIGHLY PROSPEROUS STATE OF THE CONGREGATION IN 1841 — INCIDENTS IN MR. MACDONALD'S MINISTRY — P. D. OAKEY.

THE REV. HENRY R. WEED, D. D., succeeded Mr. Faitoute. He was born at Ballston, graduated at Union College in 1812, studied Theology at Princeton, was called here in 1815, and ordained as pastor January 4th, 1816. Mr. Weed was a much esteemed minister. His labours were greatly blessed. An extensive revival of religion commenced during the first year of his settlement, as the blessed fruit of which above eighty persons were added to the communion of the church. He discountenanced the practice of furnishing ardent spirits at funerals, (it was the custom to serve them round to the assembled people,) and for many years this practice has been unknown. He also declined to baptise the children of parents, not in full communion, from which it appears that a contrary practice had prevailed. In 1822, his pastoral relation was dissolved, and he took charge of a church in

Albany. Dr. Weed is at present pastor of the Presbyterian church at Wheeling, Va. His ministry here, as will be shown in the sequel, was the beginning of a new era in the history of the church. The Rev.

SEYMOUR P. FUNCK,

who graduated at Columbia College in 1819, and studied Theology in the Seminary of the Reformed Dutch Church, at New Brunswick, N. J., was the next minister. He was ordained here March 6th, 1823. Some dissatisfaction arising in the congregation, the pastoral relation was dissolved, May 9th, 1825, and he left the place, carrying with him the warm affection of ardent friends. His removal was the occasion of a very serious dissension in the congregation. Mr. Funck never re-settled in the ministry. He died, April 3d, 1828, aged 32, and was buried at Flatlands.

The Rev. Asahel Nettleton, D. D., well known for his eminently useful labours, far and wide in the churches, was in the providence of God directed hither, during the winter of 1826, when the congregation was in a very divided and distracted state. He commenced his labours on the 24th of February, and continued them till the following November. He was in a feeble state of health, so that he did not attend many extra meetings, nor spend much time in visiting. But his labours were remarkably blessed. On the second day of July, the Lord's Supper was celebrated and seventy-two persons were added to the church, on profession; eighteen were baptized. From that day the revival received a new impulse. It was often observed, that it seemed (so great was the solemnity) like the Judgment day. A number of strangers visited the town and went home rejoicing in hope. So many from other places visited him, while here, that Mr. Nettleton thought of devoting one evening in the week to conversation with strangers.

He was instrumental in healing the divisions of the congregation. It is said, that instead of exhorting to brotherly love, and descanting on the evils of dissension as had been the uniform practice of the ministers who were sent here to reconcile the parties, he ignored their quarrels, preached on the claims of God, the wickedness of the human heart, and the duty of sinners, aiming directly at the conscience, and thus brought them to look inwardly, instead of at the sins of one another. In his sermons, outlines, and plans of sermons, published by Dr. Tyler, in 1845, may be found, it is presumed, many of the discourses which he preached here with such happy effect. The congregation wished him to take the pastoral charge, but he declined. He departed this life at East Windsor, Conn., in January, 1843. His memoirs were published by Dr. Tyler, in 1844. The Rev.

ELIAS W. CRANE,

was born at Elizabethtown, N. J., on the 18th of March, 1796. "When yet a boy from six to eight years of age, he was serious and conscientious in his morning and evening devotions." "His serious turn of mind, and his great devotion to reading, and readiness of acquisition, led his parents to entertain the idea that it was their duty to give him a collegiate education." When about sixteen years of age he entered the Junior Class in Princeton College, where he graduated in September, 1814. During his residence in Morristown, N. J., while engaged in the business of teaching, he made a public profession of his faith in Christ, and attached himself to the church in that place, then under the care of Rev. Dr. Wm. McDowell, on the 2d day of March, 1816. On the 8th of October, 1818, by the Presbytery of Jersey he was licensed to preach the gospel. December, 1819, he received and accepted a call from the church at Springfield, N. J., and was ordained January 5th, 1820. He remained here seven years, a devoted and useful pastor, and was permitted to rejoice greatly in seeing the work of the Lord prosper in his hands. In the year 1825 the Lord poured out his Spirit on that people, and very many were brought from death unto life. In the month of May, 1825, the church in Jamaica became vacant by the removal of the Rev. Mr. Funck its pastor. Mr. Nettleton, at his departure, recommended Mr. Crane to the people as a fit person to become their pastor. The great blessing he was made to this people, proves the sagacity of Mr. N. as to ministerial character. The pastoral relation of Mr. C. to the church of Springfield was dissolved, and he was dismissed from the Presbytery of Elizabethtown on the 17th October, 1826, and on the 31st of the same month was, by the Presbytery of New York, installed pastor of the church of Jamaica. Jamaica must be regarded as the chief scene of his usefulness. Here he spent fourteen years, almost the third of his whole life. "When he entered this field," remarks Dr. Murray, in a sermon preached at Elizabethtown, November 29, 1840, on the occasion of his death, and from which most of the facts concerning Mr. C. have been derived, "the cloud of mercy was withdrawing for a season, but spanned with the bow of promise that it would again return to water the seed he was beginning to sow;—when called away in the midst of his labours, the same cloud was retiring, after fulfilling all the hopes it had once inspired, glittering all over with the same bright bow, as if at once to illume and beautify his path to his rest and his reward. A few communions before his departure, it was his privilege and joy to receive nearly eighty into the church, and among them three of his own children." Mr. C. was affected with a disease, not unlike the asthma, whose violent and frequent attacks admonished him as to the manner of his departure. But he continued cheerful and constant in the discharge of his official duties, feeling that he was immortal until his work was done. On the evening of his decease, and but a few hours previous to its occurrence, he was preaching in a private house in a distant part of his congregation and exhorted his hearers with unusual fervency from the text, "But now they desire a better country, that is, an heavenly." The services were concluded by the hymn, the last he ever read or sang on earth:

> "We've no abiding city here—
> This may distress the worldly mind,
> But should not cost the saint a tear,
> Who hopes a better rest to find."

After the services were over, he returned to the bosom of his family. Mrs. C. was absent on a visit to a sister at Norwich, Conn., and he had made arrangements to leave the ensuing morning for Norwich for the purpose of accompanying Mrs. C. to her home. The family had all retired to rest, except the faithful domestic, who for years had been a member of his household, when his disease fell upon him with fatal violence. Feeling, after a few struggles, that resistance was hopeless, he committed his spirit, his wife, and his children to God, and laid him down and died, in the forty-fifth year of his life, and having just entered on the twenty-third of his ministry. He was cut down like a tree that yielded much fruit, and that was laden with blossoms, even in its fall."

The following is an abstract of the beautiful sketch given of his character, by Dr. Murray, in the sermon before alluded to. He was blessed by God with a natural disposition remarkable for its amiability and sweetness. By his severe trials and afflictions this disposition was never soured or changed. He was one of the most desirable friends and companions we have ever known. A near and dear relative relates that for twenty years, she never saw a ruffle upon his temper. And all his brethren in the ministry can say that they never met him but with pleasure, and never parted with him but with regret. His pleasant and cheerful smile always diffused pleasure around him. But it was religion which chiefly gave lustre to his character. His views of the way of acceptance with God, and of the great doctrines of grace, were clear and distinct; and he sought consolation more from resting on the great principles of the Gospel, than from excited feeling. He lived in the constant sense of God's favour and acceptance, and seemed to have little else to do than to serve God with all his might.

His character as a preacher and pastor has been highly appreciated. It was never his ambition to secure the fame of a profound scholar, or of a great theologian, or of an acute controvertist; and whilst he was a good scholar and a sound theologian, and carefully discriminated between truth and error, his great object was so to preach Christ as to lead his hearers to believe in him. We have never heard him preach a sermon of which it could not be truly said, both as to the matter and manner, that it was a sweet savor of Christ, and as ointment poured forth. His qualifications as a pastor very far surpassed those of many of his brethren. It was to him a pleasure, instead of a cross, to mingle with his people; and so frank and winning were his ways, that without repelling any, he attracted all to himself. His was an uncommonly sympathizing heart. Whilst, as a mere preacher, he has left behind him some superiors, and many equals; yet, when we regard him as a preacher and pastor, he has left behind him no superior, and but very few equals. In these respects the church has lost one of her best models.

Mr. Crane departed this life on the 10th day of November, 1840. His funeral was attended on the 14th, by a large concourse of people, who listened to an appropriate discourse by the Rev. John Goldsmith, D. D., from Phil. i. 21: "For me to live," &c. The

REV. JAMES M. MACDONALD

was installed May 5th, 1841. Rev. Dr. Spring preached from 1 Pet. iii. 15; the late Rev. Dr. Goldsmith, of

Newtown, gave the charge to the minister, and the Rev. Dr. Jacobus, of Brooklyn, now professor in the Western Theological Seminary, at Allegheny, Pennsylvania, the charge to the people. On the 16th of April, 1850, his pastoral relation to the church was dissolved, and the Presbytery, on the 28th of the same month, installed him pastor of the Fifteenth Street Church in New York. From his farewell address at Jamaica, delivered April 21st, the following summary is derived:

Perhaps days of as great spiritual prosperity as this church has ever known, have occurred since 1815. That year may, in some sense, be regarded as beginning a new era in its history. Previous to that date there are not wanting instances in which the Spirit appears to have been poured out with considerable power, as for example during the ministry of Mr. Cross, and again during that of Mr. Wilmot, and again of Mr. Mills. But previous to the year 1815, the number of communicants does not appear, at any time, to have been large. In comparison with the number of families in the congregation, the number of communicants was small. In 1762, before the revival which occurred in Mr. Mills's day, there were but twelve. In 1793, there were but fifty-eight. In 1807, there were fifty three. But soon after the settlement of Mr. Weed there was a special work of grace among the people, as the result of which about sixty were added to the communion of the church. In 1822, the year in which Dr. Weed left, the number of communicants had increased to one hundred and ninety-three. In 1827, following the revival under Dr. Nettleton, there were reported to Presbytery two hundred and sixty-three communicants. In 1831, God so smiled on the ministrations of Mr. Crane that over seventy were admitted to the communion, on profession of their faith. The church continued to increase by more gradual additions until 1839, about a year before Mr. Crane's death, when nearly eighty were received into its communion. The number reported to the Presbytery in 1841, the spring following Mr. C.'s decease, was three hundred and eighty, making an increase of three hundred and twenty-seven from the time of Mr. Weed's accession to the pastorship, and of one hundred and seventeen from the time of Mr. Crane's. This, however, only shows the number that remained, after deducting removals by death, dismissions to other churches, and otherwise. During Mr. Crane's ministry there were four hundred received on confession and by certificate, and from the beginning of Mr. Weed's ministry to the close of Mr. Crane's, about six hundred.

The above statistics serve to show the highly prosperous state of this church of Christ at the opening of the pastorate which had its commencement in the spring of 1841. Of the one hundred and seventy or eighty families in the congregation, there were not more than ten or twelve, at the most, the heads of which were not in communion with the church; and a very large proportion of the youth were also members of the church. The average age of the seventy-six received at the June communion in 1839, was less than twenty years. But God's gracious favour was so far continued during this pastorate, that an average of more than seventeen were annually received to its membership. The largest number in any single year was in 1845, when nearly sixty were received, forty-four of them on profession of their faith. Again, in 1847, the Lord granted some refreshing from his presence, and thirty-six were added during that year, mostly on profession. The congregation considerably increased. The few vacant pews found at its beginning were filled up; and, in consequence of the demand for more, the church was enlarged, and the number of pews, including those in the galleries (which were to a considerable extent rented) increased to one hundred and forty-four. These were soon all taken, and again applications for more could not be granted. The charitable collections averaged not far from six hundred dollars *per annum.* The rite of baptism was administered to one hundred and seventy-six persons, one hundred and fifty of them being infants; and eighty-eight marriages were solemnized. "I suppose I have preached," the address proceeds, "on an average, more than one hundred and fifty times every year of my ministry among you. I remember that I have officiated at about one hundred and seventy funerals, preaching in almost every instance. How often have we stood together beside the infant's grave, and from that point sought to catch a glimpse of the glory to which they had been taken! I do not forget the sympathy I received from you in those bereavements which it pleased the Judge of all the earth to bring upon my own family. I have gone with the aged, as they approached the banks of Jordan. Three of them were over ninety years of age; seven between eighty and ninety; and eight or ten between seventy and eighty. Over thirty were the victims of consumption. Several were strangers at Jamaica. One* was instantly killed by a fall from his wagon, and crushed beneath the wheels. Another,† a mother in Israel, met her Saviour in the waters of the Hudson, when the steamboat Swallow perished. One made a profession of her faith in Christ at the communion before her death, being then in blooming health. One died at the Asylum for the Insane. One was a man who had been a great opposer to religion in health, and whom I never saw in the house of God, who was penitent and heart-broken in his last sickness. One was a young man who, in a few days over a year, followed his young wife to the grave. A sprightly child of parents in humble life was drowned in a tub by the door side. One had been a communicant in this church sixty years,‡ and in her old age was a model of intelligent and cheerful piety. Another,§ a wife and mother, lingering with consumption, said of a winter during which she was wholly confined to the house and hardly expected to see the spring, that it had been the happiest portion of her life. Another was an excellent man,‖ whose snow-white locks and peculiarly beseeching tones in prayer cannot soon be forgotten, who being overtaken with sudden sickness and told only two hours before his departure that his end was at hand, was as undisturbed as if it was only a journey on which he was to start, for which he had been preparing for many weeks. And another was a man¶ of vigorous intellect and earnest piety, whose heaviest sorrow seem-

* Mr. James Baylis.   † Mrs. Ann Lamberson.
‡ Mrs. Abigail Carpenter.   § Mrs. Huntting.
‖ John Rhoades.   ¶ Nicholas Smith.

ed to fall upon him after his frame had been weakened and bowed down by years of sickness, but whose faith failed not."

* * * * *

"I have it to mention, to the glory of the God of grace, that during the whole nine years of my connection with you, there has been nothing to disturb the harmony of the congregation, or the kind feeling that has existed from the beginning between the people and minister. I know not that there is a single member of this congregation, and I may add of this community, who has ever sought, by word or deed, to injure me. I have endeavoured to live in charity with all men, and, with scarcely an exception, have met with like in spirit on the part of others. I have formed many Christian friendships here, which I do not think any thing can essentially impair, and which it comforts me to hope shall be continued and perfected in heaven. I am bidding adieu to a scene where God has graciously condescended to honour me infinitely beyond my deserts, and where, with many afflictions, I have also had many sources of happiness opened to me. I have full confidence that that God who planted this goodly vine in the wilderness, and has watched over it now, for nearly two hundred years, will continue to watch over it, and make it even more fruitful; that he will send you another minister, and I pray that he may be made more honoured and successful than any of his predecessors. Finally, brethren, farewell. Be perfect, be of good comfort, be of one mind, live in peace; and the God of love and peace shall be with you."

More than twenty ministers preceded the writer here, the greater number of them pastors; and but one of them survives. From time to time they have fallen, nearly every one of them, at some post of usefulness, faithful to their character and office, to the last. Six of them died during their pastoral connection with the church at Jamaica; five of them lie buried with their people; five of them made a sudden exit, three of them having preached on the very day of their death. The Rev.

PETER D. OAKEY

was born at New Brunswick, N. J., June 22d, 1816. He united with the First Reformed Dutch Church, September, 1830, then under the pastoral care of the Rev. Jacob J. Janeway, D. D. Graduating at Rutgers College in 1841, and completing his theological course at the Seminary in New Brunswick in 1844, he was ordained and installed pastor of the Reformed Dutch Church, Oyster Bay, in September of the same year. He resigned his charge at Oyster Bay, having been called to the Middle Reformed Dutch Church, Brooklyn, over which he was installed in March, 1847. He was installed over the church in Jamaica, May 25th, 1850, having been unanimously called almost immediately after the pastoral relation of his predecessor was dissolved.* That pastorate ceased on the 16th of April; he entered on his the following month—a striking evidence of the harmony and healthful condition of the congregation. Mr. Oakey's ministry, before he came

---

* The Rev. J. D. Wells preached from Jer. iii. 15; Rev. N. C. Locke gave the charge to the pastor; and Rev. J. M. Macdonald the charge to the congregation.

to Jamaica, had been marked with signal success. He took charge in Brooklyn of an infant church, having 20 members; at his departure, after three years, the church had increased to 150 members. Mr. Oakey's ministry at Jamaica has been blessed to the edification of the church, and a steady annual addition to the number of its communicants. He, too, bears testimony to the uniform kindness of the people to himself and his family. The following is an extract from his tenth anniversary sermon, preached May, 1860, taken from the *Long Island Farmer*, of that date:

"There have been added to the church, during the past ten years, 179 members. There have been 135 baptisms. The Pastor has solemnized the rite of marriage 98 times, and officiated at 270 funerals. He has delivered, during the ten years, about 2,000 sermons and other religious discourses. Of the whole number of communicants, but 49 have died during the period. Of this number several were over 90 years of age; 6 over 80 years; 22 over 70; 31 over 60; leaving but 18 under 60 years of age; of these but four were under 35 years."

CHAPTER IX.

Hortatory.

STATISTICS OF THE PRESBYTERIAN CHURCH IN THE UNITED STATES — INFLUENCE OF A SINGLE CHURCH — MEN DIE, TRUTH ENDURES — THE LIFE OF SOCIETY — ERROR AND SIN TRANSMITTED — LOSSES AND GAINS, OR THE TRANSCIENT AND PERMANENT IN HISTORY — SIGNS OF THE TIMES — THE MISSIONARY SPIRIT OF RICHARD BAXTER — HOPE FOR OUR COUNTRY IN ITS PRESENT TRIALS — PRINCIPLES RECEIVED FROM THE PRESBYTERIAN FATHERS — LOYALTY — RELIGIOUS INSTRUCTION OF YOUTH — FREEDOM OF CONSCIENCE — CHOICE OF RULERS — HOW WE MAY BEST SERVE THE FUTURE — KING DAVID — ABEL — THE CHAIN OF EXPERIENCE — MR. AMOS DENTON — FAITH AND PRAYER.

IN concluding this volume, it will be proper to glance at what the Presbyterian Church, in its several branches has become, in this country, since the church whose history has been sketched in the preceding pages, was established; and at the duty imposed on those who are charged with the conservation and dissemination of the principles maintained at such cost, in a former age.

In the United States there are now more than five thousand five hundred Presbyterian ministers, without including those of the Reformed Dutch Church; more than eight thousand churches; and more than seven hundred and seventy-five thousand communicants;— being considerably more than double the number of communicants, churches and ministers in the several branches of the Presbyterian Churches in Great Britain and her Provinces.* In the branch of the church, known as old-school, there are, according to the last reports to the General Assembly, two thousand seven hundred and sixty-seven ministers, five hundred and forty-five candidates for the ministry, three thousand six hundred and eighty-four churches, having more than three hundred thousand communicants. In the branch, known as new-school, there are one thousand five hundred and fifty ministers, two hundred and eighty candidates, one thousand four hundred and seventy-eight churches, with nearly one hundred and thirty-five thousand communicants. The Presbyterians have church property of larger value than any other denomination—the Methodists excepted, the two being very nearly equal in amount, it being, according to the census returns of the United States in 1850, more than fourteen millions and a half, and furnishing one church for every 4,769 of the total population. The educational interests of the country, in the higher seminaries of learning, have to a large extent been in the hands of the Presbyterian Church and her ministers.

Of course it is impossible to estimate correctly the influence of a single church, however clearly may belong to it the honour of being the first of its own name, established in the country, in laying the foundations of that which has grown into so vast a superstructure. It is difficult, indeed, to trace the influence, in promoting true religion, of the church at Jamaica, in this its own peculiar fields. Numerous evangelical churches have grown up around it, several of them, for more than a

* Wilson's Almanac for 1860.

century, sharing with it in Christian labours. Large Presbyteries now occupy the territory, including the two great cities adjacent, where there was not a single church of the Presbyterian name at the time religious worship was commenced in this place. Nor is it much easier to estimate the amount of good done when we limit our view to the confines of the congregation itself.

Godly men, one generation after another, who laboured for the establishment and preservation of this church, have passed away, but the church remains. Truth and righteousness did not take their departure from the earth with those who loved and defended them in the past. The same great fundamental principles which were so dear to holy patriarchs, prophets, apostles, and our pious forefathers are in the custody of their successors in the faith. The same faith by which Abraham was justified, justifies every believer. The law of the ten commandments, which came by Moses, is the law of the Christian Church. Even that knowledge, which is the result of experience, is not entirely lost, but has been transmitted in institutions, customs and laws; or stands recorded for our instruction in human biography. Society, like the individuals of which it is composed, has its own peculiar life and growth, which goes on, whilst one generation passeth away, and another cometh. No gulf ever divides one generation from its predecessors, or from those which follow it. The isolation of any single one, except by a mere form or figure of speech, is impossible. They may be distinct links, yet they belong to one great chain, stretching across the ages, and transmit from one to another a subtle and powerful influence. The coming one imbibes the life, and puts on the growth of that which is passing away before it wholly disappears.

Not only truth and righteousness, but error and sin, are transmitted from one generation to another. If the evil which men do died with them, long since would the fountain of supply have been exhausted, and the moral desert would be now blooming as the rose. Error survives, because of the deceivable character of man, and the imperfection of his teachers. It is truth misconceived; or, it is truth perverted; or, it is truth absolutely denied; and, because of this necessary relation to truth, it lives and will live, until the deceiver shall cease to employ it, or those who have been his dupes, shall be secured against his wiles. Let it not be supposed that the highest civilization of itself can ever expel error from among men, or withstand the corruption of the human heart. A Divine power and instrumentality are requisite for this great work. Just as Christianity, in the purity of its doctrines, and lives of its disciples, is brought to bear on the mass of evil in human society, will the work of exterminating it advance. And here, too, let us thankfully acknowledge the progress which has been made. The light which began to shine on the hill of Zion, more than eighteen hundred years ago, already shines with gladdening beams on many lands, giving joyful presage that it will yet penetrate all the dark places, and fill the earth with glory.

This view of losses and gains, as exhibited by a study of the past, is suited to check vanity, whilst it forbids despair. If we have any advantage over those who have gone before us, it is because we come after them. They have removed obstacles out of our path. If we had to contend with their difficulties, we should accomplish no more, peradventure, not so much as they. If we had lived when they did, we should have been the slaves of their ignorance and prejudices; no more enlightened and charitable than they. We are to take into consideration the age in which they lived, and judge them by their light, not ours. Can we hope to equal the greatness of their efforts in the difficulties they encountered, in contending with the difficulties that meet us, and in removing them out of the way of those who shall come after us?

We might well despair, when taking into account the slow progress which has been made for so many generations, if the entire work of bringing the world to the point where it now stands, had been committed to any single one of them; as we should certainly be presumptuous, if we supposed that all which remains to be accomplished has been committed to the one now on the stage. Each one has its allotted work; and if we perform not ours, we may fall far behind many that have gone before us.

The period in which we live has been thought, by some profound minds, to belong to an era which bears "marks of the fulness of time," as if there could be no great future beyond it, except that glorious consummation to which Prophecy has long pointed, and the Gospel so clearly tends. The ancient world lacked that perfection of moral and spiritual truth with which the Gospel has furnished us. The providence of God has opened to us doors which were effectually barred and sealed against our fathers of two hundred years ago. "Could we but go among Tartars, Turks, and heathens," says Richard Baxter, in his personal Narrative, "and speak their language, I should be but little troubled for the silencing of eighteen hundred ministers at once in England, nor for all the rest that were cast out here, and in Scotland and Ireland; there being no employment in the world so desirable in my eyes as to labour for the winning of such miserable souls; which maketh me greatly honour Mr. John Eliot, the apostle of the Indians in New England, and whoever else have laboured in such work."* Look in whatever quarter we may, we not only descry doors wide and effectually opened, but the nations that are without the Gospel, effete; and we descry no gifted race which seems endued with power to impress new elements on the history of the world. Christian nations must be, as has been said, "the last reserve of the world" to do God's work. And because it is God's work, and because they are in possession of the truth, as it is in his Son, the truth which makes men free, it shall be done. We have not the least ground for despondency, as to the final result. The delays and defeats, which vex us, are but a temporary adjournment, or perhaps the mysterious means employed for the hastening on of the day of promised peace and rest.

The trials, through which the Christian nation, to which we belong, is now passing, should be looked upon hopefully, rather than in the spirit of dejection.

* Narrative Part I. conclusion; written 1664.

Considering the long period during which God kept this great continent hidden from the rest of the world, and how it was opened just as soon as it was ready for occupation, and there were men ready to occupy it; and how the most enlightened kingdoms were sifted, for the precious seed with which to sow the virgin soil, we can not yield to the fear that He is about, at so early a stage in its history, to give the nation up to destruction. If the shadow upon the dial of our progress has seemed of late to be going back,* we can not believe it is the symbol of approaching dissolution, but rather of a prolonged and useful existence. The civil wars in England, two centuries ago, involved sufferings of which the bloody pages of its history can give us but a feeble idea; they ended in the beneficent revolution of 1688, deciding the struggle which had been kept up, for weary ages, between the monarchical and popular elements, in favour of the latter. God is sorely chastening us; but what son is there whom the Father chasteneth not? What greatness or eminent virtue is to be attained by individuals or nations, except in the school of affliction? May He grant that our present grievous troubles, like the afflictions of his own children, shall prove to be not judgments but chastisements, which afterwards yield the peaceable fruit of righteousness!

But it merits our most serious inquiry what it is we have received from the past, worthy to be transmitted to those who are to come after us; what it is we have been put in charge of specially for the future. We

* II Kings xx. 9-11.

have inherited something more than the estates of the dead—the houses they built, the acres they cultivated—to wit, *the principles they defended, and the immunities and privileges, which it cost them untold labours and sufferings to wring from the grasp of Tyranny.* The measure of our indebtedness to them is the measure of our obligation to hand down the legacy we have received, to those who have in it an equal heirship with ourselves.

What have we received from our Presbyterian fathers? We have received *the principles of loyalty to the civil government.* They even sustained a government which oppressed them. They were opposed to the violent measures which resulted in the execution of the first Charles, and were in favour of the restoration of the second. They were opposed to the usurpations of the military power and the Protector. They were opposed to whatever was in contravention of the fundamental law of the land, whether it appeared in the Charleses or Cromwell. They were supporters of the government *under* the ancient constitution of the land. Whilst they were ready to yield to the civil authority all due honour and submission, in matters temporal, in affairs concerning the commonwealth, they claimed the privilege of choosing their own ministers, and demanded that they should be ordained by their own acknowledged spiritual rulers; and persisted in their claim and demand in spite of disabilities, confiscations, and the sword. If we would prove ourselves worthy scions of such a stock, we must never relinquish Christ's headship in the church; and in the State, we must abide firmly by the Constitution, in all its parts, and the government administered, according to its provisions.

> "—— Think well through whom
> Your life-blood tracks its parent lake."

The strictest discipline in morals, and religious instruction of youth, was another of the principles of our forefathers. The Bible and the Catechism were employed in the family and in the school, as well as in the house of God, to impress on the minds of their children the principles which should govern their conduct towards God and man. These principles, submission to the powers that be in the state, freedom of conscience, the choice of rulers by the suffrage of the people, were transplanted by them to this land. They were admirably qualified by their love of liberty, their respect for law, and their fear of God, to lay the foundations of empire. May we, their descendants, be faithful to the trust committed to us, and deliver it unimpaired to the rightful heirs! They lived in times of civil commotion, but their spirit of uncharitable dogmatism and intolerance, which was the spirit of the age they lived in, has passed away. God forbid that, in these dark and bitter times which have come upon us, that fell spirit should be revived! Let us abhor that which was evil in them, whilst we cleave to that which was good.

In fine, if we would know how best to serve the future, it is by serving our own generation well. In casting ourselves forward, to live for posterity, it is not necessary to lose sight of the present interests of the world. We are not to "stop," as has been said "to dry up the fluids of present vitality, that we may embalm ourselves as mummies for posterity; yet whilst striving chiefly to act in the present, we should draw our bow with such tension as to strike within the veil of the great hereafter." Let our plans be for immediate, and if well devised, they will be for prospective usefulness. No man ever did better for men, in all time, than that Prince and Psalmist of Israel, the psalmist of God's people, of every name, of every succeeding age, in every land, who, "after he had served his own generation, by the will of God, fell on sleep." His tongue was silenced, and his right hand forgot its cunning, when the sleep of death fell on him; but his songs are echoed and re-echoed, and will continue to be, until they mingle with the hymns of the millennial morning. It is said of the very first one of our race who died, that he "yet speaketh." His voice comes sounding to us across the abysm of the past, telling us not so to magnify the present as to lose sight of the future, and commending to us that faith which gives a present realization to things hoped for, and demonstration of things not seen. It enabled him to seize hold of that great sacrifice to be made for sin in the distant future, of which the blood that stained his own altar was the type.

It is by this faith we may link ourselves to the gigantic chain of the experience of thousands of years. For it begets in all who possess it, like courage and hope, and leads to a deportment corresponding to the great and solemn revelations which are addressed to the understanding and the heart.

It constrains to a course of conduct which speaks after death has palsied our tongues and done its work on our poor bodies. The writer can truly say, and has often been constrained to say, that he never saw the life of faith more beautifully exhibited than it was in Mr. Denton, a former elder of this church, and to whom the first edition of the preceding history was dedicated. Always cheerful and hopeful, always prayerful and spiritual, always about his Master's business, always ready to speak a word in season to him that was weary, and to contribute out of his moderate means to the needy in a measure beyond many of those who have the resources of wealth, let me express the hope that he has and will continue to have many to follow him as he followed Christ. What though disease which had long been wasting his bodily strength, at length commenced its ravages on his mind and overshadowed him in his last sickness with a rayless cloud? How great and joyful must have been the good man's astonishment when, having closed his eyes for ever on the darkness of earth, he opened them on the brightness of heaven!*

---

* Mr. Denton departed this life August 9th, 1857, aged 63 years, 5 months and 8 days. The following sketch of him was published by the present pastor, Rev. Mr. Oakey:

Mr. Denton was born in the town of Jamaica, March 1st, 1794. A child of the covenant by a pious mother, he was early taught the obligation and practice of true religion.

The subject of our notice united with the Presbyterian Church in October, 1816. His consistent piety and devoted zeal pointed him out as well qualified to fill the office of ruling elder. Accordingly, having been previously called to this office by the voice of the church, he was ordained thereto on the 3d of June, 1819. How well he filled that office they who knew him most intimately can best testify. It is due to his memory to say that for 38 years, except when sickness intermitted his labours, he served the church as an elder with an affection, a faithfulness, a devotion of piety, a pure consistent christian character seldom surpassed, not often equaled. And though for awhile

It is by faith we receive the great propitiation. It is by faith that the unseen things of eternity become living and influential realities. It is CHRIST in our prayers like the angel of the Lord, ascending in the flame of the burnt sacrifice* of Israel's great champion laid aside from active duty by physical disability, yet to the last his interest was in and for the church.

Some of the traits in his character may be summed up in a few words. *He had a tender conscience.* He feared nothing so much as sin. He was very susceptible to anything in his own person or in the church that might offend the Divine Master or wound his cause. *He was of a humble mind.* He never was obtrusive in his manner. He never arrogated to himself superiority; nor was he dogmatic in the statement of his opinions. His disposition was rather conciliating, confiding, childlike; more like those of whom the Saviour said, "of such is the kingdom of Heaven." *He was charitable upon principle;* he was *liberal according to system.* If he was absent on collection days, his contribution nevertheless came. And that contribution was a fair representative of his worldly circumstances, for he felt it to be a *privilege* to "give according *as* the Lord had prospered him. *He was desirous of doing good to the souls of men.* Many can testify to his efforts in the sick chamber, and by personal conversation with the impenitent, to lead them to Jesus. And some who have united with the church traced their convictions to his conversation, or to books given them by him. "They that turn many to righteousness shall shine as the stars for ever and ever." *He was strong in his faith in God.* However little faith he may have had in *himself*, he never lost hold of his faith in God. He never permitted himself to question the wisdom or righteousness of the Divine proceedings. And in this respect, like Job, he kept his integrity to the end. And though his disease, reaching the brain, produced great mental suffering, partially thereby suspending the full enjoyment of his hope, yet in his life and character the example and power of a godly life speak out, justifying the appellation, if it may be applied to any one within the range of our knowledge, of a good man and full of the Holy Ghost. And while friends gather around his grave, the church mourns his loss, and the impenitent have lost a friend, than whom no one felt a more tender interest for them than our departed brother.

But he is gone. We can only mourn our loss, and tender our condolence to the afflicted relatives, and in the language of the apostle, exhort them "that they sorrow not, as others which have no hope. For if we believe that Jesus died and rose again; even so them also which sleep in Jesus will God bring with him."

* Judges xiii. 20.

which brings them near the throne of the LORD of all the ages and kingdoms of the world. It is a great encouragement when we remember we approach the same gracious being who heard the prayers of our own parents and ancestors, who have passed beyond the shadows amidst which we are moving to the inheritance of the promises. Our hearts are moved when we think how they prayed for their children's children, and we are blessed; how they prayed for Christ's cause and it was strengthened, and his work revived. Are we wrestling as they did to obtain the everlasting prize? and for a blessing on those who are to come after us?

ADDENDA.

I.

A list of the Towne Estate of Jemaica.

ANNO 1683	HORS	3 YE	2 YE	1 YE	OXE	COWSE	3 YE	2 YE	1 YE	SWINE	LAND	HEADS	ESTATES £ s. d.
Capt. Carpenter.......	2	1	0	0	2	5	4	3	3	1	52	2	186 00 00
John Rodes Senr......	0	0	0	0	4	2	5	2	2	0	40	1	120 00 00
Thomas Smith sen.....	0	1	1	0	2	3	3	2	2	2	45	2	145 00 00
Jonathan Deine,......	1	0	0	0	0	2	0	0	0	0	18	1	58 00 02
John Everit..........	2	0	0	0	0	3	1	4	2	0	30	1	104 00 00
Joseph Smith.........	2	0	0	0	4	4	4	2	2	0	42	2	170 00 00
Thomas Bayles.......	1	0	0	0	4	5	0	2	1	1	33	1	119 00 00
Thomas Wigens iun...	0	0	0	0	0	2	0	1	1	0	8	0	022 00 00
John Wigens.........	0	0	0	0	2	1	0	0	1	0	0	1	036 00 00
Girsham Wigens......	1	0	0	0	1	1	0	0	0	0	0	1	041 00 00
Edward Higbee.......	1	0	0	0	0	3	2	2	2	1	30	1	092 00 00
Joseph Thurston......	3	0	0	0	2	3	1	5	1	1	46	2	164 00 00
William Foster.......	2	0	0	0	0	4	2	2	4	0	35	1	116 00 00
Samuell Smith........	2	0	0	0	6	6	2	3	3	0	50	3	201 00 00
Nicholas Everit......	1	0	0	0	4	4	4	4	4	2	50	2	176 00 00
Daniel Whithed......	2	0	0	0	0	6	2	3	1	2	45	0	118 00 00
Clem Salmon.........	0	0	0	0	0	1	0	0	0	0	10	1	033 00 00
William Creed	1	0	0	0	4	6	3	0	0	0	70	1	160 00 00
Peter Stringham.....	1	0	0	0	0	3	1	0	0	0	12	1	061 00 00
Benjamin Coe........	1	0	0	0	0	4	1	1	1	0	27	1	085 00 00
Samuell Messenger....	2	0	0	0	1	3	1	0	2	0	10	1	080 00 00
Nathaniell Lynas.....	0	0	0	0	0	1	4	0	1	0	10	0	032 00 00
John Oldfield........	0	0	0	0	4	4	0	2	2	0	36	2	124 00 00
George Woolsey iun...	0	0	0	0	4	6	0	1	0	0	25	0	081 00 00
John Man............	2	0	0	0	0	3	0	4	2	1	22	2	111 00 00
Sam Mathews........	1	0	0	0	2	4	3	2	2	2	24	1	108 00 00
John Foster..........	0	1	0	0	0	1	2	0	0	0	8	1	047 00 00
Jane Foster..........	0	0	0	0	2	1	4	3	1	2	22	0	066 00 00
Richard Jones........	0	0	0	0	0	1	0	0	0	0	14	1	037 00 00
Jonathan Mills.......	2	0	0	0	2	6	1	3	3	3	16	1	119 00 00
Jonathan Wood......	0	0	0	0	0	0	0	0	0	0	0	1	018 00 00
Jonas Wood..........	0	1	0	0	0	2	0	4	0	0	5	1	051 00 00
John Wood..........	1	0	0	0	0	2	0	1	1	0	15	1	055 00 00
Elias Bayles.........	1	0	0	0	0	2	2	2	1	0	4	0	040 00 00
John Smith Jr........	1	0	0	0	1	2	1	1	3	0	8	1	065 00 00
Samuell Denton......	0	0	0	0	2	4	1	1	1	0	6	1	064 00 00
Alexander Smith......	0	0	0	0	0	2	0	2	1	0	13	1	047 00 00
Zachariah Mills.......	1	0	0	0	2	2	2	1	1	0	19	1	083 00 00

240 ADDENDA.

Rate list, etc.—Continued.

ANNO 1683	HORS	3 YE	2 YE	1 YE	OXE	COWSE	3 YE	2 YE	1 YE	SWINE	LAND	HEADS	ESTATES £ s. d.
Abell Galle..........	2	0	0	0	2	4	2	3	0	6	21	1	093 00 00
Fulke Davis..........	0	0	0	0	0	2	0	0	2	0	8	1	039 00 00
Samuell Davis........	0	0	0	0	0	3	0	2	0	1	11	1	050 00 00
John Hindes..........	1	0	0	0	0	1	1	1	0	1	6	1	048 00 00
Richard Denton.......	2	0	0	0	0	0	0	0	0	0	0	1	042 00 00
Nehemiah Smith......	1	0	0	0	4	4	3	2	1	0	22	1	116 00 00
Wait Smith..........	0	0	0	0	4	4	1	2	2	0	36	1	110 00 00
John Smith Senr......	1	1	0	0	0	3	0	2	1	1	26	1	086 00 00
John & Jos. Ludly....	1	1	0	0	6	3	2	3	1	0	30	2	151 00 00
John Carpenter.......	1	0	0	0	2	2	2	1	2	0	13	1	078 00 00
Samuell Mils.........	1	0	0	0	2	4	2	0	2	0	30	1	103 00 00
Nath Denton iu......	1	0	0	0	2	3	2	1	3	0	15	1	087 00 00
Sam Deine Sen.......	2	0	0	0	4	6	0	2	3	0	34	1	139 00 00
Sam Deine Jun.......	0	0	0	0	0	0	0	0	0	0	4	1	022 00 00
John Deine	1	0	0	0	0	1	0	0	0	0	5	1	040 00 00
Nath Denton Sen......	2	0	0	0	4	6	0	1	0	1	55	1	153 00 00
George Mills.........	0	0	0	0	0	2	0	1	0	0	4	1	034 00 00
George Woolsey Sen..	2	0	0	0	4	6	2	4	0	0	36	2	168 00 00
Widow Ashman.......	1	0	0	0	4	3	0	0	2	0	21	0	075 00 00
John Rowlifson & Fred.	1	1	0	0	0	4	0	3	3	0	16	2	104 00 00
Thomas Wellin.......	0	0	0	0	0	5	0	3	2	0	30	0	065 00 00
John Bayles..........	2	0	0	0	0	3	0	3	8	0	22	1	098 00 00
Sam Ruscoe..........	0	0	0	0	0	2	0	0	0	0	16	1	044 00 00
John Hanson.........	0	0	0	0	0	8	2	6	3	1	14	2	118 00 00
Derick Powleson......	2	0	0	0	0	6	0	3	4	0	22	1	107 00 00
Cornelius Barnson.....	1	0	0	0	0	2	0	0	0	0	10	1	050 00 00
Rich Everit..........	1	0	0	0	0	0	0	0	0	0	10	0	022 00 00
Hugh Forde..........	1	0	0	0	0	0	0	0	0	0	0	1	030 00 00
Thomas Smith iun....	0	0	0	0	1	2	0	0	0	0	9	1	043 00 00
William Bringseel.....	1	0	0	0	0	2	0	0	1	0	3	1	044 00 00
Edw Burrows........	0	0	0	0	0	1	0	1	1	0	5	1	032 00 00
Caleb Carman........	1	0	0	0	6	5	0	4	0	0	19	2	198 00 00
John Rodes iun.......	2	0	0	0	0	3	2	1	1	1	9	1	079 00 00
Tho Foster...........	0	0	0	0	0	0	2	1	0	0	0	1	032 00 00
John Carman.........	0	0	0	0	0	2	0	0	0	0	0	1	028 00 00
Tho Woolsey.........	1	0	0	0	0	0	0	0	0	0	10	1	040 00 00
John Freeman........	2	0	1	0	0	3	4	1	1	1	6	1	089 00 00
Beniamin Jones.......	1	0	0	1	2	1	0	0	0	2	6	1	053 00 00
William White.	1	0	0	0	0	1	0	0	0	0	3	1	038 00 00
Hope Carpentor.......	1	0	0	0	2	1	0	1	1	0	4	1	055 00 00
Randolph Evans......	0	0	0	0	0	0	0	0	0	0	9	0	000 00 00
Barnet Caterlin.......	0	0	0	0	0	0	0	0	0	0	0	1	018 00 00
John Foster..........	1	0	0	0	0	0	0	4	0	0	0	1	046 00 00
Jerem Hubard........	0	0	0	0	0	2	0	0	0	0	6	1	034 00 00
Daniel Denton..	2	0	0	0	0	2	1	0	0	0	0	1	056 00 00

ADDENDA. 241

II.

Return of Marriages Christenings and Burials in the town of Jamaica, for Seven Years preceding 1688.—Doc. Hist. III. 197.

	MARRIAGES.	CHRISTENINGS.	BURIALLS.
Capt. Carpenter, . . .	3	0	0
Joseph Smith, . . .	1	1	0
John Oldfield, . . .	1	2	0
Mr. Woolsey, . . .	1	0	1
Will ffoster, . . .	1	0	1
Samll Smith, . .	3	2	0
John Everett, . . .	0	3	0
Zachary Mills, . . .	0	0	1
Alexander Smith, . . .	0	4	0
Rich Jones, . .	0	1	0
Edward *Burons* .	0	2	0
Nehemiah Smith, . .	0	0	1
John Heines, . .	1	1	1
John Carpenter, . .	0	3	0
Saml Mills . . .	2	2	0
Nath Denton Senr . .	3	0	0
John Rodes, . .	0	3	0
John, *Ludlom* . .	0	1	0
Nath Denton, . .	0	4	1
George Woolsey, . .	0	3	1
Tho: Smith Senr, .	1	2	1
Tho: Smith Junr, .	0	1	1
John Smith, . .	0	2	0
Rich: Rodes, .	0	0	1
Ralph Hunt, . . .	1	0	0
Theadory .	0	2	1
Derrick Poulson .	0	3	1
Rich Everett . .	1	0	0

11

242 ADDENDA.

	MARRIAGES.	CHRISTENINGS.	BURIALLS.
Samll Mathews,	1	0	0
Nicolas Everett,	1	4	1
Jonas Wood,	0	4	1
ffrederick	0	3	0
John Baylie,	1	0	0
John Hanson,	0	0	1
Elias Baylie,	0	3	0
Abell Gale,	1	0	1
Jonth Dean,	0	0	1
Samll Dean,	3	0	1
Nath Lynas,	0	4	0
Wait Smith,	0	3	0
Danll Denton, Junr,	0	0	3
Joseph Thurston,	1	8	1
John Wood,	0	2	0
Mr. Whitehead,	0	0	1
Mr. White,	0	0	2
Hope Carpenter,	0	1	1*
Danll Denton Senr	—	—	—
Tho: Wellen,	—	—	—
Will Creed	—	—	—
John ffoster,	—	—	—
John Man,	—	—	—
Will Sallierd	—	—	—
Fulk Davis,	—	—	—
Mr. ffreeman,	—	—	—
Samell, Ruscoe.	—	—	—
Jonth: Mills,	—	—	—
Beniemin Coe,	—	—	—
Tho: Wiggins,	—	—	—
Widdow, Ashman.	—	—	—
Edward Higbee,	—	—	—

* The remaining figures of the MS. are obliterated.

ADDENDA.   243

Widdow Davis, . . — .... — .... —
Samll Denton, . . — .... — .... —
Widdow Messenger, . . . — .... — .... —
Rich: Wright, . . . — .... — .... —
Peter Stringam, . . . — .... — .... —
Jeremiah Hubbard, . . — .... — .... —

This is what we can Remember hath hap'n'ed within 7 years.

ffor ye number off horse & ffoot & how armed & provided an account is alreddy given by ye Military officers:

By order from ye Commissioners
By DANLL DENTON Clerk

To Maior Thomas Willet, Sheriff.

———•••———

III.

Rate List for £51 of Jamaica feb 4, 1708-9.

	£	s.	d.	q.w		£	s.	d.	q.w
Cornelius Baise	0	3	3	0 0	William Cornell	0	0	7	0 0
Widow Coe	0	3	6	3 1	Gershom Wiggins	0	6	9	3 1
John Carpenter, Jr.	0	3	8	2 0	Simum Bloome	0	5	10	2 0
John Brass	0	3	0	1 1	John Bleuw	0	5	8	2 2
Andrew Gaile	0	4	10	0 2	William Golder	0	3	3	3 3
Daniel Coe	0	6	4	2 2	Samuel Higbie	0	4	10	1 3
Nathan'l Smith	0	2	1	2 4	Thomas Thurston	0	0	4	0 0
John Cokefair	0	8	1	1 4	John Coe	0	0	5	0 0
Joseph Coe	0	5	3	1 3	William Bloodgood	0	0	1	2 0
John Mills	0	4	5	1 1	Justice Mastin	0	0	1	2 0
Jonan Mills, Sr.	0	4	1	1 1	John Gray	0	0	5	0 0
Jonan Mills, Jr.	0	0	2	0 0	Anthony Waters	0	17	5	2 3
Powel Amberman	0	4	5	2 2	Johanas Bruer	0	5	9	1 3
Samuel Seitmore	0	4	6	3 3	Obadiah Wilkins	0	1	11	2 0
Daniel Whithead	0	3	9	0 0	Richard Betts	0	0	10	0 0
John Cleare	0	4	9	0 0	Hope Rodes	0	3	6	2 2
John Talman	0	1	0	0 0	Jonan Dean, Jun	0	4	10	1 3
Eliacam Hedger	0	0	5	0 0	Benjamin Smith	0	4	3	0 4
John Hendrickson	0	0	3	0 0	Nicolas Everit, Jr.	0	2	1	0 0
Johanas Eldertson	0	0	3	0 0	John Hanson	0	17	6	1 2
Christian Snedicer	0	0	3	0 0	Hanse Bargin	0	2	9	1 1
William Johnson	0	7	1	0 0	Tunis Hanson	0	0	2	0 0
Charles Randall	0	0	10	0 0	William Creed, Sen.	0	9	7	1 3
Richard Everitt	0	0	4	0 0	Widow Okly	0	2	9	0 4

244　ADDENDA.

Rate List, etc.—Continued.

	£	s.	d.	q.w		£	s.	d.	q.w
John Garison	0	0	7	0 0	Jacob Lowese	0	1	11	2 0
John Rodes	0	7	10	1 1	Jos. Oldfield	0	7	2	2 2
Mrs. Woolsey	0	1	9	0 0	Sam'l Thurston	0	3	11	1 3
William Ludlum	0	5	11	2 0	Hope Mills	0	5	6	2 0
John Gaile	0	16	8	0 0	Dan'l Bayles	0	4	0	1 3
John Morehead	0	2	4	2 2	John Messenger	0	2	8	0 0
John Wright	0	0	7	00	Abm. Lot	0	8	1	0 2
Adrian Hegeman	0	1	2	0 0	David Forman	0	1	10	3 1
Nathaniel Higbe	0	7	1	1 3	Wait Smith, Jr	0	3	3	0 0
Sam'l Denton (Smith)	0	5	10	0 0	Nathan Smith	0	2	6	2 4
Elias Doughty	0	0	7	0 0	Nicolas Stillwell	0	5	1	0 2
Daniel Smith	0	5	1	2 2	Peter White	0	5	10	2 2
Thos. Welling	0	7	3	3 3	Justice Robt. Reade	0	2	5	2 0
Sam'l Smith (red hd)	0	7	11	3 1	Josiah Wiggins	0	9	4	3 3
Jos. Carpenter	0	0	2	0 0	Sam'l Smith (Cord)	0	6	9	3 3
Nath'l Denton, Jr	0	6	0	0 2	Ebenezer Smith	0	2	1	1 1
Sam'l Bayluys	0	7	7	0 4	Jonas Dean, Jr	0	0	2	0 0
Wm. Creed, Jr	0	9	10	1 1	Nath'l Denton, Jr	0	10	0	3 1
Thos. Whithead	2	15	1	1 3	Daniel Dean	0	4	2	1 1
Capt. Geo. Woolsey	0	7	3	1 1	Samuel Clows (Clerk)	0	1	6	0 0
John Smith, Jus	0	10	11	2 0	Sam'l Mills, Jr	0	6	0	0 0
Thos. Humphres	0	1	4	0 0	Thos. Howel	0	2	6	0 0
Rem Durland	0	9	11	0 4	John Foster (Comber)	0	1	4	0 0
Garret Durland	0	9	9	0 4	Gabrill Luff	0	3	11	0 0
Peter Garason	0	8	5	2 2	Jos. Smith	0	11	5	2 2
Jacob Ramson	0	10	7	0 0	James Denton	0	0	3	3 3
Johanas Williamson	0	8	1	2 0	Widow Goldin	0	0	1	2 0
John Snedicer	0	7	1	0 0	Zachariah Mills	0	5	0	0 0
John Lamberson	0	7	10	2 0	John Carman	0	0	10	0 0
Theodorus Polchemus	0	19	7	1 3	Sam'l Mills, Sr	0	4	8	1 3
Jacob Colyer	0	1	6	0 0	Jos. Ludlum	0	3	8	0 0
Eldert Lucas	0	12	5	2 4	John Ludlum	0	8	8	0 0
Jehonas Bukout	0	1	4	0 0	Jas. Lewis	0	0	5	0 0
Hendrik Lot	0	16	5	2 2	Waite Smith, Sr	0	9	7	0 2
Jacob Johnson	0	3	7	1 3	Neh. Smith, Sr	0	4	11	2 4
Dow Johnson	0	12	2	1 3	Neh. Smith, Jr	0	2	9	1 3
John Deane	0	4	1	3 1	Capt. John Carpenter	0	6	3	2 4
Samuel Deane	0	4	7	0 4	Daniel Bull	0	1	8	0 0
Hendrick Brass	0	4	2	2 2	Thomas Smith, Jr	0	4	10	3 3
Tunes Huff	0	2	0	2 0	Abell Gaile	0	3	8	1 4
Peter Hendrickson	0	0	4	2 0	Thos. Gaile	0	5	6	0 4
Garitt Johnson	0	8	11	2 4	Neh. Gaile	0	2	3	0 0
Garitt Clason	0	16	10	0 4	Wm. Moss	0	3	0	2 4
John Okey	0	12	4	2 0	Jonan Waters	0	11	0	0 0
John Weson	0	0	7	1 1	Doc Beckman	0	3	4	2 0
Samuel Durling	0	0	7	2 0	John Smith, Jr	0	4	2	2 4
Stephen Stephenson	0	8	2	2 2	Jos. Burton	0	3	5	2 4
Benj. Thurston	0	18	6	0 0	Sam'l Fisch	0	4	8	0 0
Benj. Wiggins	0	5	6	0 0	Hope Carpenter	0	7	10	3 3
Wm. Carpenter	0	4	11	0 0	Jonas Wood, Jr	0	10	10	0 0
John Probasco	0	8	4	1 1	Timothy Wood	0	1	10	1 1
Elias Baylies	0	5	6	1 1	Thos. Wiggins	0	6	4	0 4
Samuel Carpenter	0	8	1	3 1	Charles Williams	0	0	11	0 0
Wm. Brinkley	0	0	5	3 1	John Woolsey	0	5	11	1 3

ADDENDA.   245

Rate List, etc.—Continued.

Hend'k Hegeman	0	11	5	2	4	Sam'l Smith, Sr.	0	6	3 8 1
Thos. Burus	0	4	11	0	0	Mrs. Whithead	0	4	9 1 1
John Burus	0	1	4	0	0	Doct. Ocquart	0	2	0 0 0
Sam'l Denton	0	1	4	0	0	Francis Sawyer	0	0	7 0 0
John Foster, Jr	0	6	3	3	1	Justice Everitt	0	9	10 1 3
Wm. Jones	0	5	3	2	0	Noah Smith	0	0	2 0 0
Charles Smith	0	1	8	0	0	Thos. Petit	0	2	6 1 3
Thos. Woolsey	0	5	5	1	1	George Cimbal	0	0	2 0 0
Jonas Wood, Jr	0	0	2	0	0	Justice Whithead	2	11	10 2 4
Solomon Carpenter	0	2	5	0	0	Joseph Fanton	0	0	2 0 0
Thos. Smith (Cord)	0	3	10	0	0	Andrew Mariner	0	1	8 0 4
Richard Oldfield	0	13	6	0	2	Widow Hinksman	0	0	3 0 0
Wm. Oldfield	0	8	0	2	4	Widow Hadlock	0	3	2 2 0
John Pearce	0	0	5	0	4	Thos. Waters	0	6	2 0 4
Frederick Van Lew	0	17	10	2	2	Amos Smith	0	5	4 2 0
John Everitt	0	7	8	0	0	Edward Hare	0	0	4 2 0
David Waters	0	5	1	3	3				

The above rate being £51 16s 9½d, whereof £50 3s 1d to be paid to Col. Abm. Depeyster, Treasurer of the Colony, and the remainder £1 13s 8d to remaine to ye townes use   made by us

           THOS WATERS } *Assessors*.
           AMOS SMITH }

TOWN RECORDS, III. 58 to 60.

Remarks on the foregoing List.

The Whitheads were the two richest, and now not one of the name can be found hereabouts.

The denominations of money are, £. s. d. qrs. and *wampum*. I suppose 5 wampums were a farthing.

We have here *all* the taxable inhabitants of the town of Jamaica.

We learn there were two doctors, one Bloodgood and one Urquhart, perhaps the *father* of the Rev. Mr. Urquhart. John Urquhart occurs in 1696.

We see the odd affixes to persons of the same name, as Smith, *Cord, i. e.*, cordwainer or shoemaker; Smith, *Red hd, i. e.*, red haired, red head; Foster, *Comb*, whether it means wool *comber*, or what, I can't guess; Smith, *Pond*, who lived at Beaver Pond; Sam'l Denton, *Smith, i. e.*, blacksmith.

Dan'l Bull was the one who caused the riot in Jamaica, while McNish looked on and encouraged the non-payment of church dues to Poyer. He was supervisor.—Doc. Hist. III. 285.   H. O., JR.

IV.

LETTER OF THE REV. GEORGE HALE.

Pennington, N.J., February 5th, 1862.

Rev. J. M. Macdonald, D. D.

DEAR SIR,—The township of Hopewell, in which the village of Pennington lies, was originally settled about the year 1700, and principally by emigrants from Long Island. These emigrants were the founders of the First Presbyterian Church of Hopewell of which I am now the pastor and which formed part of the old "congregation of Maidenhead [Lawrence] and Hopewell" mentioned as early as 1709, in the minutes of the Presbytery of Philadelphia.

Some of these were from Jamaica. Within view of the spot where I am now writing, is the farm conveyed (as the parchment deed before me states) on "the 17th of November, 1699, to Edward Burrowes of Jamaica on Long Island." This land was first occupied by his son Thomas Burrowes, who took an active part in favor of the "old side" in the controversy which agitated the Presbyterian church in 1737–8, &c. In the call for the services of the Rev. John Guild in 1739, are found his name and those of his five sons. Three of his descendants have been elders of this church, and one of them is the Rev. George Burrowes, D. D., now of San Francisco, California.

Opposite to the farm of Thomas Burrowes, on the north side of the road, is the land purchased by George Woolsey also of Jamaica, and now in possession of his descendant of the fourth generation, George Woolsey, a deacon of this church.

Adjoining the farm of Thomas Burrowes is land once the property of John Muirheid, who was married to

"*Rebekah Bailey*" at Jamaica, November 22, 1706. Their oldest child Jane, was born August 29, 1710 and "baptized by Mr. George McNish." It is recorded that all their other children, seven, were baptized in infancy. Two of his posterity, each bearing the name of their ancestor, "John," have been ruling elders of this church.

A portion of the last mentioned tract was bought by *John Carpenter* of Jamaica, and occupied by him and three generations following, each of the four bearing the name "John" the third being for many years a ruling elder in this church, and the fourth dying unmarried just as he had reached manhood. Between the farm of Mr. Carpenter, and a line fence, which is but a few rods distant from here, is the purchase of *John Welling*, also of Jamaica, two of whose grandsons have been ruling-elders, and a great grandson a deacon of this church.

In addition to the above, Thomas Smith, John Everit, Eldad Davis, Jonas Wood, Caleb Carman, Samuel Everit, and Andrew Foster, are believed to have immigrated hither from Jamaica, Long Island.

Two of the early settlers married daughters of the Rev. John Prudden, once pastor of the Presbyterian church of Jamaica:—viz, Nathaniel Moore of Newtown, the husband of Joanna Prudden, and Elnathan Baldwin, (of the Hempstead Baldwins) the husband of Kezia Prudden.

From Hempstead came John Mott, John Johnson and William Cornwell.

From Newtown, came Ralph Hunt, whose son Nathan, was long a ruling elder here, and whose daughter Charity became the wife of the Rev. John Guild, the pastor for nearly fifty years of this church. In this family there have been at least three ministers of the Gospel, five ruling elders, and numerous professors of religion who have been pillars of this church and a blessing to other Presbyterian churches. John Titus also was from Newtown. Through his seven sons and two daughters, most of whom settled in this vicinity, he has become the ancestor of a posterity more numerous probably than that of any early inhabitant of this county. Seven of his descendants have served the people as ruling elders and three as deacons, besides those who have been office-bearers in other churches.

Ephraim Titus, one of the original settlers from Newtown, was a ruling elder here; and through the marriage of his two daughters, one to a Phillips of Lawrence, and the other to a Green, of Ewing, his descendants are numerous,—among whom may be mentioned the Rev. Enoch Green, once pastor of the church of Deerfield, New Jersey.

Other immigrants, who came directly from Newtown hither, were Timothy Titus, John Hunt, Sackett Moore, Robert Blackwell, John Burroughs, John Reed, William Read, John Keetcham, Benjamin Keetcham, Andrew Smith, John Smith, Jonathan Sticklin, Thomas Combs, John Field, Gershom Moore, Simon Sackett, Jonathan Furman, Samuel Furman, and doubtless others.

It is probable that the family of Stevenson, of Amwell, on the north, Reeder, Scudder, Severance, Reed, Sackett, Fish, &c. of Ewing, with those who bore the name of Hunt, Smith, Davis, Phillips and Lawrenson of Lawrence, were also originally from Newtown, Long Island.

There is no evidence, either documentary or traditional, that the Christian people who settled the region, occupied by the churches of Lawrence, Ewing, Pennington, Trenton, and Titusville, were not Presbyterian from the beginning; and their Presbyterianism seems to have been brought with them from Long Island. The first Presbyterian record we have of this "people of Maidenhead and Hopewell" is in the minutes of the Presbytery of Philadelphia, May 11th, 1709, where "Mr. Smith is ordered to go to them, and confer with them on such matters as shall be propounded to him by them, concerning his being called to be their minister."

There are some names which denote that the people were in part descended from Hollanders, as Hoff, Ringo, Debough, Vanhook, Hendrix, and two at least are of French origin, La Rue, and Vannoy, [Huguenots?]

If this meagre sketch can aid you in your investigations it will be gratifying to,

Yours as ever,
GEORGE HALE.

V.

Showing the Presbyteries with which this Church has been connected.

This church belonged to the Presbytery of Philadelphia, from 1711 to 1716. It was set off to the Presbytery of Long Island, which was organized at Southampton, April 17, 1717, and was the first Presbytery constituted in the province of New York. May 24, 1738, the Presbytery of Long Island was united with the eastern part of Jersey, under the name of the Presbytery of New York, under the jurisdiction of which this church continued, until the ministry of Mr. Mills, who became a member of the Suffolk Presbytery. On the 20th of May, 1774, in the Synod of New York and Philadelphia, "a reference was brought in from the Presbytery of New York, praying the advice of the Synod, whether the congregation of Jamaica, on Long Island, whose late minister, the Rev. Mr. Mills, belonged to the Presbytery of Suffolk, may be taken under their care as they formerly were, and had never been dismissed. The Synod allowed that the

11*

above congregation be taken under the care of the Presbytery of New York." (Minutes of Synod, p. 454.) Accordingly, by the last named Presbytery, Mr. Burnet was ordained here in 1774. But Mr. Faitoute says, that at the time he came here a dispute had existed some time, whether this church belonged to the Presbytery of Suffolk or the Presbytery of New York; the Synod, in 1789, decided that it belonged to the Presbytery of New York, which body proceeded to install Mr. Faitoute. In 1790, the Presbytery of Suffolk was dissolved, and a new one formed under the original name of the Presbytery of Long Island, and this congregation was attached to it. It was organized at Jamaica, November, 1790. Dr. Buell was appointed to preach. In 1809, the minister and congregation of Jamaica requested to be detached from the Presbytery of Long Island, and placed under the care of the Presbytery of New York, which request was granted. This church has been attached to the Presbytery of Nassau since Nov. 7, 1855, at which date said Presbytery was organized.

VI.

Catalogue of the Ministers of the Church.

Zechariah Walker,
John Prudden,
William Woodruff,
George Phillips,
Jeremiah Hobart,
John Hubbard,[1, 2]
Francis Goodhue,[2]
George McNish,[2]
Robert Cross,
Walter Wilmot,[1, 2]
David Bostwick,[1]
Elihu Spencer, D. D.,
Benoni Bradner,
William Mills,[2]
Matthias Burnet, D. D.,
George Faitoute,[2]
Henry R. Weed, D. D.,[1]
Seymour P. Funck,[1]
Elias W. Crane,[2]
James M. Macdonald,
Peter D. Oakey.

[1] Ordained when settled here.   [2] Died pastors of this church.

VII.

Elders of the Church.

Mr. McNish, at the meeting of Presbytery in 1716, gave reasons for not bringing an elder with him, which were sustained. At the first meeting of the Synod of Philadelphia, in 1717, John Rodes (Rhodes) was present as an elder, who was, I have no doubt, from Jamaica. In 1737, Philip Tanner was present in Synod as an elder, who may have been from Jamaica. Daniel Smith, an elder of this church, was present in 1720. He died on the 15th day of October, 1754, having been born in 1663 or 1664. By his last will and testament he gave the Register, which is now in use by this church. Elias Baylis was present for the first time in Synod in 1734. As we have no Records of Session, and no Register extending back of the middle of the last century, it is probably impossible to form a complete list of the Ruling Elders of this church. With the exception of Messrs. Rhodes and Tanner, respecting whom there may be some doubt, the following are known to have been Ruling Elders in this church:

John Rhodes,
Philip Tanner,
Daniel Smith,[1]
Sam'l Smith, Esq.[1]

Elias Baylis,
Joseph Skidmore, Esq.,
Daniel Baylis,[2]
Sam'l Smith, Jr. Esq.[1]

[1] Acting as Elders in 1744.

[2] Daniel Baylis, is supposed to have come from England. He had five sons, who were all elders of Presbyterian churches. Isaac was an elder of the Huntington church; Daniel, of the Goshen Church; Oliver and Elias, of the Huntington church; Thomas was an elder of the Jamaica church. Several of his grandchildren are at this time officers of Presbyterian churches. Thomas Baylis, an elder, and Abraham Baylis, a deacon of the Second Presbyterian church in Brooklyn, and Daniel Baylis, one of the elders of the church in Jamaica, are of this number.

252 ADDENDA.

Increase Carpenter,
Nehemiah Smith,
Nicholas Smith,
Samuel Denton,
Benjamin Thurston,
Benjamin Everitt,
Richard Creed,
William Ludlam,
Thomas Baylis,
Abraham Burtis,[1]
Benjamin I. Smith,[1]

Hon. Eliphalet Wickes,[2]
Amos Denton,[2]
Nathan Shelton, M. D.,[3]
Charles S. Lord,[3]
John Carpenter,[3]
Nathaniel Carpenter,[3]
Jas. H. Reeve,[4]
Daniel Baylis,[4]
Hon. James Rider,[5]
Laurens Reeve,[5]
John D. Shelton, M. D.,[5]

VIII.

Deacons.

Daniel Smith,
Elias Baylis,
Samuel Denton,
Nicholas Smith,
Michael Skidmore,

Othniel Everitt,[5]
Laurens Reeve,[7]
James Rider,[7]
Wm. L. Denton,[5]
Latham M. Jaggar.[5]

IX.

Trustees of the Church.

Benj. Thurston,	1791	David Lamberson,	1791
Benj. Everett, Esq. Pres.	1791	Daniel Ludlam, Esq.,	1791
Jacob Carpenter, Pres.	1791	Daniel Smith,	1791
Nicholas Everitt,	1791	Wm. Ludlam, Esq. Pres.	1791

[1] Elected Feb. 23, 1817.
[2] Elected June 3, 1819.
[3] Elected May 13, 1821.
[4] Elected Feb. 21, 1847.
[5] Ordained Oct. 18, 1857.
[6] Ordained Jan. 13, 1819.
[7] Ordained Sept. 22, 1833.

Stephen Herriman,	1791	Gen. Van Wyck Wickes,	1827
Ephraim Baily,	1791	David Bergen,	1827
Daniel Higbie,	1793	John Rhodes, Jr.,	1827
Joseph Robinson,	1793	Daniel Baylis,	1827
Bernardus Hendrickson	1793	Laurens Reeve, Pres.,	1829
Nehemiah Everitt,	1794	Samuel Higbie,	1829
Eliphalet Wickes, Esq.,	1795	Nich's S. Everitt,	1830
Samuel Mills,	1796	Thomas Smith,	1831
Benj. Everitt,	1798	James Baylis,	1831
James Denton,	1802	James Herriman,	1833
Simeon Smith,	1802	Benj. Bergen,	1833
Henry Mills,	1805	Daniel Baylis,	1837
Othniel Smith,	1805	Amos Denton,	1842
Dan'l Ludlum, Jr. Pres.	1805	Wm. Ludlam,	1843
Benj. N. Smith,	1805	Hon. James Rider,	1845
John Rhodes,	1810	Jacob Bergen,	1849
Richard Creed,	1813	John B. Smith,	1859
Thomas Baylis,	1817	John D. Shelton, M.D.,	1860
David Lamberson, Jr.	1817	John J. Armstrong,	1860
Daniel Smith,	1817	Isaac S. Hendrickson,	1861
Michael Skidmore,	1818	Waite S. E. Ludlam,	1861
John Rider, Pres.,	1824		

X.

Number of Communicants annually reported as far back as can be ascertained.

[Up to the year 1826, the year ends on the first of October; from 1827 to 1861, on the first of April.]

YEAR.	TOTAL IN COM.	YEAR.	TOTAL IN COM.	YEAR.	TOTAL IN COM.	YEAR.	TOTAL IN COM.
1807	46	1821	184	1835	328	1849	420
1808	47	1822	193	1836	325	1850	419
1809	49	1823	196	1837	316	1851	445
1810	51	1824	201	1838	328	1852	456
1811	53	1825		1839	327	1853	464
1812	58	1826	197	1840	392	1854	470
1813	55	1827	263	1841	380	1855	484
1814	54	1828	262	1842	373	1856	480
1815	53	1829	270	1843	369	1857	493
1816	118	1830	276	1844	368	1858	504
1817	147	1831	278	1845	404	1859	513
1818	160	1832	333	1846	403	1860	519
1819	169	1833	338	1847	417	1861	529
1820	177	1834	335	1848	419		

In 1793, there were fifty-eight communicants. In 1762, there were but twelve, whose names are thus given by the Rev. Mr. Mills: Benjamin Hinchman; Nehemiah Denton; Deborah Denton, his wife; John Carman, and his wife; Samuel Denton; Dea. Elias Baylis, and his wife; Mr. (John) Messenger; Obadiah Smith, and his wife; Elizabeth Smith, (Justice Smith's wife.)

It is proper to state, that in the above list there is a number who have been long absent, and their places of residence being unknown they have not been reported to Presbytery since 1854.

XI.

List of Ministers who have gone forth from this church to preach the Gospel.

The following Ministers, either by baptism or communion, have been members of the Jamaica Church. They are given without reference to the order of their licensure; the date of their connection with the church extending back about thirty years; there being no record preserved of any who may have studied for the Ministry previous to that date.

	Entered on Ministry.
Rev. Charles S. Lord	—
" Thomas S. Wickes	1816
" Daniel Higbie	1836
" William B. Reeve	1836
" Frederick W. Shelton	1847
" Frederick M. Noll	1837
" Jeremiah S. Lord, D.D.	1840
" Samuel L. Lamberson	1829
" Nicholas E. Smith, D.D.	1845
" Abraham Francis	—
" William Mack, D.D.	1831
" Thomas Wickes	1834
" Henry Wickes	—
" John Wickes	—
" Geo. F. Hendrickson	—
" Martin Ryerson	1844
" John Hall	—
" Charles Furman	—
" James Smith	—
" John H. Mills	—

		Entered on Ministry.
Rev. Wilson Phraner	. . . .	1850
" E. N. Crane	. . . .	1852
" Benjamin S. Everett	. . .	1858
" Joseph T. Duryea	. . .	1858
" Sam'l Hendrickson (col'd) Missionary to Liberia.	. . . .	—

There are also two young men now in course of preparation for the gospel ministry.

XII.

List of Vestrymen, under the Act of 1693, (as far as can be ascertained) from 1702 to 1722, chosen by the Parish of Jamaica, arranged alphabetically.

Berrian Peter 1714–22
—— Nicholas 1717
—— Jno 1702
Bass Abm. 1716—not present
Bloom Barent 1716 — not present
Bayles Elias 1714–18
—— Sam'l 1708
Burroughs Thos & Jos 1709
—— Jas 1712
Bull Dan'l 1708–18
Betts Dan'l 1720
Bloodgood W^m 1702
Brinckerhoff Derick 1720
Carpenter Jno 1709
—— Hope 1702–09
—— Jos. 1714

—— Sam'l 1705
Coe Jno 1702–19
— David 1709–20
— Robert, 1705
— Sam'l 1709–19
— Jona. 1714
Cornelius Elias 1709—erased
Dean Sam'l son of Jona. 1720
Denton Nath'l 1702–9
Everet Jno 1705–20
—— Nich. 1713
Fitch Sam'l 1712–19
Fish Sam'l 1719
— Jona 1713–20
Furman Josiah 1716
—— Jona. 1712
Glean Anthony 1709

Glenn W^m 1702
Gale Jno 1717
Hazard Thos 1709-20
—— Jas 1709
—— Nath. 1713-18
—— Jona. 1705
Hougton Jno 1713
Higbie Nath. 1715
—— Sam'l 1705
Huff Peter 1714-20
Ketcham Jos 1716
Ketcham Sam'l 1709
Lawrence W^m 1710
—— Dan'l 1705
—— Thos 1718
Ludlum Henry 1716
Messenger Jno 1720
Mills Zach. 1709
Moor Gershom 1709
Moss W^m 1714
Monfort Peter 1715
Morrell Jos 1713
Oldfield Rich. 1714-18
—— W^m 1712
Petit Thos 1716
Roe David 1717
Renne Jas 1714-18
Reeder Jacob 1714
Ryder Jurian 1713
——Stephen 1713-18
Sackett Jos Jr. 1712

—— Jos 1702
Skidmore Sam'l 1709
Smith Dan'l 1710-20
—— Eben. 1712
—— Nehemiah Jr. 1702-22
—— Sam'l (Scoon) 1715
—— Nathan 1716
—— Jeremy 1717
—— Amos 1712
—— Thos 1702
Skillman Thos 1717
Titus Silas 1712-19
——Content 1702
Talman Jno 1705
Thurston, Benj. 1710
—— Sam'l 1712
Van Liew Jno 1712
Van Wyck Jno 1716—not present
Waters Anthony 1705-10
—— Jona. 1710-17
—— Thos 1713
Woolsey Geo 1709
Wood Timothy 1714
——Jonas 1720
Woodward Nath. 1720
Wright David 1702-9
—— Henry 1705
—— Jona. 1709-19
Willet Thos 1702

XIII.

Cotemporary Ministers of Jamaica.

DUTCH REFORMED CHURCH.

1702–5	Ministers from N. York and Kings Co.
1705–41	Bernardus Freeman*
1705–41	Vincentius Antonides*
1741–48	John Henry Goetschius
1742–54	Johannes Arondeus*
1754–60	Thos Romeyn
1766–72	Hermanus L. Boelen
1775–6	Sol. Froeleigh, D.D.
1781–4	Martinus Schoonmaker*
1785–97	Rynier Van Nest
1792–1824	Zach. H. Kuypers
1802–50	Jacob Schoonmaker, D.D.
1835–49	Garret J. Garretson
1851–	John B. Aliger

CHURCH OF ENGLAND.

1702	Patrick Gordon—Died before induction.
1704–9	Wm Urquhart
1709–32	Thos Poyer
1732–55	Thos Colgan
1757–66	Sam'l Seabury
1769–90	Joshua Bloomer
1790–95	Wm Hammel
1796	(2 months) Chas Seabury
1797–1802	Elijah D. Rattoone
1803–4	Calvin White
1805	Geo. Strebeck
1806	Andrew Fowler
1807	John Ireland
1808	Edmund D. Barry
1809	Timothy Clowes
1810–30	Gilbert H. Sayres
1830–	Wm L. Johnson, D.D.

* Resided in Kings County.

XIV.

The First Indian Deed for the Township now called Jamaica, referred to on page 26.

Be it known unto all men by these presents that we whose names are underwritten, have sold and set over from ourselves, our heirs, executors, administrators or assigns unto Mr. Richard Odell, Nicholas Tanner, Richard Ogden and Nathaniel Denton, their associates, heirs, executors, administrators or assigns a certain tract of land beginning at a great swamp lying on the west side of Rockeway neck, and so running westward to a river lying on the east side of a neck of land which Mr. Coe hath hired of the Indians, which river is called by the Indians, Wauweebheag, the north line running near unto or about the path that goes from Hemsted to Midlburroug,* with all the uplands & meadowing within the aforesaid bounds, with all privileges & appurtenances thereunto belonging. In consideration whereof the aforesaid Mr. Richard Odell, Nicholas Tanner, Richard Ogden, Nathaniel Denton & their associates shall give unto these whose names are underwritten, two guns, a coat & a certain quantity of powder & lead. In witness whereof we have subscribed our hands this 13th of September Anno Domini 1655. *Their marks.*

Witnesses.	
DANIEL DENTON	RACKQUAKEK +
RODGER + LINAS	RUNNASUK +
CASPEROUW +	AUMERHAS +
ADAM, or	CAUMENUK +
ACHITTERENOSE +	CHACHANAT +
	ASKASETONE +
	WAUMETOMPACK +
	MANGUAUOPE +

* Newtown.

APPENDIX

CONTAINING AN

ACCOUNT OF THE CELEBRATION OF THE BICENTENNIAL
ANNIVERSARY OF THE

First Presbyterian Church,

JAMAICA, L. I.,

HELD ON THE 7TH, 8TH AND 9TH OF JANUARY, 1862.

PREPARED BY THE

COMMITTEE OF ARRANGEMENTS.

APPENDIX.

PRELIMINARY ARRANGEMENTS — OPENING EXERCISES — MURAL TABLETS — SERMON BY DR. MACDONALD — INTERLOCUTORY MEETING OF MINISTERS IN FORMER CONNECTION WITH THE CHURCH — SERMON BY REV. J. M. KREBS, D. D. — SERMON BY REV. W. P. BREED — COMMUNION — LETTERS FROM DR. WEED AND OTHERS — CONCLUDING ADDRESS BY THE PASTOR, REV. P. D. OAKEY — "NEW YORK OBSERVER" "PRESBYTERIAN"

AT a meeting of the Session of the First Presbyterian Church, Jamaica, L. I., held August 31st, 1861, the Moderator having stated that on January next would occur the two hundreth anniversary of the founding of the church, it was unanimously

"*Resolved*, That from a sense of gratitude to God for his preserving care over us as a church for so long a period of time, the occasion should be celebrated with appropriate services; and that the Trustees and Deacons be invited to meet with us on Wednesday, September 4th, at 3 o'clock P. M., to take measures for carrying the same into effect."

The Elders, Trustees and Deacons held a meeting in the Lecture Room, September 4th, the Pastor in the chair. The meeting was opened with prayer, and Latham M. Jaggar appointed Secretary. The following Resolutions were adopted:

"*Resolved*, That it is highly proper, in thankful remembrance of God's goodness, and due to the history of the past, that the Bicentennial Anniverary of this church should be suitably observed.

Resolved, That the Pastor, Laurens Reeve and John D. Shelton, M. D., be a committee to make all necessary arrangements."

Also on motion of the Pastor, the following preamble and resolution were adopted:

"*Whereas*, The Rev. J. M. Macdonald, D. D., when pastor of this church, published its history to the year 1847 inclusive, therefore

"*Resolved*, That the Rev. Dr. Macdonald be invited to preach the historical sermon."

It was also voted to erect mural tablets to the memory of those who had been pastors of the church.

John J. Armstrong was subsequently added to the committee.

The following invitation was printed and circulated through the mail and by the press:

DEAR SIR:

With the close of the present year a period of two hundred years will have elapsed since our forefathers established divine worship in this place, and laid the foundations of the Presbyterian church of which we are members, and which has continued to the present time. It has appeared proper to us, their descendants and representatives, that an occasion so rich with happy results and remembrances should not be permitted to pass without some suitable commemorative exercises. We propose, accordingly, to celebrate it with appropriate services expressive of gratitude to GOD, who has thus far helped us. We wish to summon together from far and near our friends and kindred who have, as ministers or fellow Christians, held church relations with us, to unite with us in a social Christian re-union and a season of religious services, to commemorate an event which should awaken in every heart grateful emotions.

Providence permitting, the services will commence the 7TH OF JANUARY, AT 3 O'CLOCK P. M., with a commemorative sermon by Rev. J. M. MACDONALD, D. D. Communion services on Thursday afternoon.

Please let us know, as soon as convenient, if we may expect the favor of your company.

Yours very respectfully,

P. D. OAKEY,
LAURENS REEVE, } Committee.
DR. JOHN D. SHELTON,

JAMAICA, L. I., Nov., 1861.

The following invitation was sent to the different pulpits in the vicinity:

The Presbyterian Church of Jamaica contemplate celebrating their two hundredth anniversary with appropriate exercises, commencing on Tuesday, January 7th, at 3 o'clock P. M., with a commemorative sermon by the Rev. Dr. Macdonald. This congregation is respectfully invited to participate in the exercises.

By order of the Session,

P. D. OAKEY, Moderator.

The following was the order of exercises adopted by the committee:

"Services to commence Tuesday, January 7th, at 3 o'clock P. M., by the Pastor dedicating the mural tablets, to be followed with the commemorative sermon by Rev. Dr. Macdonald. Wednesday morning a meeting for free conversation by the ministers present who have been born in this church, or who have commenced their religious life or education in connection with it. The afternoon to be appropriated to social receptions and calls. Wednesday evening a sermon by the Rev. Dr. Krebs, of the Presbytery of New York. On Thursday morning a sermon by the Rev. Wm. P. Breed, of the Presbytery of Philadelphia;* in the afternoon the communion, administered by the oldest minister present."

On Tuesday afternoon, January 7th, at 3 o'clock, a very large congregation assembled in the church. After the invocation by the pastor the Scriptures were read and a very appropriate prayer offered by Rev. N. E. Smith, D. D., of Brooklyn. The Bible used on this occasion was the oldest pulpit Bible belonging to this church, which has been preserved, being an Edinburgh edition published in 1769. On the fly leaf is the following inscription in the hand-writing of the Rev. Mr. Burnett: "This Bible belongs to the Presbyterian Church in Jamaica, Long Island. April 20, 1776."—An important period in American history—when Washington was in New York city, preparing its defences; and but a short time before the adoption of the immortal Declaration of Independence of the United States.

* The Jamaica Church was one of the original churches of the Presbytery of New York, which was well represented by Rev. J. M. Krebs, D.D. The Rev. W. P. Breed was appointed by the Presbytery of Philadelphia as their representative, the Jamaica Church being one of the earliest members of the mother Presbytery, or, as asserted by one qualified to judge, "the mother of the mother Presbytery."

After prayer the following address, dedicatory of the mural tablets just erected, was made by the pastor:

"To-day dates an epoch in the history of this church. The spirit of that history is upon us. The associations of the past gather around us. We summon from their graves the generations of our fathers according to the flesh who have here engaged in the services of the sanctuary, and our fathers in the ministry who conducted these services. For two hundred years they and their descendants, as a united church and congregation, have in this place worshipped the God of their fathers. But 'your fathers, where are they? and the prophets, do they live for ever?' As sacred to the memory of those who here 'laboured in the word and doctrine,' as a memento of proper affection for them 'who being dead yet speak,' as a matter of gratitude to God who so early in the history of this country here planted this church, and gave to it a succession of able and faithful ministers, as in every way fitting the occasion we celebrate, we this day inaugurate these exercises by dedicating these mural tablets to perpetuate their names, and cherish the influence, which if living they would have imparted.

"These stones are our Ebenezer—hitherto hath the Lord helped us. They will be a link, binding the present to the past. Their perusal will not fail to awaken profitable musings in the reflecting mind, carrying anticipatory thoughts to the grave, and to the place where are the spirits of just men made perfect, and where the earthly worshipper shall ere long join his hallelujahs with the songs of those who have gone before. And they will speak with the uniform testimony of the church's experience that God in covenant is a God to them that fear him and their seed after them in their generations. The evoked voice of these tablets, as read from the spirit of the past, will say to the guardians of the Sacred Desk: preach the Gospel, the truth as it is in Jesus; and to the responsibilities of those who enjoy Gospel privileges, 'Take heed how ye hear.' And the abiding effect which we would leave as the engraved sentiment of these stones is in the words of Paul to the Hebrew Christians concerning their deceased Pastors: 'Remember them which have the rule over you, who have spoken unto you the word of God; whose faith follow, considering the end of their conversation: Jesus Christ, the same yesterday, and to-day, and for ever.'

"But we turn from the dead to the living. There is a connection between the two. As the descendants by family ties or church relation, of those whose memory we revere, we extend to you our cordial greeting and welcome. We welcome you to a participation in these exercises. Many of you here will revisit the scenes of your childhood, and revive youthful impressions and friendships. Some of you here began your heavenward journey, and consecrated yourselves to your lifelong work in the service of God. Here at the altar of your early consecration may you receive a fresh baptism for your holy work. And your souls mingling with kindred spirits, and communing with thoughts of the past, be sweetly bathed afresh with the light of Divine Love, and spiritual joy. We welcome you to our homes and hearts. Mingle your prayers and praises with ours. We have looked forward to this season with prayerful interest as a means of grace. And now may the Divine influence of the ever blessed Spirit be shed copiously upon these exercises and their participators, and to the triune God of our salvation, the Father, Son and Holy Spirit, shall be given the glory evermore. Amen."

The Rev. Dr. Macdonald then preached a very able and interesting historical sermon from Eccles. i. 4: "One generation passeth away, and another generation cometh; but the earth abideth for ever." This discourse, which was requested for publication, constitutes the main body of this work.

On Wednesday morning, at half-past ten, a large audience assembled in the church, to engage in a conference meeting of the old friends who had come to join in the festive occasion. The pastor stated that this was a meeting of the friends from a distance, to be under their particular care, and conducted as they thought most fitting. He therefore called upon them to appoint a chairman from their own number; whereupon Dr. Macdonald was selected to preside. The chairman stated that the meeting would be left mainly to shape itself. He then called on the Rev. John Wickes, pastor of the Congregational Church of Brighton, N. Y., to offer prayer. The presiding officer said that there were three persons there who had been acting elders of this church more than forty years. He would call on one of these, his venerable friend, Dr. Nathan Shelton, to address them. The Dr. made some brief and appropriate remarks, telling of his hearing fifty years ago of one of the female members of this church who was very much in prayer, and on one occasion kneeled down at bedtime to pray, and became so engaged that when she closed, to her surprise it was daylight.

Following the Dr. was the Rev. J. Wickes, son of Van Wyck Wickes, Esq., a former resident of the village. He told of his love for the place and congregation, and though this was not the place of his spiritual birth, yet it was here at that altar that he was dedicated to God in baptism by his pious parents. He gave his testimony to the fidelity of God to his covenant, and found verification of this in the experience of his father's household. God hath brought one after another of them into the fold; and parental faith and covenant vows with the baptismal seal had not been in vain.

Dr. Macdonald then, by a happy reference to the Rev. Elias W. Crane, a departed Pastor of blessed memory, introduced his son, the Rev. Elias N. Crane, of New Vernon, N. J., who addressed the audience interestingly, referring to the happy days of his youth; especially to the precious privileges of the Sunday School, and the faithful superintendent, who for more than thirty years has presided and labored and prayed there. He read also an old paper on which were the names of the officers appointed at the organization of the first Temperance Society in Jamaica, in the year 1827, thirty-five years ago. They were as follows:

President—Van Wyck Wickes.
Vice Presidents—Eliphalet Wickes, Nathan Shelton.
Secretary—Elias W. Crane.
Treasurer—James Rider.

Managers—J. Rhodes, Jr., C. Smith, L. Reeve, G. Creed, N. Carpenter, W. J. Johnson M.D., D. Bergen and M. W. Fox.

Mr. Crane was followed by Rev. B. S. Everitt, of Blackwoodtown, N. J., who appeared as the descendant of the first founders of the church, as the representative of the rural district, and being also one of the two last that have gone forth from the membership of the church to preach the Gospel; having been in the ministry but three years, and consequently, as he looked at his audience saw very few unfamiliar faces. He, too, added his testimony to the inestimable value of Sabbath School instruction and the sure blessing of God that will follow fidelity on the part of parents to their covenant obligations.

The next speaker was the Rev. Dr. Nicholas Everitt Smith, (altogether a Jamaica name) of Brooklyn, N. Y. He spake of the old stone church that stood in the Main Street, where now Union Hall Street enters it. He exhibited a diagram of the church and told how his father (now ninety-four years old) saw a man who bet he could ride on horseback at full speed in at the west door and out of the east of that old church, and how the bettor actually performed the feat.

The next speaker was the Rev. Mr. Breed, Pastor of the West Spruce Street Church, Philadelphia, who came as the representative of the Old Mother Presbytery of Philadelphia, and gave its congratulations to all on this interesting occasion, and though he came here a stranger yet he found his heart so warmed and touched by the interesting exercises to which he had listened that he really felt as one of them, a member of the same household, having with them a common Saviour and Father.

Rev. Dr. Krebs, of Rutgers Street Church, New York city, came to represent the Presbytery of New York, and the Rev. Wm. B. Reeve, that of Long Island, each of which made brief and engaging remarks. The services closed by the reading of letters from Rev. Dr. Phillips, of New York city, and the Rev. Dr. Henry R. Weed, of Wheeling, Va., the oldest living pastor of the church, and others, with a brief address and prayer by the Rev. Daniel Higbie, (another child of the church,) of Orange County, N. Y.

LETTER OF REV. H. R. WEED, D. D.

Mr. Laurens Reeve, *Wheeling, Nov. 11th, 1861.*

My Dear Friend,—Your favour of the 20th September, was duly received and its contents awakened memories of great interest in my early ministry. To no period of my life does my mind recur with greater pleasure than to the time I spent in the dear old church of Jamaica, and should I be so happy as to find my final home in our heavenly Father's house, I expect to meet many there whom I was permitted in the ardor of my youth successfully to point to "the Way, the Truth, and the Life." Later events, too, I have witnessed of a soul stirring character in your congregation, that have left an indelible impression on my mind. Indeed, the history of that church is one of great interest from early times. Its old records and the traditionary accounts current among the elder members in my day, were such as pertain to no other church in our connection, and fully justify the commemoration you contemplate. I trust the occasion will be profitable to all concerned, and redound to a new display of that glorious grace that has eminently distinguished the history of your venerable old church.

Let me say, in conclusion, that while I feel flattered by the invitation to attend, and by the kind remembrance of all surviving friends among you, my age and infirmities forbid me to indulge the hope of being with you.

Please give assurances of my affectionate regard to all inquiring friends, and believe me,

Very truly yours,

H. R. WEED.

LETTER OF REV. THOMAS WICKES.

P. D. OAKEY, ETC.,   *Marietta, Ohio, Jan. 2d,* 1862.

GENTLEMEN,—I received your kind invitation to participate in the celebration of the 200th Anniversary of the founding of the Presbyterian Church of Jamaica. Be assured that it would afford me the highest gratification to be present with you on this most interesting occasion, meeting again those whom once I knew so well, and with them reviewing all the previous memories of the past, and the goodness of our God. Never shall I forget Jamaica, though for many years separated from it. It is my birth-place in a double sense, the scene of my natural and spiritual birth. I remember its Sabbath School, where one of your number was my loved teacher. I remember its sanctuary and its consecrated place of prayer. I remember some of its precious revivals of religion there experienced, for which I have such reason to thank God and rejoice.

The first minister whom I recollect was Dr. Weed, now labouring within 80 miles of me at Wheeling, where he is finishing his earthly work by a pastorate of more than 25 years. I well remember the grief that was awakened by the announcement of his intention to leave. It made a strong impression upon my youthful mind.

Mr. Nettleton came in 1826, and with him came the Spirit of God in mighty power. Those scenes I remember well. It was the first outpouring of the Spirit of which I knew. It was not however until the revival of 1831, that I was brought to a knowledge of Christ, and enabled to devote myself to his service. With the history of the church for the last 25 years or more, I have not been so familiar. With sincerest pleasure however would I be with you on the coming week, were it in my power, and participate in all the interests of the occasion. You have my sympathies and prayers as one of the spiritual children of that church honoured also of Christ, with the work of the ministry, and a pastorate over the Congregational Church in this place of 22 years, the close of the present month.

May the Lord abide with you still, making that church his joy and crown, from which a multitude of faithful ones shall be raised up to be found worthy of Christ, at his coming and kingdom.

Yours very sincerely in the bonds of Christ,

THOMAS WICKES.

LETTER OF REV. W. W. PHILLIPS, D.D.

REV. AND DEAR BRO., *New York, Jan.* 3d, 1862.

I thank you for the invitation which has been sent me, to be present at the celebration of the 200th Anniversary of your church. It would gratify me very much to accept it. I have found however that, as I am situated, it will not be in my power to be with you. It appears from our records that the church at Jamaica did at one time very reluctantly, and against their consent furnish the 1st church in New York, then in Wall Street, one of their most acceptable pastors, Rev. D. Bostwick. Your church has been a remarkably favoured one, and furnishes a most interesting history. How many precious souls have there been gathered into the fold above? What an instance of faithfulness on the part of our common God, to preserve a people called by his name and to dwell with them, giving them tokens of his presence, and displaying the riches of his grace for 200 years! Yet it is not strange, since he has made with them an everlasting covenant ordered in all things and sure. May his presence abide with you evermore, and your experience of his past favours be as the first fruits only of what is in reserve for you.

Affectionately and truly yours,

Rev. P. D. Oakey.   W. W. Phillips.

LETTER OF THOMAS S. WICKES, ESQ.

Laurens Reeve, Esq.   *Poughkeepsie, Jan. 1st,* 1862.

Dear Sir,—I had the favour of receiving a few days since, a circular, to which your name with others was appended, inviting me to be present at Jamaica on the 7th inst., to join with others in celebrating the first founding of the Presbyterian Church in that place. The design seems highly appropriate, and did my health permit, I should be very happy to participate in those services. As it is, I cannot at present leave my home.

Many associations connect me with the Jamaica Presbyterian Church. I delight to think of those days of mercy, which God has shown so abundantly there—of the many honoured names, written upon the history of that church, whose memory is blessed.

God grant that the recollections of the past may be full of cheer and encouragement for the future.

With sentiments of kind regard and Christian fellowship, I remain, yours,

Thomas S. Wickes.

76   APPENDIX.

EXTRACT OF A LETTER FROM REV. E. N. CRANE.

Rev. P. D. Oakey: *New Vernon, Dec. 17th*, 1861.
Dear Bro.,—   *   *   *   *   *.   *   *

As you may suppose, the occasion would be one of great and peculiar interest to me. Most of my father's ministerial life was spent at Jamaica, and there he rested from his labours, and lies in the graveyard beside my mother. There I was born and baptized and passed my childhood and early youth. There I, and my three sisters and a brother professed our faith in Christ and united with God's people, and there I made one of my earliest efforts to preach the Gospel. Well do I love Jamaica and the old church, though so little associated with them of late years. My heart will ever pray for the peace and prosperity of Zion there. Ever may her "walls be called Salvation and her gates Praise."   Yours fraternally,

E. N. Crane.

In the evening the Church was again crowded, when Dr. Krebs delivered the following Exordium and Sermon:

EXORDIUM REMOTUM.

It was formerly the custom in the Reformed Dutch Church, at some time in the service previous to the *sermon*, to prepare the way for it by what was called the "Exordium Remotum." I shall take the liberty, on the present occasion, of following the example. Under other circumstances, I would not presume to offer the suggestion which I now design to throw before you. I hope to be justified at this time, speaking in the midst of your rejoicings, and welcomed among you as almost one of yourselves.

Two passages of Scripture I commend to your consideration.

"Moreover, I will appoint a place for my people Israel, and will plant them, that they may dwell in a place of their own and move no more."—2d SAMUEL vii. 10.

"Enlarge the place of thy tent, and let them stretch forth the curtains of thine habitations: spare not, lengthen thy cords, and strengthen thy stakes: For thou shalt break forth on thy right hand, and on thy left."—ISAIAH liv. 2, 3.

Home, Peace, Increase. These are the elements of blessing indicated by these passages. Precious to us as individuals, as families, as a people, as citizens or as Christians, as a civil community or as a Church. Dear is the hearth-stone and the homestead where God setteth the solitary in families; and goodly and pleasant is it for brethren to dwell together in unity, sitting in peace under their own vine and fig-tree and none to make them afraid. Sweet, too, to go to the house of God in company with them who are likeminded, heirs of like precious faith, the associates of our childhood, the guides, the acquaintance with whom we took sweet counsel together, the familiar friends whose countenances greet us in the walks of life, whose sympathies are cherished amid the associations of worship and communion in the same holy truths and songs of praise and labours and cares, in the same sanctuary and enjoyments of the same ministrations. Dear, too, to patriotism and piety the contemplation of the purposes and promises of security and enlargement in reference to the people to whom we belong, an inheritance both for possession and for communication, a prosperity which grows within our borders and around them, till the wilderness and the solitary place are glad for us and the desert rejoices and blossoms as the rose. Thus does Jehovah promise Israel, and thus, especially, He declares His purposes in regard to the security and enlargement of that holy nation, the generation which He has chosen and ordained to be a royal priesthood to minister the sacrifices of His praise, and to make all men see what is the fellowship of the mystery which from the beginning of the world hath been hid in God who created all things by Jesus Christ, to the intent that now unto the principalities and powers in heavenly places might be known by the Church the manifold wisdom of God.

Here, too, is an implication of the interest we ought to take in all that relates to this great cause and of our personal obligation to promote it: an obligation which rests not on ministers only, but on all the people of God.

This interesting anniversary may be used, I think, to suggest large illustration of the duty and the privilege to which you are come who have entered on the inheritance transmitted to you by two centuries. Other men have laboured, and you have entered upon their labours. Your heritage is a responsibility. By accepting it and improving it you will show yourselves worthy children of worthy progenitors. I recognize gladly, and congratulate you while I recognize, the prosperity you enjoy and the service and success of those whom you have sent forth to till other fields, of which we have had example to-day in your sons who have returned to tell you of their ministries elsewhere, and in the reports that have been brought you from others whose blessing also comes back to you. For a recompense in the same, be ye also enlarged.

This commemoration is well. But does it not become you to make the occasion *monumental?* Whether you should engage in the work of Church extension in *one form* rather than in another, you are better able to judge than I am. But I have heard that the place in which you worship is too strait for your increasing numbers. Why should you not signalize your grateful zeal *by erecting on this sacred spot another edifice of more enduring material, more tasteful and convenient, and of ampler accommodation,* while the building in which we are now assembled may be removed and still devoted to kindred uses?

Do not be startled at this *broad hint.* Do not too readily conclude against it by alleging that this house will answer all your need for a good while to come. You may think so: others will not accept your decision. Your pleasant village is growing. It is attracting residents from the neighbouring metropolis. It is destined to be girdled with tasteful villas and to be enlarged with new accessions. Already you are compelled to deny or to restrict the accommodation of those who desire to worship with you. You cannot long afford to act upon a narrow and short-sighted policy. The overflowing population will seek accommodation elsewhere—and it may be, for such things have been—you may find organizations and churches growing up altogether separated from you, with fruitful rivalries and jealousies, which might be prevented forever by a timely provision for the increasing numbers who are now desirous only to be joined with you even as they are in the Spirit, *joying and beholding your order and the steadfastness of your faith in Christ.* Now, therefore, thank God and take courage. *The joy of the Lord is your strength.*

SUBSTANCE OF SERMON.

"The joy of the Lord is your strength."—NEHEMIAH viii. 10.

To be sorrowful under calamity is neither unnatural nor unsuitable,—especially to be sorry for our sins. Yet, is it consistent with cheerfulness in view of the grace that saves. Grief may be indulged immoderately and untimely. Upon the return of the Jews from captivity and the restoration of their worship, they were glad; but as they listened to the law they felt their sins, their hearts sunk, and they wept aloud. They were dissuaded from this excess, and were reminded of all the mercy which had forgiven their sins and restored them to the privileges they had inherited from their fathers, and they were exhorted to give themselves up to holy festivity and to display kindness to the destitute as a token of their prosperity and gratitude: and it was added, "Neither be ye sorry, for the joy of the Lord is your strength."

The joy of the Lord. God is often said to rejoice over His people. His delight is in them. They are to Him a holy satisfaction; as are faithful children to their parents. And if this were what is meant by the "joy of the Lord" in the text it would be equally true as a declaration of the cause of our strength and the element of our joy, our safety and defence.

But it is rather used subjectively, to express that joy which we have from the Lord and in Him. Since it is God's joy in His people in saving and blessing them which furnishes joy to their own souls. And this affection of theirs is the "joy of the Lord," because (1) It comes from God. He imparts it—He produces it. It is His gift through Jesus Christ, and it is the work o the Holy Spirit. It is divine in its nature, like that which God himself feels in objects that are good. It arises from a sense of the mercies of God—all His favour in redemption, in the blessings of His covenant, His kindly providence, all the portion He has prepared for his people. (2) We have this joy *in* God. "We joy in God through our Lord Jesus Christ, by whom now we have received the atonement [or the reconciliation]." By virtue of our reconciliation to God, Jehovah becomes our portion, our dependence, hope and trust and love. Once it was not so. The Christian did not then know God, nor Jesus Christ. He was opposed to God; he was jealous and afraid of God; he saw no form nor comeliness in Christ; He trusted in himself, and looked for his portion in his fleshly idols.

A change has come. He has become acquainted with God, and is at peace. He has fellowship with the Father and with His Son. Jesus is precious. The love of God is shed abroad in his heart by the Holy Ghost. He delights himself in the Lord, in His supremacy and holiness, in His law and grace, in His holy providence and exceeding great and precious promises. He walks with God. He looks to Him to supply all his need from the riches of His glory in Jesus Christ, and his hope of heaven is that there he shall be for ever with the Lord.—As *Asaph*, "Whom have I in heaven but thee, and there is none upon the earth that I desire beside thee;." or as *David*, "Thou art fairer than the children of men;" or as the *Church*, "Thou art the chiefest among ten thousands and altogether lovely."

This joy is our strength. It fortifies the believer in his attachment to the great truths of the gospel. Men without an experimental knowledge of the doctrines of grace, disparage and deny them. But let one feel those truths in their effects upon the heart; let him realize his guilt and his depravity, and cry out in anguish, " What must I do to be saved?" let him realize the grace and power of Christ to save him; let him taste the joy and peace of believing and the attraction of the love of God shed abroad in his heart by the Holy Ghost; let him bask in the light of the knowledge of the glory of God by Jesus Christ, and adore with grateful wonder the sovereign mercy which begot him anew by His resurrection to the lively hope of the immortal inheritance;—let him *feel* all this, and you have before you a man to whom *all* the truths of the gospel are precious and nourishing as the very life of the soul. You cannot make him relinquish them. He knows whom He has believed; and the joy of his salvation anchors his soul fast to all the counsel of God.

It is an element of our growth in grace. " Unto you that fear my name shall the sun of righteousness arise with healing in his wings: and ye shall go forth and grow up as calves of the stall." Diseased by sin and enfeebled, we begin the Christian life in weakness: we are as those who are recovering from sickness, while the genial influence of the sun and the sweet breath of heaven animate the convalescent and impart life and bounding joy and invigorate all the powers. A merry heart doeth good like a medicine. Let the Christian be joyful in the Lord. All his faculties shall work in harmony; his soul shall grow in knowledge, love, and purity and power. Even as when the circulation flows buoyantly through the veins, the blood briskly fulfils its course, health mantles the cheeks, the spirits bound, the limbs play, the active powers develope in healthful and vigorous growth; even as the skipping heifer fatted at the stall furnishes an image of happy life rejoicing in the freedom as well as the fatness of the open pastures.

This joy is our support under trials. A wounded spirit who can bear? It is weak and wasted, and incapable of exertion and of hope. But if the heart be joyous—if it knows the joy of the Lord, it regards affliction as light, and patience performs its perfect work. Joseph in the prison, Daniel in the den of lions, the Hebrew children in the burning fiery furnace, Paul and Silas bleeding in their midnight dungeon, David in the valley of the shadow of death,—all have supports and comforts, and they learn even to glory in their tribulation, which was producing the peaceable fruits of righteousness and begetting hope that should never be ashamed nor confounded. "Thy statutes are my song in the house of my pilgrimage."

This joy is our guard and defence against temptation. The heart that is destitute of it is exposed and open to the fascinations of sin, and in its vacant or troubled hours has no resort but worldly and sinful recreation. But the Christian has meat to eat the worldling knows not of. Thus preöccupied and fortified he opposes his godly joy to the incantations of the charmer that would allure him to transgression. The joy of the Lord has an expulsive power, and it meets the full tide of temptation and rolls it back:

> "God is my all-sufficient good,
> My portion and my choice;
> In him my vast desires are filled
> And all my powers rejoice.

> "In vain the world accosts mine ear
> And tempts mine heart anew,
> I cannot buy your bliss so dear,
> Nor part with heaven for you."

"There be many that say, Who will shew us any good? Lord lift thou up the light of thy countenance upon us. Thou hast put gladness in my heart more than in the time that their corn and their wine increased." "We will remember thy love more than wine."

This joy is our wealth, enabling us to make sacrifices of worldly ease and possessions, at the call of duty. Men who brood over their sorrows become terribly selfish. They have little thought for the woes of others. Morose and churlish they do not, cannot, understand, how it can be more blessed to give than to receive. But a joyous, is apt to be a lavish spirit. It takes a pleasure in doing good. It will divide its crust with the famishing, and rise at midnight to comfort the weary. It has always enough for contentment, yea, enough and to spare. It may be poor, but it makes many rich—with a cup of cold water, a kind look, a tear, a prayer—all it has to give. It loves to do good just in proportion as it is like God. The ever-blessed God is the most bountiful giver in the Universe.

This joy is our energy and efficiency in duty, and a source of our help and success in enterprize. Grief and fear depress a man, and hide from his view all encouragements. There is always a lion in the way. Moses cannot rouse his countrymen in Egypt; they hearkened not to him for anguish of spirit and for cruel bondage. The disciples cannot watch with their Lord, but sink into sleep for overmuch sorrow. David says, "Restore unto me the joy of thy salvation, *then* will I teach trangressors thy ways, and sinners shall be converted unto thee." And he resolves, "I will run the way of thy commandments when thou shalt enlarge my heart." Joy disposes a man to action like the bubbling and bounding life of a healthful, happy child. It sees encouragements and finds resources. It is ready for service. It can testify of God's faithfulness and love. It has good success: as when God honoured the praises of his people, and gave Jehoshaphat the victory over the Ammonites—for when he encouraged Judah to believe in the Lord their God, and the singers went out before the army, not playing *dead marches*, but singing, "Praise the Lord, for his mercy endureth forever," so that when they began to sing and to praise, the Lord set ambushments against their enemies and they were smitten.

Finally, this joy is the strength of God's people in their dying hour. It removes the bondage and the fear of death. See,—the timid woman, who has apprehended the parting with beloved friends, and shrunk from the thought of judgment, finds supports and comforts in the presence of that Friend who sticketh closer than any brother and in the assured hope of entering upon the joy of the Lord forever. The little child, that trembled with vague fear of the cold church-yard and the dread mysteries of the world beyond the grave, is more than consoled with the sweet promises of the Good Shepherd who folds the lambs in his bosom, and expects with sweet hope the call of that dear voice which said, "Suffer the little children and forbid them not to come unto me, for of such is the kingdom of heaven."

> "Jesus, the vision of thy face
> Hath overpowering charms;
> Scarce shall I feel death's cold embrace,
> If Christ be in my arms.
>
> "Then while ye hear my heart-strings break
> How sweet my minutes roll;
> A mortal paleness on my cheek,
> But glory in my soul."

Would you then be strong in the faith, useful, beneficent, pure, comforted in life and death, rejoice in the Lord always. So, too, shall you honour your religion and commend it. Of all persons in the world, a Christian is the most obliged and has the best right to be happy. Sulky and sullen tempers only disgust and repel. Cheerfulness is a hymn of praise; and whoso offereth praise glorifieth God. But guard against losing this joy. Sin makes broken bones, and hides God's countenance. Grieve not the Holy Spirit. But follow on to know the Lord, then shall thy goings be as the morning. The path of the just is as the shining light that shineth more and more unto the perfect day. Let the superiority of the Christian's portion be appreciated and sought after. The true Christian is not that moping, melancholy, feeble creature the thoughtless worldling deems him. He has joy, he has strength, both in acting and suffering, while you despond and lie inactive: and he is honouring his Maker and enjoying Him, while you are vainly dreaming of selfish, earthly, sinful pleasure. What is the mirth of fools? "I said of laughter it is mad. There is no peace to the wicked." But how shall we get this true joy? "We joy in God through our Lord Jesus Christ, by whom now we have the atonement." Let the Christian always resort to Him. In Him the most sorrowful abject may find comfort. Let the sinner turn from the paths of sin. "Ho every one that thirsteth, come ye to the waters. Why spend ye your money for that which is not bread, and your labour for that which satisfieth not? Come unto me all ye that labour and are heavy laden, and I will give you rest." He will *give*—salvation is free in Christ; He will give *rest*—O, the precious repose for the sin-burdened and sin-weary—rest! rest! rest in the bosom of God! joy! joy forever!

Come then—let not conscience make you linger—nor of fitness fondly dream—think not of buying the *gift* of God—of offering a price for the grace of the Lord Jesus Christ. Come *thus* to the mercy-seat:

> " Just as I am, without one plea,
> But that thy blood was shed for me,
> And that thou bidst me come to thee,
> O Lamb of God I come."

On Thursday, at half-past nine A.M., the friends assembled in the Lecture Room to spend an hour in prayer and conference, having reference especially to the World's concert of prayer, which was that week being observed by the Evangelical churches. Here the Rev. Wilson Phraner, (another child of the church,) of Sing Sing, N. Y., made some appropriate and forcible remarks.

At half-past ten, a large assembly gathered in the church to listen to a Sermon from the Rev. William P. Breed, of Philadelphia.

SERMON.

"Wherefore, seeing we also are compassed about with so great a cloud of witnesses, let us lay aside every weight, and the sin which doth so easily beset us, and let us run with patience the race that is set before us, looking unto Jesus, the author and finisher of our faith."—HEBREWS xii. 1, 2.

The more strictly doctrinal portion of this epistle terminates with the eighteenth verse of the tenth chapter, and the hortatory begins with the next verse.

In the first exhortation *faith* is thus mentioned. "Let us draw near with a true heart in full assurance of faith." In the thirty-eighth verse, this faith is declared to be the principle of spiritual life. "The just shall *live* by faith."

In the first verse of the following chapter, faith is defined. "Now faith is the substance of things hoped for and the evidence of things not seen." The rest of this chapter consists of a list of illustrious examples of the power and achievements of this faith in the sphere of practical life, as in the experience of Abel, Noah, Enoch, and the rest. And our text is a rational and forcible exhortation, based upon what has gone before.

"Wherefore, seeing what faith is, and what it has done let us, committing ourselves to its influence, run the race set before us, looking unto Jesus."

In a passage so opulent in treasures, the chief difficulty lies in making such a selection of points for a single discourse as to avoid, on the one hand, crowding and thus confusing the vision, and on the other, omitting those whose prominence and importance are essential to any other than a merely fragmentary view of the text.

A little attention however in this case obtrudes upon the view as the most prominent object, "The race set before us," with a cloud of witnesses on the one hand, and Jesus, faith's author and finisher, on the other, as stimuli to the racers. Each one of these three objects therefore, demands more or less of our attention.

First, Look at The Cloud of Witnesses.

The rhetorical figure of a cloud as a type of multitude, could hardly fail of frequent recurrence in the literature of all nations. Accordingly, Homer writes of "a cloud of Infantry." Livy says, "The King hurled a cloud of horse and foot upon the foe;" and Isaiah asks, "Who are these that fly as a cloud, and as the doves to their windows?"

Nor is the figure less impressive than it is apt. Who has not gazed with rapt interest upon a cloud in a summer afternoon—black but comely! At first no bigger than a man's hand, it rises and spreads its sable wings till at length they cover and darken half the hemisphere, and pile their cumulative masses up to the skies, the very type of majesty and multitude!

And now suppose every constituent atom of that vapory mass replaced by a glorified spirit, Abraham, Isaac, Jacob, David, Samuel and the Prophets: You are compassed about with a great cloud of witnesses! Now listen to the exhortation—"Ye candidates for eternal bliss, blood-bought, blood-washed, vow-laden, think that all those celestial eyes are fixed upon you, watching the banner of the cross committed to your hands to see whether it is waving in victory over a prostrate, or trailed in the dust beneath the feet of a triumphant foe; watching for the ark of God entrusted to your custody, to see if it be safe within its peaceful curtains at Shiloh, or whether it has fallen into the hands of heathenish Philistines!

Beyond all doubt such an exhortation were quite intelligible, and to every true child of faith, spirit-stirring. Still, we are persuaded that this view by no means exhausts the meaning of the sacred writer. Had it been his chief aim to impress it upon us, that we were the objects of constant celestial scrutiny, there was a truth to this effect nearer home and much more effective.

For indeed there is One that watches us day and night, at home and abroad, scanning our thoughts, sifting our motives, making record of our ends and aims, and this, not as a mere spectator, but as a gatherer of testimony for the judgment-seat of Christ! "Whither shall I go from thy Spirit? or whither shall I flee from thy presence? If I ascend up into heaven thou art there! If I make my bed in hell, behold thou art there! If I take the wings of the morning and dwell in the uttermost part of the sea, even there shall thy hand lead me and thy right hand shall hold me!"

Nay, my brethren, those bright hosts are summoned in clouds around us, as witnesses of another kind! They are witnesses *upon the stand*, giving testimony! And the point of their testimony is the validity of a scriptural, Christian faith, and its power to bear its subjects through all life's toils, trials, and temptations to the very end! Thus they declare, it did for them, thus we are to infer it will do for us.

Under its inspiration Noah, amidst the sneers and jeers of his cotemporaries, built a great ark, to shield him and his from an overflowing flood, beneath a sky undarkened by a threatening cloud, and upon a continent that since the world began had neither known nor feared aught of overflowing floods!

By faith Abraham set out with his family and flocks to go, he knew neither why nor whither, "on a fools errand" as his heathen deriders would say, and at the bidding of a groundless fancy.

And what shall I more say? For the time would fail me to tell of Gideon, and of Barak, and of Samson, and of Jephtha; of David also and Samuel, and the prophets; who through faith subdued kingdoms, wrought righteousness, obtained promises, stopped the mouths of lions, quenched the violence of fire, escaped the edge of the sword, out of weakness were made strong, waxed valiant in fight, turned to flight the armies of the aliens."

And now saith the Spirit, in the presence of this cloud of worthies, bearing such testimony to faith's exhaustless and invincible power, let us, with a faith like theirs in origin—like theirs in kind, and, if we will Beloved, like theirs in degree also,—let us run the race set before us, looking unto Jesus!

In the Second place consider, "The Race set before Us."

1. These words may be considered as pointing to the Race set before the Whole Christian Church.

Uttered centuries ago, the exhortation still rings in the ears of the church of Christ, urging her to apply herself with all diligence to the solution of the great problem assigned to her of discipling the nations! As Moses set up the brazen serpent where every bitten Israelite in the camp could see it, so the church is to bear the cross onward and upward, from height to height, "Excelsior!" her constant motto, until, with redoubled emphasis and significance, the cry may ring forth from its lips—"Look unto me and be ye saved all ye *ends* of the earth."

How this problem has been understood and practically treated by the church is significantly hinted in certain statistics attributed to Sharon Turner. During the first century, he tells us the church gathered under discipleship half a million of souls. The second century made this half million, two millions. The third century increased the number to five millions; the fourth to ten; the fifth to fifteen; the sixth to twenty; the seventh to twenty-five; the eighth to thirty; the ninth to forty; the tenth to fifty; the eleventh to seventy; the twelfth to eighty; the thirteenth, the dark thirteenth reduced the number to seventy-five; the fourteenth, regained the lost ground, and restored the number to eighty; the fifteenth advanced it to one hundred; the sixteenth to one hundred and twenty-five; the seventeenth to one hundred and fifty-five; the eighteenth to two hundred, and the nineteenth, thus far to three hundred millions!

Now, whatever may be said of the character of this nominal Christianity in the mass, and admitting that these figures can only be approximatively accurate, yet is there enough in this general view to encourage and exhilarate the soul, and assure us from the lips of history itself, that the day is drawing on when the millennial bells will announce that the kingdoms of this world have become the kingdoms of our Lord and of his Christ!

And it by no means weakens this assurance to bear in mind that no other religious system in the world can lay claim to anything like such a population in any sense under its sway, excepting perhaps that of the Buddhists—that not one of all these false systems of religion is aggressive—that palsied with age, they all feel the discouraging premonitions of coming dissolution—further still, that every one of these great systems is assailed and penetrated at many a point, by our religion which, though so many centuries old, is yet in the dewy morning of its youth, and last, but not least, the grasp with which Christianity has seized the reins of power among the nations. Treaties between high contracting parties, legislation in Congresses and Parliaments, and the great thoughts that pervade our literature and rule the age are mainly what they are by reason of the religion of Jesus!

Away then with apologies for the tardy growth of Christianity! The mushroom may spring up in a night, but yonder oak, that hardly bows its proud head to the tornado, has been gathering strength for a century! And assuredly the steady growth of a plant through more than eighteen hundred years, demonstrates a vitality that must strike its roots down, till they take the very planet in their embrace, that must lift its top into eternal sunshine, and spread its branches until all the nations find shelter beneath and food upon them!

2. In the solution of this general problem, there is also A RACE SET BEFORE EACH GENERATION OF CHRISTIANS.

And before us, as members of the generation living in the middle of the nineteenth century, there lies a large and important work of *Aggression* and *Defence*.

Our generation is peculiarly one of Christian Aggression. Never before were all barriers so prostrated in the church's path. But a few years ago a potent director of the British East-India Company declared that he would more willingly send fifty devils to India than fifty missionaries. And now where is the power of that company? Once a Governor-General of India forbade the Christian missionary to set foot on Indian soil, and what became of him? Like Julian the Apostate, breathing out his life on Parthian plains, he too had reason to cry—"O, Galilean thou hast conquered!" One and the same vessel bore him in disgrace from Madras to Ceylon, and returning, carried from Ceylon to Madras the missionaries he had persecuted! And now what a vast, unforbidden chorus of Macedonian voices calls thence in our ears! A grand and impressive truth is set to music in the immortal lines of Heber:

> "From Greenland's icy mountains,
> From India's coral strand;
> Where Afric's sunny fountains
> Roll down their golden sand;
> From many an ancient river,
> From many a palmy plain,
> They call us to deliver
> Their land from error's chain."

And never were men so our brethren and neighbours as they are now. Who is my neighbour? He to whom I may send a message, and in half an hour receive reply! But he may live in New Orleans or Nova Scotia. If our fellow men, two hundred miles away are starving, are they sufficiently our neighbours to oblige us to send them bread? But Ireland is nearer to day than was such a community twenty years ago.

Beloved, the triumphs of the human intellect, under the blessing of God, have laid the heathen world on the doorstep of the Christian church!

But a work of *Defence* also lies before us. For we have a foe of immeasurable cunning and immeasurable malice, immeasurable resources, and terrible energy. "The devil is come down unto you, having great wrath, because he knoweth that he hath but a short time."

Ours is a day in which the current sets strongly in for the cold, cheerless shores of Unbelief. The grim divinities of Doubt and Denial, exhumed for the thousandth time, are again set upon their pedestals, and all the world called on to fall down before them. "We seem to be slowly coming round through sublime byways of intellectual superiority and sentimental faith, to the old mean era of cavilling and criticism, the age that finds humbug in every thing—the puny, debased, narrow age of unbelief." The Church even has been menaced with invasion. The Christian world has recently been startled by the discovery of a conspiracy in the bosom of the venerable Church of England, to pour poison into the "pure water of life that flows out from the throne of God and of the Lamb."

Further, this is a day of unusual cultivation, pride and power of intellect; and marshalled on the side of the foe are found no little solid learning, profound research and keen logical acumen. Besides these are troops of sciolists, whose smattering of knowledge and overweening self-conceit render it harder to convince one of them than "seven men that can render a reason."

Whole universities, too, lend their power to the unhallowed work of undermining the faith once delivered to the saints. Never was the infidel library so well replenished. Volume after volume, the ever-recurring Quarterly instinct with Infidelity, and furtive scraps in the omnipresent magazine and newspaper, allure and ensnare the unwary, satisfy and fortify the sceptic, and form a barrier behind which the ribald wag their heads and affect to defy the armies of the living God. Even Science has been suborned to lie against the Holy Ghost, and the stars in their courses to fight on the side of Sisera. And that no stone might be left unturned, an imbecile necromancy has been evoked, and, in its mutterings, Paul under the rapping table made to contradict Paul at the Areopagus.

Now the race set before the Christians of this generation is, in the midst of all this, and in spite of all this—the enemy coming in like a flood—not only to save the cross, but to give it the victory; not only to retain the ground already won but to add new kingdoms to its sway.

3. Then there is A RACE SET BEFORE US AS AMERICAN CHRISTIANS.

Ancient History furnishes us with examples of two classes of nations; those which, destitute of true religion, have assailed it in other nations, and those which, once having it in possession have become apostate.

The doom of the former was thus written by Moses. (Gen. xii. 3.) "I will bless them that bless thee and curse him that curseth thee." And Ezekiel (xxv. 12, 13) records particular applications of this law. "Thus saith the Lord God, because that Edom hath dealt against the house of Judah, by taking vengeance, and hath greatly offended. Therefore, thus saith the Lord God, I will also stretch out my hand upon Edom, and I will cut off man and beast from it; and I will make it desolate from Teman; and they of Dedan shall fall by the sword."

And Babylon and Nineveh and Egypt, where are they?

But it fares worse with apostate nations! When the unclean spirit, once gone out of man, returns again, the last state of that man is worse than the first. "So," said the Saviour, "shall it be unto this generation."

And so it was with that generation—for under the whole heaven hath not been done as was done upon Jerusalem.

But our country must be ranked, if with either, with the apostate. It has never been the assailant of religion; on the contrary we have been from the first a Christian nation. The first act of Columbus, after leaping upon these western shores, was to set up a cross. The first sounds the wolves and Indians heard on our New England coast from the lips of the white man, were sounds of prayer and praise to the Triune God. The name of Jesus has been invoked in our Congresses and great political assemblies from the first to this hour. Appeal was made to Him on the battle field before the conflict and in thanksgiving for victories. Our legislation, so far as it has borne at all upon religion, has been Christian in its character. High authority has declared Christianity to be a part of the common law of the land. The Sabbath is distinctly recognized and annually days of devout thanksgiving to Almighty God are appointed in nearly all our commonwealths. In our land Gospel institutions have sprung up like willows by the water-courses. Revivals of religion, like that of Pentecost, have been enjoyed. Church edifices stud our territory from limit to limit. From our shores the most successful of Christian missionaries have gone to bless the heathen world. And this day we behold an army of five millions of communicants enrolled under the banner of evangelical religion; and as the Sabbath sun moves in majesty from the Atlantic to the Pacific, he sends down his beams upon more than four millions of children in

Sabbath-schools, grouped around more than four hundred thousand teachers! Our land furnishes a home for some thirty thousand or thirty-five thousand ministers of the Gospel, who preach, with more or less regularity, in some sixty thousand houses of worship, of various classes; sometimes a school-house, sometimes a court-house, and sometimes a church edifice, built for the purpose. Bible societies, tract societies, colporteur agencies, and other societies—Christian and benevolent, (supported by an annual voluntary contribution for all religious purposes of from twenty to twenty-five millions of dollars) make up a world of hallowed activities that set the broad seal of Christianity upon our national character, and make it impossible for us not to be either permanently Christian or basely apostate. The only alternative left us, is either, with hands at once impious and ungrateful, to tear up the deep-rooted cross and cast it into the sea, and thus hang the millstone of divine wrath about our nation's neck; or to go forward, ploughing and planting, until at the name of Jesus the whole aggregate Republic shall bow the knee in heartfelt devotion!

The race set before us then, as *American Christians* is, at whatever cost, to make our land a tabernacle of Immanuel. Infidelity and wickedness in every form must be met and thwarted. The emigration from other lands must be Christianized; the neglected youth must be gathered into Sabbath-schools, and in every valley, on every hill-side, and along all water-courses Gospel ordinances must be enjoyed.

While Alexander was thundering at the gates of Tyre, the terrified inhabitants, fearing lest their god should desert them, assembled in the public square, and there had the statue of Apollo chained to his pedestal.

The folly of the heathens may teach us wisdom. We must secure the permanent residence of Immanuel in our midst, or we are lost. We must bind him fast, not with iron chains, but with the bands of a man— the ties of love for a Christian people.

4. AGAIN THERE IS A RACE SET BEFORE US AS PRESBYTERIAN CHRISTIANS—Christians holding as distinctive tenets the equality of the clergy, the coöperation of the Ruling Elder in the government of the church, and courts of review and control.

With our sister-denominations we have no quarrel. God forbid! We bid "God speed" to as many of any name as "sensible of their lost and helpless state by sin, depend upon the atonement of Christ for pardon and acceptance with God; such as desire to renounce their sins, and are determined to lead a holy and godly life." There is room for all and work for all.

Still, will any chide us for entertaining the conviction that there lies a peculiar race before a church like ours in a land like ours; a church, between whose form of government and that of the nation analogies so striking exist—both enjoying in felicitous counterpoise the right and privilege of free thought and private judgment on the one hand, with the predominance of an ultimate, venerable and potent authority on the other; a church historically and notoriously not one whit more Republican in the form of its government than in its spirit and tendencies; always ready in her clergy to bless and pray for, and in her membership to carry and fight under the banner of Republican liberty, and hence always looked on with cordial disfavour by high monarchists. "You are aiming at a Scot's Presbytery," snarled King James at the Hampton Court Conference in 1604, "which agrees with monarchy as well as God and the devil. Then Jack, and Tom, and Will, and Dick shall meet and censure me and my council. Then Will shall stand up and say it must be thus; then Dick shall reply and say nay, marry but we will have it thus."

In this, this Scottish Solomon only followed Queen Elizabeth who "hated Presbytery because it held principles inconsistent with allegiance to her crown." And in this he was followed by Charles the First, who wrote: "Show me any precedent wherever any Presbyterial government and regal was together without perpetual rebellions." And Dryden has left his testimony in no very amiable lines:

> "So Presbytery and its pestilential zeal,
> Can flourish only in a commonweal."*

A church always taking high ground in favour of general education, under a government whose very life depends on general education as one of its essential conditions; a church embracing such a proportion of high character, talent, learning, zeal and piety—before this church we say there is a peculiar and honourable race set by her Master, and well will it be for her and for the world if, like true children of Issachar, they "have

* Smythe's "Ecclesiastical Republicanism."

understanding of the times to know what Israel ought to do."

The race it has already run demonstrates that her race is only just begun. While Louis XIV. was filling France with profligacy, and emptying her of citizens and wealth; while the Marlboroughs and Peterboroughs of England were winning renown for her abroad, and at home, amidst bitter and endless wranglings of Whig and Tory factions, Swift, Pope, Addison, Steele, and others were filling her libraries with a brilliant and deathless literature; while the American colonies were harassed with controversies with their selfish old mother for their rights, and their borders tormented with the miseries of a savage warfare, God, in his quiet but resistless providence, was moving on, sowing the seeds of Presbyterianism on these western shores. Two hundred years ago signs of Presbyterian vegetation here and there appeared. At Jamaica, in Maryland, New York and Philadelphia, churches sprang into existence.

About 1695, weekly religious worship began to be held in a litte stocking-store with a sign above the door, "C & N Jones," on the northwest corner of Chestnut and Second Streets. Nine Baptists and perhaps as many Presbyterians (Presbyterians in reality if not yet in name) and a few Episcopalians, formed that seminal congregation.

Since that day of small things how many precious souls have gone from these churches with so humble an origin, to join in the song of Moses and the Lamb on high! And to-day Philadelphia rejoices in some two hundred and seventy Evangelical churches, numbering perhaps one hundred thousand communicants. Of these churches seventy are Presbyterian, thirty-three Old-School, eighteen New-School and nineteen of other names.

And you heard in the sermon two days ago, what an aggregate of Presbyteries, of ministers and of communing members are now arrayed under the two Assemblies in our land, equipped with a noble array of schools, colleges and theological seminaries, and with a powerful machinery for the propagation of the truth in fields domestic and foreign.

Before the Presbyterian Church, thus endowed, there is set a race which includes at least the duty of demonstrating to the world the superior efficacy of our ecclesiastical system in spreading the Gospel among men, in subduing sinners to King Emmanuel, in developing all the graces of piety, and training the branches of the messianic vine to the production and maturing of all the rich "fruit of the Spirit, love, joy, peace, long-suffering, gentleness, goodness, faith, meekness, temperance."

FINALLY. THERE IS A RACE SET BEFORE US AS INDIVIDUAL CHRISTIANS.

There is a race set before each believer peculiar to himself, which no one can run either for him or with him.

Of all the thousands of vessels that have left New York for Liverpool, no two ever pursued just the same path. And of all the Pilgrims that have made the voyage to heaven, no two ever followed in just the same track.

The experience of each one was marked with decided peculiarities.

God sets the race before us, and He never repeats himself in nature or in grace. He makes no two stars, no two flowers, no two dew-drops, no two grass-blades, no two human faces, no two courses of human experience alike.

The race of one lies among the allurements, temptations, and sometimes persecutions of wealth and high social position; that of another, through the toils, cares and hard trials of extreme poverty. Having supped upon his hard crust, hardly earned, the son of penury retires to his hard bed to sleep. The early dawn finds him again at his task, or in anxious pursuit of employment. And so his life wears on to the end. At length he dies, and the undertaker hides his poor body among the long grass in some obscure nook in the field, and soon no one of all earth's thousand millions knows or cares that such a human being ever lived and sinned and suffered and died!

The race of one is very short, a few brief suns bringing it to the close; that of another runs on almost through the century. The race of one lies in the bustle and excitement of public life; of another through paths of almost unbroken bodily sickness. To one is appointed a race amidst scenes of general Christian defection, and he cries out with the prophet, "I, even I alone am left, and they seek my life to take it away;" while the career of another is like that of a Whitefield, a continued succession of revival scenes. One finds his way to bliss through the sorrows and glories of martyrdom, another through years of fearful bereavement and sorrow, and another still passes to the cold river's verge, through the Dark Valley, through the grim horrors of Doubting Castle and the merciless beatings of Giant Despair. Each one, we repeat, has his own appointed race to run.

Run then, Beloved, the race set before you! Grieve not, envy not, repine not, wish it not otherwise than it is. Say with Rutherford, "If it were come to an exchange of crosses I would not exchange my cross with any."

Indeed, there is something both of selfishness and folly in the wish that our race were other than it is; folly, for we each have ills the balm for which lies only in the path marked out for us; selfishness, for some one must run this very course. The religion of Jesus must have this particular illustration of its power. Heaven's choir cannot lack the song that you are learning to sing. The tapestry of grace, weaving here below to be the wonder and admiration of the universe, cannot lack that particular figure and colour that your peculiar experience is adding. Some one must weep these tears, bear these burdens, do these works, and you are the only one just qualified for the task. Run then with patience and diligence the race that God hath set before you!

And now, beloved brethren, as we near the close of these refreshing exercises, let us all as members of the great Church of our Redeemer, as participants in the honours and duties of this passing generation, as Christian citizens of our beloved America, as Presbyterian Christians and as individual believers, each with his own salvation to work out with fear and trembling

—let us all, I say, set out anew in the race set before us, looking, as we run, on the one side at the witnesses, and on the other unto Jesus!

For our text seems to place us, as it were, in a parenthesis between the two. First we look at the witnesses, as the text commands, and as did the saints of old. "Our Fathers trusted in Thee. They trusted and Thou didst deliver them. They cried unto Thee and were delivered—they trusted in Thee and were not confounded."—Ps. xxii. 4, 5.

But should any be disposed to add with the Psalmist, "Yes, but we are very different from our fathers;" "I am a worm and no man, a reproach of men and dispised of the people." "The Patriarchs trusted and were delivered, but we have not the faith of the Patriarchs." Then look away to Jesus, the author and finisher of your faith, and He can increase its power till mountains shall flow down at its presence!

It is as if two separate divisions of Napoleon's army were fighting under his eye, each with his own opposing force, the one nearer and the other more remote. The remoter one is victorious at the first onset, but the nearer one wavers. The officer in command, trembling lest disgrace befall his flag, cries to his men, "See how your comrades chase the foe!" "Ah," they murmur in reply, "we are fewer and weaker than they."

Seeing now that the case is desperate, as a last resort he cries, "Behold, your Emperor is looking at you!" Every face is turned, and catching fire from the glance of that eagle eye, like a tornado they sweep the enemy before them!

So let us on in the race set before us—looking at the

cloud of witnesses, now more numerous by hundreds of thousands than when this exhortation was penned —embracing in addition to the more ancient worthies, the blessed army of confessors and martyrs of early Christianity, and then the Luthers, Calvins and Knoxes; Baxters, Bunyans and Owens; Tennents and Davies; Brainards and Paysons; yes, and others too, whom we have known and loved in the flesh! We saw how they lived; we saw how they struggled with ill; with what preternatural patience they endured! Racked with pains we heard them cry, "Thy will be done!" Bruised and crushed they still exclaimed, "We glory in tribulations also!" The dark chamber of adversity they made to echo with the shout, "Although the fig-tree shall not blossom, neither shall fruit be in the vine; the labour of the olive shall fail, and the fields shall yield no meat; the flock shall be cut off from the fold, and there shall be no herd in the stalls: yet will I rejoice in the Lord; I will joy in the God of my salvation!" And we saw how they died! Some as the infant falls asleep on its mother's bosom, and some as Elijah went to heaven in a chariot of fire!

Yes, blessed witnesses, we take your testimony, and here before the Triune God, and before the angels, and in view of all the toils, and sorrows and triumphs of believers in every age, we solemnly promise to heed this exhortation, and from this good hour to run more resolutely, more diligently, more patiently, the race set before us, looking unto Jesus, the author and finisher of our faith. Amen and amen!

The closing services of the Anniversary were on Thursday, commencing at half-past two P. M. It was the Communion season. Dr. Krebs conducted the exercises, assisted by Dr. Macdonald and Rev. Mr. Breed, with a few concluding remarks and prayer by the pastor. "It was a time the solemnity, the delight, the profit of which language fails to convey, and was a fitting close to the series of interesting services, such as would be appropriate to very few churches in this country."

The Committee would here acknowledge their obligations to Professor Andreu, organist, and the choir for the music throughout the Anniversary. Their performances aided much to enhance the pleasure and interest in the occasion.

AN APPLICATORY ADDRESS

SUBSEQUENTLY DELIVERED

BY THE PASTOR TO THE PEOPLE OF HIS CHARGE.

"The Lord our God be with us, as he was with our fathers."—1 Kings viii. 57.

"Beloved of God, called to be saints; grace to you, and peace from God our Father, and the Lord Jesus Christ."

DEAR BRETHREN,—God has favored us. Our recent anniversary exercises have left their impress upon our minds. The congratulations received; the satisfaction expressed; the elevated spiritual enjoyment acknowledged by all; the reluctance to leave the place where lingered so many sweet and sacred associations, and the full heart and tearful eye when those from a distance spoke the parting word—all accumulated the evidence that it was a "high day" in the annals of our Zion, and that we did not mistake the indications of Providence calling to its observance.

But the more important that occasion, and the more delightful those services, the greater subsequent responsibilities do they impose upon us. They have tended to fix the gaze of the religious world upon us. They have served to raise this church to the hill top of public observation. A more than local interest gathers around the place, where, it is believed, God, in his all-wise purposes, planted in its continuance, the First Presbyterian Church in America.

For the purpose of retaining these impressions, and of appreciating our responsibilities, as they are understood by the Christian world, and as due to God, I would offer for your consideration a few thoughts which, it may be hoped, will tend to strengthen the *practical* effects of the services in which, as a church, we have been so pleasantly engaged. He who was among "the chiefest of the apostles," sought the will of God at the throne of grace. And in what way can we so suitably express our gratitude to God, and our readiness to do his will, as in the form of earnest prayer for grace to be equal to our position in the world, in the church, and in our obligations to the Great Head of the church, who in the past has gone before us "in a pillar of a cloud to lead us in the way, and a pillar of fire to give us light," and whose Covenant of mercy has spanned the future with the bow of promise?

Such a prayer I find Solomon offered. With the children of Israel he was engaged in dedicating a new temple to the service of God. That temple was at once a monument of their gratitude and liberality. They were children of a blessed ancestry. God had led their fathers through a "waste and howling wilderness." They had been "brought forth also into a large place," and safely settled in the land the Lord had given them. By the good hand of the Lord upon them, temporal and spiritual prosperity, in a distinguished manner, had marked their career. How much is all this like our own nation! King Solomon could say with Asaph — and we might also almost literally adopt the same language—"Thou hast brought a vine out of Egypt; Thou hast cast out the heathen and planted it. Thou preparedst room before it, and didst cause it to take deep root, and it filled the land. The hills were covered with the shadow of it, and the boughs thereof were like the goodly cedars. She sent out her boughs unto the sea, and her branches unto the river." Descendants of parentage so highly blessed of God; enjoying the worship of the true God for so many successive generations; living to see the church of their father spread from river to sea; assembled in a new house of worship, the most splendid the world ever saw: well might the Children of the Covenant, so greatly favored, through the mouth of the Royal Preacher offer the prayer, "The Lord our God be with us, as He was with our fathers."

This prayer may certainly be considered relevant to the condition of our church and congregation at the present time. God *was* with our fathers. Brethren, if you call to mind the difficulties incident to the settlement of a new territory, the hardships, the poverty, the sickness, the dangers, the weakness of even good men, the proneness of all to error, and to all this add a persistent effort of the Colonial Government to destroy this church in its form of worship and doctrine, there will be no room to doubt the fact of God's special providence with the early founders of this church. Amid all these pressures would this Church have subsisted for two hundred years without divine interference and preservation? Believe it who may. We say with adoring gratitude: The Lord Jehovah was with our fathers. They paused before they commenced the toils and trials of the wilderness, and at the threshold of all sanctuary enterprises with Moses prayed, "Now, therefore, we pray thee, if we have found grace in thy sight, show us now THY WAY, that we may know thee: and consider that this nation is thy people." And God answered their prayers: "My presence shall go with you, and I will give thee rest." The spirit the fathers manifested; their inclination to the service of God; "their coming together in a church way;" their uniform regard for the ordinances of God's house; the fruits of their labors and prayers which are this day present to our consciousness, all attest the same truth—*God was with our fathers.*

Their *faith in God*, and their *zeal for his cause* bear the same testimony. "Abraham believed God," and one of the greatest evidences of his faith was, at the call of God, to go from his "country," his "kindred," and his "father's house," into a strange land. The early settlers of this country did this very thing. They left their "country," their "kindred," and their "father's house." Conscience was trammeled, liberty of worship was suppressed, and under the light of the guiding star of Faith and Hope, they said farewell to childhood's early scenes, launched their bark upon the boisterous deep, and with a cheerful voice sang as they sailed:

"His call we obey, like Abram of old,
Not knowing our way, but faith makes us bold;
For though we are strangers, we have a good guide,
And trust in all dangers, the Lord will provide."

But their faith and zeal led them to do more than this: *they made provision for the future.* They were men of the covenant. The blessings which they enjoyed they wished to transmit to their children and their children's children. The more religion a man has the less selfish he is, and the greater will be his sympathies for others. And especially will those in covenant with God feel upon them the binding force of parental obligations, and the duty of providing for the spiritual welfare of their children, after their own heads shall lie low in the bed of death. No man liveth to himself. Not for themselves alone did our fathers brave the dangers of the deep; not for themselves alone did they fell the ancient forest; not for themselves alone did they build houses of worship—they had faith in God. They saw this great wilderness peopled with a multitudinous population—a happy, free and independent people. For them they labored, for them they prayed, and for them they established the institutions of the gospel. It was faith in the future and in the God of the future that gave vigor to their purpose, courage to their hearts; and the results of the seed sown has evidenced the correctness of their faith, abounding in a harvest to the praise of God's grace, the grandest and most glorious the eye of the world ever rested upon. In our faith in God, in our zeal for his glory, and the future welfare of his church, God be with us as he was with our fathers.

For the attainment of this, let the petition of Solomon be ours. *We must pray.* We must earnestly, habitually pray. The life of the Christian is in proportion to his *closet devotion.* If I had to compress all I had to say in one sentence, it would be, *Live the life of prayer.* Prayer is a realization of dependence upon God. We stand in our place this day, and, at the footstool of God's throne, say, Our fathers would have been nothing if God had not been with them. None were more conscious of this than themselves. Their whole history is replete with the evidence that they *looked to God.* Every step of progress was marked by prayer. And we would not be their worthy successors in church privileges, if, like them, we did not feel that our springs are in God. "And we desire that every one of you do show the same diligence to the full assurance of hope unto the end. That ye be not slothful, but followers of them who through faith and patience inherit the promises."

We claim not perfection for man in his best estate while a sojourner on earth. Solomon, in the sentiment of his prayer, did not mean to intimate that their fathers were exceptions to the common laws of human infirmity,—that David, that Jesse, that Moses or Jacob or Abraham had never erred. The prophet makes the direct acknowledgement "our fathers have sinned." But the petitioner meant that as "heirs according to the promise" "of like precious faith through the righteousness of God and our Saviour Jesus Christ," "that ye be like minded, having the same love, of one accord, of one mind." The prayer is *as* Thou wast with our fathers, be with us. Thou didst give them the grace of self-sacrifice, give us the same grace. Thou didst give them the grace of perseverance, so give us the same grace. Thou didst give them wisdom, give us wisdom. Thou didst give them zeal for thy glory, impart the same to us. What thy providence was to them, leading, protecting, controlling, be Thou to us. Wherein thy Spirit did work in them, in like manner work thou in us. The Lord our God be with us, as he was with our fathers. "So that *ye come behind in no gift*, waiting for the coming of our Lord Jesus Christ."

Dear Brethren, "all anniversaries have their force and their joy in this, that they are the registry of growth!" And as we survey the growth of the past, these anniversary exercises would fail in one of their most important effects did they not serve to awaken emotions of gratitude to God who *has* been with us and our fathers. By the mouth of Moses God commanded Israel: "Thou shalt remember all the way which the Lord thy God led thee these forty years in the wilderness." Memory of divine favors will inspire grateful thoughts. And if as a church we look back two hundred years we cannot be otherwise than sensible of God's goodness, and our duty of thanksgiving. For such a history,—for the characters composing that history—for the tokens of the divine presence, radiant with the displays of God's saving grace up to this very moment of our existence, we have great reason to say with hearts of adoring love; "Lord thou hast been our dwelling place in all generations." "Give unto the Lord the glory due unto his name."

It is a scriptural injunction to be "followers of them who through faith and patience inherit the promises."

To imitate the virtues of those who have gone before us is no less a duty than that of gratitude for their godly example. When Paul speaks of "forgetting the things that are behind" he does not mean that the record of the past should be effaced from the mind. If so, why was the faculty of the memory created? Where then would be the rich results, and incomparable benefits of experience? But I understand the apostle to caution us against *relying* upon the past as though nothing further was to be attempted; making the past a pillow to rest our heads upon in ease and quietness. If this were the only result, then the past would be a snare and sin. If we could gather together before us in one depository, all the virtues of our ancestors, their merit could not be imputed to us. And so far from excusing *us* from the obligations of the present they are of no more value than the mouldering dust of their lifeless remains. We hold in reverence the importance of the past. But the more important the historic character of the past, the heavier the weight of responsibility resting upon us to sustain its dignity, and, by carrying it forward, secure its amplest fruits. It is in the rich fruition of their graces in our hearts and hopes and labors, that "the memory of the just is blessed," and their devotion, love, joy and faith become ours. "Know, therefore, that the Lord thy God, he is God, the faithful God, which keepeth covenant and mercy with them that love him and keep his commandments to a thousand generations."

Beloved in the Lord, as a church and congregation we stand on high vantage ground. The dust of sainted generations, of Pastors, Elders, Deacons, Trustees, Members, male and female, are at our feet. "They rest from their labors, and their works do follow them." We cull from their departed ashes gems of immortal truth to enrich our spiritual treasury. They cleared away the rubbish and paved a well-beaten path after the "good old way" easy and safely for our feet to walk in. They "labored, and we have entered into their labors." And as they made history for us, so we are making history for those who are to follow us. In the great drama of life every one has a part to act. "And though one may have a more splendid and another a more obscure part assigned him, the actor of each is equally responsible." In one hundred years from now our descendants will meet to review our actions, as we have those of our ancestors. Not one of us shall be at that meeting. Long, long before that time each one of us shall have gone to his account. Shall we in our generation fill a bright page in our church relation? Brethren, the answer of that question is in ourselves. "Our fathers had the tabernacle of witness in the wilderness," but their "dust has returned to the earth," "their sepulchres are with us unto this day." And as we enter upon the third century of our existence, it appears to me that every particle of their sleeping dust is instinct with life, and from the memory of their cherished graves, and from their glorified spirits around the throne, as a great cloud of witnesses, comes a united voice into the living ear of those upon whom the present responsibility rests; "*Be faithful to the Past—be true to the Present—be just to the Future.*" And the influences of their history, sparkling with rays of light, as stars in the milky way, emitted from the Sun of rightcousness, converging into one focus, emblazon as upon the very face of the heavens—as the express will of God—as the teachings of the past, that which must ever be the Christian's, the church's motto—*Go forward.*

> "'Tis God's all animating voice,
>   That calls thee from on high:
> 'Tis his own hand presents the prize
>   To thine aspiring eye.
>
> " A cloud of witnesses around
>   Hold thee in full survey;
> Forget the steps already trod,
>   And onward urge thy way."

" Blessed *be* the Lord, that hath given rest unto his people Israel, according to all that he promised: there hath not failed one word of all his good promise, which he promised by the hand of Moses his servant.

"The Lord our God be with us, as he was with our fathers: let him not leave us, nor forsake us:

"That we may incline our hearts unto him, to walk in all his ways, and to keep his commandments, and his statutes, and his judgments, which he commanded our fathers."—Amen.

From the New York Observer, of January 16th, 1862.

BI-CENTENARY COMMEMORATION

AT JAMAICA, L. I.

Tuesday, Wednesday and Thursday, (January 7, 8 and 9, 1862,) will long be remembered by the people of Jamaica, Long Island. Agreeably to the comprehensive preparations made for the commemoration of the settlement and the planting of the Presbyterian church at that place two hundred years ago, the exercises were continued through those three days; and the spirit with which they were carried on, would only have been satisfied had they continued three days longer. It was a "holy convocation to the Lord." The dwellings of a hospitable people were thrown open for the reception of their guests—their own returned children—and for the interchange of friendly greeting and intercourse; and in them was heard abundantly the voice of prayer and praise.

The Commemorative Discourse was delivered on Tuesday by the Rev. Dr. Macdonald, now of Princeton, the predecessor of the present worthy and successful pastor at Jamaica, the Rev. Peter D. Oakey. Dr. Macdonald's discourse occupied two hours in the delivery, and was heard by the crowded assembly with continued interest until the close. It did not need his own felicitous apology for its length, that it was but in the proportion of an hour to a century. It will be printed uniform with the author's interesting volume,

"The History of the Presbyterian Church at Jamaica, L. I.;" and no abstract, therefore, is given here. It was rich in research; in historical detail; in quaint incidents of the olden time; in clear and logical argument and proof of the antiquity and of the decided Presbyterianism of the Church from the beginning, of its trials and persecutions, its pastoral succession, its seasons of refreshing, its emigrant development and relation to the history of the Church and the country at large, and—last, but not least—its opportunities and its obligations to preserve and to extend its influence in all time to come.

On Wednesday morning there was a festival of good things;—Dr. Macdonald presided. More than twenty ministers have gone out directly from this church, especially in its later years; of these a goodly number were present. There were no formal services, each in turn came forward and contributed his reminiscence and memorial with the simplicity, frankness and unction, which had free scope in this family gathering. The Rev. Dr. Nicholas Everitt Smith, pastor of the Reformed Dutch Church in Harrison street, Brooklyn, and the Rev. Benjamin S. Everitt, pastor of the Presbyterian Church at Blackwoodtown, N. J.,—descendants of Nicholas Everitt, one of the original members of the church,—were baptized here, although the former of them was in infancy removed by his parents to the Rutgers street congregation, New York, where he claimed as his spiritual father the Rev. Dr. Krebs, its pastor, now present. The Rev. Mr. Wickes, pastor of a church, near Rochester, spoke in behalf of himself and of his brother, also a minister. The Rev. Elias N.

Crane, pastor at New Vernon, N. J., son of the former beloved pastor, Elias W. Crane, and the Rev. Wilson Phraner, of Sing Sing, brought their affectionate tribute. The Rev. Dr. Henry R. Weed, of Wheeling, Va., (the eldest surviving minister of the former pastors of Jamaica,) and others, unable to be present, sent letters. As this congregation was first brought into a regular "church way," and that way was in an important legal document referred to "according to the rules of the Gospel in this town,"—*i. e.*, Presbyterian—it is not a child, but the mother even of the "mother Presbytery." George McNish, (settled A. D. 1710,) cotemporary of Francis Mackemie and John Hampton, (who was imprisoned by the Colonial authorities in the old church at Jamaica, for preaching the Gospel,) was one of the original members of the Presbytery of Philadelphia, (1706–1716,) and was the *eighth* pastor at Jamaica. Mr. McNish and the church of Jamaica were set off subsequently to form the Presbytery of Long Island—the first Presbytery in the province of New York. Afterwards the congregation became a part of the Presbytery of New York, and in 1855 it was attached to the new Presbytery of Nassau. Representatives of these Presbyteries were also present:—The Rev. Mr. Reeve, of Long Island; Mr. Wm. P. Breed, of Philadelphia, and Dr. Krebs, of New York. These brethren also spoke. Mr. Breed could not claim to be a descendant of Jamaica, but he also, as well as Dr. Smith, recognized as his spiritual father the pastor of the Rutgers street Church, (which relation may be claimed by about twenty-five ministers of the Gospel,) he would feel as if he belonged here too. Dr. Krebs had come on behalf of the Presbytery, which, for a long time after the foundation of Jamaica, had not yet come into existence, as indeed there was no church in New York until the beginning of the eighteenth century, but was now multiplied into six or seven Presbyteries with their many scores of churches and pastors. But he would not now speak of this. His own church was for many years familiarly spoken of as the "Long Island Church in New York." Many of its members were drawn from the Island and from Jamaica, even in his own day. And he had been so intimately connected with them in intercourse with their pastors and with themselves in the enjoyment of their hospitality, and in preaching the Gospel to them in their own place, as well as by the marriage of his own child with the descendant of one of their oldest families, still numerous and dwelling there, that he felt as if he also was their kinsman. He spoke with especial eulogy of that man of God—the Rev. Elias W. Crane—and enlarged on the happy combination of means of grace, in the " home, the school, and the church," which God had so signally blessed.

No attempt is made to report these speeches. Reference was made to the presence of three ruling elders still in office, after forty years' service, and to the Superintendent of the Sunday-school, Mr. Laurens Reeve,* still labouring in that vocation after thirty-three years.

---

* [Elder Laurens Reeve has been superintendent of the village school for thirty-three years; Elder John Carpenter was superintendent of the Foster's Meadow school for thirty years; and Elder Nathaniel Carpenter, of the Springfield school, for twenty years.—COM.]

The venerable Dr. Shelton was called upon and gave some pleasant recollections of the early days, not only of fifty-five years ago, but through old people with whom he had conversed in his early life among them. He was able also to speak of what *they* had seen and told him of nearly one hundred and fifty years ago. For three hours this free and unrestrained outgushing of the heart went on—some speaking only with tears, where the tide of feeling choked utterance—till the time itself gave out, and the people, who would fain have lingered, were forced to disperse. None who were there will ever forget that scene. A volume only could describe the interesting details, nor could any written record describe the heavenly and tender feelings of the scene.

On Wednesday evening Dr. Krebs preached, and on Thursday morning Mr. Breed, and on Thursday afternoon the Lord's Supper was administered. Thus fitly concludes this delightful anniversary. The people had remembered their fathers and the grace of God that was with them; and now, crowning all, they kept with joy the feast in remembrance of Him "of whom the whole family in earth and heaven is named," by whose death they and their fathers were made heirs together of the grace of life.

It may be mentioned as an affecting incident, that there came also messages and greetings from sick beds of members of the church, who felt that they were standing on the verge of Jordan; and that one of the more aged members of the church was actually dying,* while we, unaware of that fact, were singing the hymn,

* Nathaniel Ludlum.

"Come let us join our friends above," which contains these stanzas:

> "One army of the living God,
> To his commands we bow;
> Part of the host have crossed the flood,
> And part are crossing now.

> "How many to their endless home,
> This solemn moment fly!
> And we are to the margin come,
> And soon expect to die!"
>
> A Guest.

From the Presbyterian, January 25, 1862.

THE JAMAICA BI-CENTENARY.

We can hardly realize that any thing human in America can be two hundred years old. But we have just celebrated the Two Hundredth Anniversary of a Christian church at Jamaica, Long Island, and in all probability the oldest Presbyterian church on this continent! That Father Makemie was an adopted son of Presbyterianism in America, and not its father, is manifest from the fact that, long anterior to his arrival in this country, this church existed, and without doubt as a Presbyterian church; and when, in 1707, he was arrested by the amiable Lord Cornbury, he was imprisoned in the old stone church at Jamaica.

It was about 1655, while Peter Stuyvesant was Governor of New York, that seventeen persons, some from Hempstead, Long Island, and some from New England, formed this settlement. They were a virtuous, godly race. The town records for February 27, 1658, say: "It is y^s day voted by this town that no person shall sell, or give to any Indians within, or about ye said town, any strong licker, much or little, more or less, upon the forfeiture of fifty guilders." The original name of the town was "Yemacah," of Indian origin. As early as 1662, public worship was regularly established, to which the citizens were called by "the sound of the church-going" *drum*. And on January 22, 1663, it was "voted by the town that

Abraham Smith shall have thirty shillings a year for beating the drum upon Sabbath days," etc.

It would seem that longevity has become a confirmed habit with persons and things in Jamaica. The church two hundred years old; three of the ruling elders more than forty years in the eldership; the superintendent of the Sabbath-school more than thirty years in office, and able to count more than twenty ministers of the Gospel who have once been in connection with his school, and an uncommon number of venerable, silver-headed patriarchs in the congregation!

The commemorative services were commenced on Tuesday afternoon, the 7th inst., at half-past three o'clock, with a most instructive discourse of a historical character, by the Rev. Dr. James M. Macdonald, formerly pastor of the church, and now of Princeton, New Jersey. The house was crowded, and at the close of the service all withdrew with the deep conviction that such an anniversary could not have had a more instructive and appropriate beginning.

On Wednesday morning, at half-past ten o'clock, the congregation again assembled for free conference and prayer. Dr. Macdonald was called to the chair, and a most touching and impressive service it was. Before our eyes on each side of the pulpit, was a marble tablet, containing the names of all the deceased pastors of the church, beginning with Zechariah Walker, in 1662. Here and there, in the same pew, might be seen the grey-haired patriarch, with his white cravat and venerable mien, and the son, in the vigor of manhood, evidently ready to endure hardness in the service of either Church or State, and the flaxen-haired, bright-eyed grand-daughter, the flower in the grass beneath the aged tree. Children of the church were there from a distance, several of whom came to tell the story of their labors as ambassadors of Jesus Christ.

The first who spoke was the venerable Dr. Shelton, now more than two score years a ruling elder in that church. Among other things, he told of a pious woman of the congregation in former days, who, one night before retiring, bent the knee in prayer at her bedside, and when she rose to lay her head upon her pillow, to her astonishment, she found the daylight streaming into the windows! She had spent the whole night in prayer!

Following him, came several "children of the Church," now ambassadors of Christ, with their stories of hallowed and touching reminiscences. The Rev. Mr. Weeks, from the vicinity of Rochester, New York; the Rev. Elias N. Crane, the Rev. Mr. Everitt, and the Rev. Mr. Higbie—all these brethren spoke in the most earnest manner of God's faithfulness as a covenant-keeping God; and all bore repeated and explicit testimony to the value of Sabbath-school instruction, as illustrated in their own experience.

As the exercises continued, every heart was moved, and tears flowed freely from aged and youthful eyes, and when Mr. Laurens Reeve, Superintendent so long of the Sabbath-school, was called upon, his emotions utterly forbade utterance.

The representatives from sister churches and Presbyteries were now called on; and the Rev. Dr. N. E. Smith of Brooklyn, now of the Dutch church, responded in a happy address. His father, now ninety years old, was formerly a member of the Jamaica Church, and could narrate many curious incidents in its history. The old square stone church stood in the middle of the road, and, besides the usual door before the pulpit, had two others in the sides of the building, opposite each other, and connected by an aisle. One summer Sabbath, when the people were engaged in worship, and these two doors standing open, a worthless fellow, at a neighbouring tavern, made a bet that he would ride on horseback in at one of these side doors, and out at the other—which bet he won! The effect on preacher and hearer, of the sudden apparition of a man on horseback in the midst of the congregation, may be imagined.

The Rev. W. B. Reeve, of the Presbytery of Long Island; the Rev. W. P. Breed, of the Presbytery of Philadelphia, the venerable mother of all our Presbyteries; and the Rev. Dr. Krebs, of the Presbytery of New York, made appropriate gratulatory addresses.

On Wednesday evening, Dr. Krebs preached on the text, "The joy of the Lord is your strength." Thursday morning, Mr. Breed preached from Heb. xii. 1. In the afternoon, the sacrament of the Lord's Supper was celebrated, and it added no little to the solemnity of the occasion, to reflect that the generations of two centuries had refreshed themselves at that table on their way to the marriage-supper of the Lamb. This was the closing service; and, altogether, the occasion was of a most refreshing and delightful character, and will not soon be forgotten by any who were permitted to participate in its sweet solemnities. May many a godly generation yet enjoy the precious means of grace in the venerable old church at Jamaica!   B.

At a meeting of the Elders, Deacons, and Trustees, held January 27th, 1862, the report of the Committee of arrangements was accepted and adopted. It was "Resolved that our thanks be presented to the Brethren who have come to assist in the anniversary exercises; that a new edition of 500 copies of the history of the church be published, and that the Rev. Dr. Macdonald be requested to complete it for the two centuries of the churh's existence; that a narrative of the anniversary exercises be published as an appendix to the same, and copies of the sermons preached on the occasion solicited for publication." The Committee of arrangements were authorized to carry out these resolutions, and Latham M. Jaggar, was appointed treasurer of the publication fund.

www.ingramcontent.com/pod-product-compliance
Lightning Source LLC
Chambersburg PA
CBHW030729230426
43667CB00007B/648